Advance Praise for
Fermenting Revolution

With equal pulls of humor and history, O'Brien toasts the dedicated
good-beer activists who've battled the homogenous evil of "globeerization"
and brought "beerodiversity" back to communities across the land.
Pop a cool one and enjoy this empowering and enlightening book.

— Jim Hightower, author of *Thieves in High Places*
and publisher of *The Hightower Lowdown*

Fermenting Revolution is a lively, sometimes humorous, sometimes
horrifying, and always illuminating tale. It's a tale that needed to be told.
As Chris says, "More so than ever before, the world today needs beer."
I'll drink to that!

— Sam Calagione, Owner, Dogfish Head craft Brewery

Fermenting Revolution is full of surprising facts and puts a whole new
perspective on the act of making and drinking beer. If you like beer,
you'll love this book. And if you want to save the planet, you'll
be glad to know the work starts and ends with beer.

— Fran Korten, Publisher, *YES!* magazine.

You don't need to be an alumnus of the fraternity Tapa Kega Day to
enjoy this funny and comprehensive book. It is the one book that
will make you an expert on beer's important role in history
and its potential for social change today.

— Kevin Danaher, Cofounder, Global Exchange

Reading this book is like one of those great beer-drinking sessions with
good friends where, at the end, you feel like you've solved all the world's
problems — and all it took was drinking local and organic beer!

— Amelia Slayton, former Greenpeace campaigner,
founder of Seven Bridges International

Part history lesson, part political polemic, and wonderfully opinionated, *Fermenting Revolution* is a book destined to spark great philosophical conversations over chalices of real beer. It's a book that will make you think about where your beer comes from, who made it, why it was made, where it fits into a healthy global society and what joys it can bring you and the people around you. O'Brien shows us why the unexamined beer is not worth drinking, but the examined beer can bring enlightenment.

— GARRETT OLIVER, Brewmaster of the Brooklyn Brewery, author of *The Brewmasters Table*, Counselor for Slow Food International

Drinking beer may strike you as an odd way to save the world, but Chris O'Brien tells you how to do it with intelligence, humor, and style. Along the way, you'll learn about 10,000 years of beer history as well as brewing and drinking lore from around the world. It's a fresh look at man's oldest beverage that will help you quench your thirst for social justice.

— STEVEN RAICHLEN, author of *The Barbecue Bible* and *How to Grill*, and host of "BBQ University" on PBS.

A great read on the history of beer and how it has been an integral part of shaping the different cultures in the world. Chris raises the reader's awareness of the modern day environmental, agriculture and social issues with facts, and how mass industrialization has taken the taste out of beer.
Here is proof that running a sustainable brewery is necessary and profitable, and building our local economies will bring balance back to the world. Cheers to local craftbrewing and returning to being a localvore.

— MORGAN WOLAVER, Co-founder Wolaver's Organic Ales

The reaction against the corporate homogenization of the entire globe began, believe it or not, with beer. One of the few environmental and social indicators pointing in the right way is that the number of small breweries has exploded in the last couple of decades,. Chris O'Brien tells this and many other stories in mellow and charming fashion; read it with a pint of something local in one hand.

— BILL McKIBBEN, author of
Deep Economy: The Wealth of Communities and the Durable Future

Fermenting Revolution

Christopher Mark O'Brien

How to Drink Beer and Save the World

Fermenting
Revolution

Christopher Mark O'Brien

NEW SOCIETY PUBLISHERS

Cataloging in Publication Data:
A catalog record for this publication is available from the National Library of Canada.

Cover design by Diane MacIntosh. Cover Photo: iStock Photos, Douglas Freer. All interior photos, unless otherwise indicated, by Christopher Mark O'Brien.

Printed in Canada. First printing August 2006.

Paperback ISBN 13: 978-0-86571-556-1
Paperback ISBN 10: 0-86571-556-4

Inquiries regarding requests to reprint all or part of *Fermenting Revolution* should be addressed to New Society Publishers at the address below.

To order directly from the publishers, please call toll-free (North America) 1-800-567-6772, or order online at www.newsociety.com

Any other inquiries can be directed by mail to:

New Society Publishers
P.O. Box 189, Gabriola Island, BC V0R 1X0, Canada
1-800-567-6772

New Society Publishers' mission is to publish books that contribute in fundamental ways to building an ecologically sustainable and just society, and to do so with the least possible impact on the environment, in a manner that models this vision. We are committed to doing this not just through education, but through action. We are acting on our commitment to the world's remaining ancient forests by phasing out our paper supply from ancient forests worldwide. This book is one step toward ending global deforestation and climate change. It is printed on acid-free paper that is **100% old growth forest-free** (100% post-consumer recycled), processed chlorine free, and printed with vegetable-based, low-VOC inks. For further information, or to browse our full list of books and purchase securely, visit our website at: www.newsociety.com
NEW SOCIETY PUBLISHERS   www.newsociety.com

Dedication

To all beer crafters for conjuring the gift of fermentation.

Contents

Thanks for All the Beer

Thanks to my family, Mom, Dad, Molly, Tim, Katy, Sharon, and to Seung-hee F. Lee. Without your love and support I would not have been able to complete this book

Thanks to all the folks who have shared beer and knowledge: Dave Bonta, who provided invaluable feedback on this book; Steve Breyman; Mike and David Bronner; Sam Calagione, for beer and benevolence; Graham Chennells for letting me brew Zululand's first Wandering Keg; Pat Conway for great beer at Great Lakes; Jim Dorsch for the column in American Brewer; Rob Hanson for homebrewing excellence; Bill Harris for someday investing in my certified fair trade line of beers; Anthony Hayes for being South Africa's most generous homebrewer-host; Eric Hesse for teaching me that good beer isn't for yuppies; Don Hubman; Dave Jeffries (for whom I am sure in heaven there *is* beer); the Jackman family; Andy Myers; Stephen Morris for sharing insight into the book publishing world; Ben Murphy; Peter and Cathy Kiddle; Schumacher College; the Beer Institute; Marie Kere; Jim Parker for all the articles in New Brewer and Zymurgy; Andy Ricker; Amelia Sleyton for better brew for a better world; Chris and Jodi Treter for being the number one beer activists!; Craig and Nicole Tower for hosting the Malian leg of my research; Morgan Wolaver for pioneering organic beer in America; Carol Stoudt; and everyone else who has ever shared a beer with me.

Introduction

B eer is sublime in its simplicity and spiritual in its boundless complexity. It is a democratic drink, but it is also complicit in the tyranny of civilization.

Sometimes beer delivers the best life can offer, while other times it is insufferably disappointing. In this book, I attempt to illuminate some of beer's virtues and to encourage a move away from the corporate-led global industrial capitalism that debases beer-drinking culture.

Fermenting Revolution is not an ordinary "beer book." It is not a technical guide to brewing or a history of brewing, at least not in a strict sense. It's not a beer adventure tale, or an academic study of beer or brewing during a specific period in a particular place. Even though beer is mentioned on virtually every page, this book is about more than beer. It is also about saving the world. But neither is it an "environmental book," per se. For example, it is not about saving the alligator snapping turtle in Mississippi, although I do briefly cover that topic. *Fermenting Revolution*, as its subtitle suggests, is about how to drink beer *and* save the world. Maybe I'm a hopeless victim of the age of multitasking, but I love doing these two things at the same time.

After years of consuming it, beer took me by surprise when I realized it could do more than muddle my consciousness. Beer nurtures and soothes, inspires and excites. It can be creative and fulfilling, both spiritually as well as materially. Beer is diverse and yet unifying. It is the past, the present, and the future. Beer is the nearest I have ever come to finding God.

I realize that last sentence makes me sound like a lunatic, but such is the lot of a zealot.

So as is the wont of a zealot, I will proceed with due hyperbole. More so than ever before, the world today needs beer. In the age of globalization, we humans have become capable of the wholesale destruction of life on Earth. We are in bad need of some life-affirming energy to counterbalance our penchant for mass annihilation. With global climate change dominating the headlines, and ever-worsening prospects of a military debacle pitting America against developing nations and the Middle East, we face questions about the very survival of our species. And as a wise friend once said to me, beer seems to have all the answers.

What this book proposes is a vision of the world where there is greatness in something common. It is a manifesto for building a better world with beer. In short, my thesis is this: beer is good for people and the planet. This book is my attempt to explain how and why.

Fermenting Revolution is filled with meanderings, postulations, proclamations, controversial claims, and radical ideas. Kind of like a good rap session among friends over a couple of beers. Truth be told, I drank more than just a couple of beers while assembling this one-point platform of the Fermenting Revolution. And now that you have it in your hands, I hope we might become friends over the next couple of hundred pages. Consider it our own beer-infused bull session. And feel free to tell me what you think by visiting my Website: <www.beeractivist.com>.

I've tried hard not to weigh you down with loads of scientific mumbo-jumbo, including just enough to establish that my assertions of beer as the planet's best ameliorative are affirmed by so-called "objective" researchers. For the most part though, I've stuck to good, honest, bar-thumping beer proselytizing. Here and there you will find some facts and figures, thrown in to satisfy the scientifically-minded, but rest assured, these are only the most selectively chosen numerical forays.

Much of what you will read here is not original. I really only have one idea, and you've already heard it: beer is saving the world. But mostly what I have chosen to do is tell two well-worn stories as one brand-new tale. There must be thousands of books about beer and many more about saving the world. But I haven't come across a single one yet that combines the two.

I began envisioning this book when I was working for a group called Co-op America. Their mission is to harness the power of the marketplace to promote social justice and ecological sustainability. During my years there I had the great pleasure of working with hundreds of small-business owners who are trying to save the world. Some of their companies have become household names, like Patagonia and Ben and Jerry's, but most are tiny and unknown. Though small, these micro-business entrepreneurs have spawned a whole new generation of "green" and "fair trade" businesses. Sustainable businesses embody the simple idea that business is an endeavor meant to sustain us, not harm us. Business activities should be conducted according to the same ethical and moral principles that guide everyday life. Basically, people and the businesses they build should help people and sustain the planet, not exploit people and damage the Earth. The craft-brewing revolution is part of this sustainable business phenomenon and serves as the inspiration for this book.

There is a distinct gender theme in this narrative: beer used to be "feminine" and now it is "masculine." At the risk of stating the obvious, this is a simplification based on generalizations and I implore you to read it as such. References to gender traits should be read with the caveat that I believe more in the human will than I do in determinism, and I don't think there are many innate differences between men and women, other than some minor biological quirks. Even these, I believe, are less than we make them out to be. Generally speaking, society has invented the roles assigned to women and men, and we have the power to reinvent them if we so choose. So when I characterize women as more cooperative and compassionate, as I do, I do not mean to imply that this is innate, or that it applies to all women (imagine!), nor that it somehow makes women better than men. Neither do I mean to imply that men never display these virtues. But I do think these generalizations stand up to the test of the real world. I don't know exactly why most women are more cooperative than men. Is it nature or nurture? I'm really not sure, although I tend to think it's the latter. Regardless, that is not the debate I intend to address. Rather, "feminine" traits being what they generally are agreed to be, I attempt to make the case that human society would benefit from a stronger feminine influence in beer-drinking culture. I hope this assertion might provoke some debate. And again, I encourage you to get in touch via my Website. We can continue the debate — over beers, I hope.

Directly related to the gender dialogue is the great globalization debate. The masculinization of beer is part of globalization. Beer has inspired mystical transcendence while also unlocking the secrets of nature's bounty. For millennia it has empowered women while nourishing the human body as well as spirit. But beer plays both sides of the fence, and when society shifts toward centralized authority and industrialized production, beer becomes a tool of exploitation and injustice. Organized religion, centralized politics, and industrial capitalism have used beer as a tool of enslavement. Today, beer can be found serving the masters of corporate industrial capitalism as well as engendering community power, a shift toward sustainable production, and a return to healthful drinking. Small brewers are offering solutions while corporate brewers continue blindly down the dead-end path of exponential growth.

The world is undergoing two revolutions, one with bad global corporate beer, and one with good, local beer. To put a new spin on Emma Goldman's famous quote: If I can't drink good beer, it's not my revolution. So here's to all the beer activists fermenting revolution!

Part I

Is, Was, and Ever Shall Beer

CHAPTER 1

In the Beginning, There Was Beer

"Beer, the cause of, and solution to, all of life's problems."
— Homer Simpson

Earth and the Primordial Brew

This is a story about how beer is saving the world, so let's start with how beer and the world were created. The story of beer begins when the sun was born in a burst of nuclear fire about 4.5 billion years ago. A little later the clouds of dust and gas surrounding the sun gathered into the masses we know as planets. Then a couple of dozen million years later, Earth collided and merged with another giant celestial body and formed, more or less, our current planetary home.

About a billion years more and the ideal conditions for life emerged, allowing tiny little life forms resembling blue-green algae to cover the planet. Today, brewers are growing blue-green algae on their brewery wastewater. The algae actually thrive on the "waste" contained in the water, a remarkable and sustainable synergy. When they first appeared on earth, these little life forms needed two things in order to grow: water, and the ability to manage energy, a process called metabolism. The first step in metabolism is fermentation. Water and fermentation are also two of the main elements required to make beer. But now we're skipping ahead by billions of years.

Somewhere around two billion years ago, yeast made the scene. Yeast cells are fungi, which are eukaryotes, the first complex cells to evolve on

Earth. Oddly, human beings are more closely related to yeast than to more seemingly complex organisms, such as corn. By about five million years ago, the original blue-green algae had evolved into, among other things, the earliest ape-like ancestors of humans. It took another million years for them to start walking upright. The earliest finds of barley, a choice brewing grain, come from the Paleolithic period, about two million years ago. About 100,000 years ago people started doing the things we think of as marking the emergence of human civilization. For example, we started creating art and developing language. We're not exactly certain when, but sometime thereafter, people started fermenting alcoholic beverages.

Only a little over 10,000 years ago did people start domesticating crops and building urban civilizations. Barley and wheat were probably the first food crops to be intentionally cultivated by humans on a large scale. They became the staples of the oldest known civilizations, around Mesopotamia in the Fertile Crescent. Not coincidentally, the first physical evidence of beer comes from this same period, though some anthropologists think humans were drinking it much earlier.

A Brewster, a Baker, and a Barley Malt-Maker

It must have been a hard slog through those first four and half billion years, but we finally made it and damn if we weren't thirsty. Our thirst was unequivocally for beer. Anthropologists such as Thomas W. Kavanagh, PhD, now speculate whether the desire for a secure supply of beer might, in fact, have motivated people to intentionally cultivate grain crops and settle down in one place. The earliest known urban civilizations, throughout Eurasia and northern Africa, based their agricultural production on wheat and barley crops that were used to make beer and bread. Places like Mesopotamia (modern-day Iraq) and Egypt emerged as the first known economic superpowers, power that was based largely on their trade in barley and beer. Less is known about northern China, but recent evidence suggests that people in its earliest urban settlements were making beer around this time too. Beer could have been the foundation on which the first settled human civilizations were built.

The main argument for beer as the inspiration for settled agriculture goes like this: Both bread and beer, like most things, were first discovered by accident and then perfected by trial and error. Someone chewed some grains, spit them out, and left them in the rain. The sun then dried them and, voilà, the humble beginnings of bread. As one might imagine, this bread would not have been particularly spectacular in its gustatory appeal. Beer may have been discovered in a similar way, with a small but important twist. Some wild-harvested grain was accidentally sprouted by

> "Alcohol brought us together as an organized society."
> — Gene Ford, The Benefits of Moderate Drinking, summarizing the research of University of Pennsylvania anthropologists Solomon Katz and Mary Voigt.

rain water. Wild yeast proceeded to devour the fermentable sugars inside the grains and thus created the alcoholic beverage we call beer. Matters of taste aside, the alcohol contained in this accidental beverage must have made beer considerably more alluring than a very primitive piece of hard, dry bread. The fermented grains would have provided urban settlements a more digestible source of nutrition than the hard bread, and the alcoholic buzz would have provided a pleasurable experience. It's not hard to imagine that people would have immediately set to work devising ways to produce this beverage more consistently.

It may have taken a few tries, but eventually our ancestors struck on the combination necessary to make this intoxicating porridge. Now they needed to figure out how to ensure a steady supply of fermentable grains so they could make it often and in abundance. Eventually they began intentionally cultivating grain crops and returning to areas where they had established fields. Grain and beer were in huge demand so their value increased, allowing the people who produced them in surplus to establish a sedentary way of life, trading barley and beer for other natural resources like timber and stone for building, and metals like copper that could be fashioned into useful implements. Finally, they settled down into relatively stable beer-drinking lifestyles. With a steady supply of beer in place and non-agrarian trades and crafts emerging, the first urban centers grew. This all sounds like plausible theory, I should think, especially for those readers who, like me, have a strong predilection for beer.

> "The mouth of a perfectly contented man is filled with beer."
> — Egyptian inscription, 2200 BCE.

Funerary statue of a female brewer, circa 2500 BCE, on display in the Egyptian Museum in Cairo. She would have been expected to continue brewing for her household master in the netherworld.

A Civilized Drink

Sumeria, Babylon, and Egypt quite literally grew their complex societies on beer. The earliest evidence of written language comes from the Uruk people in the fourth millennium BCE. This archaic written language was used primarily for counting and measuring important things, like beer (what else?). For example, Hammurabi, King of Babylonia

"Fermentation and civilization are inseparable."
—John Ciardi

in the 18th century BCE, conquered the Sumerians and composed one of the first known legal codes. The Code of Hammurabi enacted, among other laws, rules regarding beer and taverns. It fixed a fair price for beer and required brewers — who, at the time, were all female — to bring disorderly customers to the palace to be summarily punished. Failure to do so was itself punishable by death.

Babylonian city life revolved largely around the temples. The temples employed many laborers and paid these workers with daily rations of barley, oil, and beer. In turn, the deities of the temples required daily libations of beer at their altars. There is even evidence that the temple priestesses were themselves brewsters. However, during the end of the Late Babylonian period, brewsters were forbidden from entering the temples. There is reason to think this was a move by male rulers to eviscerate the power of spiritual brewsters (female brewers) and supplant them with a more hierarchical and domineering male power structure — the beginnings of the patriarchy.

According to Gwendolyn Lieck, in *The Babylonians*, "It has been calculated that the calories supplied by the most standard rations of beer and barley exceed those advocated by the United Nations in modern times … Beer was … nutritious, due to the malt, [which was] rich in vitamins and minerals. Since particular care was taken to ensure that the water used for brewing was clean, it was generally safer to drink beer than the water from nearby canals. As such it contributed substantially to the general well-being of the working population, combining nutritional value with a source of safe liquid, all with the added benefit of the mood-enhancing properties of alcohol." The Babylonians also concocted a variety of beer-soaked foods and created beer-based health tonics to treat ailments. One account explains that the Babylonians brewed at least 20 distinct types of beer.

Beer Money

Barley is the first known form of currency in Babylonia. In fact, most wages were paid in barley and beer. Much of the commerce of ancient civilizations was dominated by private merchants who extracted maximum profit from their trading. As urban civilizations grew, profit-seeking eventually resulted in the overexploitation of natural resources, degrading the environment and impoverishing farmers as the merchant class sought to increase its wealth and power. Women were engaged in this commerce too, dominating the tavern-keeping trade as well as the beer-brewing craft itself. Taverns were already important social places, serving as public meeting places for locals and travelers alike, and providing women with a valuable role in the economy.

Egypt's Great Pyramid of Giza is believed to be the largest one ever constructed. It was built both on and by beer. Pyramid laborers were served beer three times daily. Frequent festivals and holy days provided ample occasions for the lower classes to escape their daily grunt work and enjoy food and beer. The Pharaohs buried inside these mysterious tombs were sent on their way to the afterlife with copious supplies of food and drink. Chief among them was beer. Many of the pyramids and temples contained offering rooms that were literally filled with jugs of beer. But people were afraid these stores would be insufficient to see their inhabitants through all of eternity; they depicted beer offerings on the walls of the tombs, so that the Pharaohs would

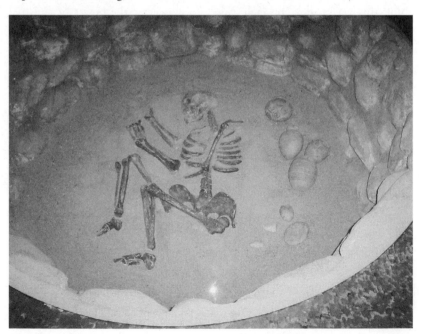

Skeletal remains of an ancient Egyptian buried with beer jug offerings.

never run dry. The Egyptian Book of the Dead extols the virtues of beer, including a lengthy list of varieties like "beer of truth" and "beer of eternity." In fact, most human civilizations have held beer in high regard, considering it healthful, fun, and even sacred.

Here's Spit in Your Beer

One of the great mysteries of agriculture is the emergence of corn, aka maize, as a domesticated crop. What is puzzling is that ear corn, as we know it today, lacks a known non-domesticated predecessor. It's closest relative is *teocintli*, which means grain of the gods in the Nahuatl tongue. But it would have taken millennia of widespread cultivation for ear corn to have evolved from this plant. No one could have known that this practical product would appear in the future, so teocintli's long-term intentional cultivation is difficult to explain. One theory is that the edible ear of kernels was an unintentional byproduct and that it was the starchy stalk that people originally sought. This stalk would have been easily fermented into an alcoholic drink, but it is only speculation to suggest that this was the motivation behind the domestication of corn.

In any case, the cultivation of corn eventually led to the plant we know today with its ear of kernels. And we do know that these kernels have been used for at least a thousand years, and probably much longer, to ferment a beer called *chicha*. *Chicha* is brewed by chewing grains of corn and then spitting them into a pot. Enzymes in saliva break down the corn's starches into fermentable sugars, and wild yeast, or yeast from a previous batch, initiates the fermentation. Just like beer in Egypt, *chicha* was the economic driver behind the success of the Incan Empire about 500 years ago.

People native to the Amazon region and Panama are known to have produced fermented beverages using similar means, chewing up manioc, maize, or plantains, spitting it into pots, and fermenting the results into a drink called *cauim*. Then there is the Hohokam civilization of the desert Southwest, built around fermentable agave plantations in one of the driest regions of the Earth ever to support large-scale agriculture and urban life. The plant and the utensils used for fermenting *pulque* and distilling mescal were central elements in Mesoamerican iconography and the worship of a female deity named Mayahuel. Alcoholic agave drinks were incorporated into many rituals and consumption was restricted to designated occasions and individuals.

Gaia

These complex ancient civilizations are remarkable in themselves, and the fact that they brewed beer (and other fermented drinks) is even more intriguing. But the simple fact that life on Earth exists at all, and that it *continues* to exist, is even more stunning. Every ancient civilization was eventually destroyed. Babylon crumbled. Ancient Egypt disappeared. Rome collapsed. What went wrong and how did humans manage to pull through? Basically, nature's systems were overburdened by human demands, and power became too consolidated. This combination of environmental devastation and unjust rule eventually unraveled every great society. During the Industrial Age this cycle was repeated and social movements like Communism and Anarchism emerged as countervailing forces against hierarchical aristocracies. For the moment, democracy provides some hope that we may be able to avoid a repeat of the hubris that brought down earlier societies, but only time will tell — after all, ancient Greece and Rome were purportedly democratic too. The contemporary sustainability movement is striving to steer society away from environmental disaster. If history is any indication, the planet will manage to survive, but the question is how well Homo sapiens will fare.

Modern experts like atmospheric scientist James Lovelock and microbiologist Lynn Margulis have explained how the planet and the living things on it work together to maintain conditions that are conducive to life. This theory, called the Gaia Hypothesis, helps explain how life persists on Earth. In 1969, Lovelock hypothesized that Earth acts something like a living organism, with its living and nonliving components acting in concert to create an environment that continues to be suitable for life.

In this Gaia postulation, life is no mere accident, nor is it a passenger on the planet. Life and the material environment evolve together. The long-term chemical stability of Earth is regulated by the collective activity of life on the planet. When first hypothesized, these notions were considered radical and were strongly opposed by the scientific establishment. For one thing, they seemed to contradict Darwinian evolution. Lovelock has since shown how the two theories are compatible and today Gaia is widely accepted in the scientific community, inspiring new research around the world, helping especially in understanding climate change.

Gaia theorists hold that Earth's surface environment is a self-regulating system, composed of all living organisms, the atmosphere, oceans, and surface rocks, which sustains conditions favorable for life. It postulates the evolution of life and the evolution of Earth's surface and atmosphere as a single process, not separate processes as taught in biology and geology. Organisms evolve by a process of natural selection, but in Gaia they do not merely adapt to the environment, they change it. Humans are clearly changing the atmosphere, the climate, and the land surfaces, but other organisms, mostly microscopic, have in the past made changes that were even more drastic. The appearance of oxygen in the air two billion years ago is but one of them.

Gaia theory has proven critical in understanding the process of global climate change and has prompted discoveries that may help curb its progress. One important implication of Gaia is that, overall, individual life forms adapt toward the benefit of life in general, collectively maintaining a hospitable atmosphere for life's own continuation. Gaia does not contradict the Darwinian survival-of-the-fittest theory, but serves as an extension of it, somewhat as relativity did for Newtonian physics.

What About the Beer?

At this point, you must be wondering what all this has to do with beer. In layman's terms, Gaia suggests that Earth continuously calibrates its systems to maintain life. Humans are doing dangerous things to lots of those systems, like the ozone layer, the climate, the oceans, the soil, and the air. As the planet makes adjustments in order to maintain favorable conditions for life, it may well "adjust" humans right out of the equation. This might seem like just desserts, since our own irresponsible behavior is creating the conditions unfavorable to our own continued survival. But let's get to the beer now.

As Homer Simpson once said, "Beer is the cause of and solution to all of life's problems." And in a way he is right. If beer created urban society, which then led to large-scale exploitation of nature, which may now be leading us toward our own extinction, then beer must bear some of the blame. On the other hand, beer could be part of the solution. Many brewers and beer drinkers are now helping to reverse, or at least slow down, the negative trends associated with our modern consumer lifestyles, and innovating sustainable ways of living. And that, beer-drinking Earthlings, is the topic of this book.

Beer Is Divine

"In heaven there is no beer. That's why we drink it here."
— German-American drinking song

Some folks believe that one day God will come down from the heavens and save the world. The book in your hands is about how beer is already doing just that. But the two ideas — god and beer — are actually connected quite intricately. I do realize that religion is one of the deadly no-no's when it comes to friendly beer talk, but surely an exception can be made for the religion of beer.

You have already read a scientific version of how beer and the planet got here. We all know that people of certain religious persuasions have other ideas about how the planet was created, but what about all the religious stories that explain the creation of beer? There are many, and to my beer-biased mind they are a bit less troublesome than the religious controversies regarding the creation of the world.

"From man's sweat and God's love, beer came into the world."
— Saint Arnold, Bishop of Metz

Drink the Beer, Destiny of the Land

Inebriation in general, and beer drinking in particular, has been a core tradition in religions around the world throughout much of history. As we saw in the opening chapter, Sumerians were the first humans known to build an urban civilization. Since their society was profoundly dependent on beer, it is not surprising that beer was also central to their spiritual beliefs. The foundation story for the Sumerians and the Babylonians was the epic of Gilgamesh. In it, there is a wild man named Enkidu who lived with the beasts, and is thought to be a literary representation of early nomadic man. The epic relates how Enkidu attained self-awareness by drinking beer, eating bread, and having sex. By doing so, he left the wild behind, became human, and attained a cultured state. Later in the epic, Enkidu's sometime-nemesis, sometime-compatriot Gilgamesh meets Siduri, a fermentation goddess who tries to dissuade him from seeking immortality, urging him instead to enjoy the pleasures of human life.

Sumerians came to believe that their main purpose in life was to worship and provide for the gods — not hard to understand why, since the gods

Enkidu knew nothing
Of eating bread,
Of drinking beer.
He had never learned.
The harlot made her voice
    heard
And spoke to Enkidu,
"Eat the food, Enkidu,
The symbol of life.
Drink the beer, destiny of the
    land."
Enkidu ate the bread
Until he had had enough.
He drank the beer,
Seven whole jars,
Relaxed, felt joyful.
His heart rejoiced,

His face beamed,
He smeared himself with oil
His body was hairy.
He anointed himself with oil
And became like any man,
Put on clothes.
He was like a warrior,
Took his weapon,
Fought with lions.
The shepherds could rest at
    night;
He beat off wolves,
Drove off lions.
The older herdsmen lay down;
Enkidu was their guard,
A man awake.

— The Epic of Gilgamesh, translated by N.K. Sandars,
Penguin Books, 1972

gave them beer. Note the line in the epic about beer being the destiny of the land. Is this supporting evidence that the purpose of settled agriculture was to produce beer? In any case, the Sumerians knew beer was good and wanted to ensure the continued happiness of the gods and goddesses so that they would continue providing them with beer. As a symbol of appreciation, the gods required offerings of food and beer for their own refreshment. Enki was the god of water, and not only was he believed to have saved the human race from the great flood (an early source for the story of Noah), but he was also a formidable beer drinker. One of his daughters was Ninkasi, to whom a hymn was inscribed on clay tablets nearly four thousand years ago. The Hymn to Ninkasi praises her beer-making ability and describes her method of brewing, making her the earliest known beer goddess.

The Mistress of Inebriety Without End

The myth of the great civilizing Egyptian god Osiris credits him with teaching humans to brew beer. Since Pharaohs were considered both human and divine, it seems appropriate that they were sent off with large caches of beer. Tomb paintings depict guests at banquets drinking to the point of disgorging and then being carried home.

Sekhmet was an ancient Egyptian goddess of beer, and was the daughter of the supreme sun god Ra, the divine ruler of Upper Egypt. In one mythic tale, Ra became angry with the people of Lower Egypt for their lack of worshipfulness and sent Sekhmet to punish them for three days. As she began her slaughter, Sekhmet grew bloodthirsty and nearly wiped out the entire human race in one day. Ra saw that his daughter had gone too far and tried to stop her. When she ignored his command to cease the rampage, Ra resorted to some clever beer-drinking chicanery. He mixed pomegranate juice with a vast lake of beer so that it resembled blood. Sekhmet saw this great goblet of blood and guzzled it down, becoming so drunk that she fell asleep for two days, allowing her three-day limit to expire and thus sparing the rest of humanity. After this, Sekhmet transformed into the loving, kind, and gentle goddess Hathor who was thenceforth worshipped as the Egyptian goddess of beer and called the Lady of Drunkenness. She also symbolized love and destruction and was a patron of dance and music. As part of their spiritual practice, her worshipers got drunk on beer.

It is said that Hathor greeted the souls of the dead in the underworld, and proffered them refreshments of food and drink. A hymn to Hathor calls

Beer goddess poetry is a literary niche whose popularity has declined somewhat in recent centuries but was all the rage with the ancients. The Hymn to Ninkasi, inscribed on a nineteenth-century BCE tablet, contains praise for the goddess of beer and includes detailed brewing procedures.

Hymn to Ninkasi
Borne of the flowing water ... [text missing in original]
Tenderly cared for by the Ninhursag,
Borne of the flowing water ... [text missing in original]
Tenderly cared for by the Ninhursag,

Having founded your town by the sacred lake,
She finished its great walls for you,
Ninkasi, having founded your town by the sacred lake,
She finished its great walls for you.

Your father is Enki, Lord Nidimmud,
Your mother is Ninti, the queen of the sacred lake,
Ninkasi, Your father is Enki, Lord Nidimmud,
Your mother is Ninti, the queen of the sacred lake.

You are the one who handles the dough, [and] with a big shovel,
Mixing in a pit, the bappir* with sweet aromatics,
Ninkasi, You are the one who handles the dough, [and] with a big shovel,
Mixing in a pit, the bappir with [date]-honey.

You are the one who bakes the bappir in the big oven,
Puts in order the piles of hulled grains,
Ninkasi, you are the one who bakes the bappir in the big oven,
Puts in order the piles of hulled grains,

You are the one who waters the malt set on the ground,
The noble dogs keep away even the potentates,

Ninkasi, you are the one who waters the malt set on the ground,
The noble dogs keep away even the potentates.

You are the one who soaks the malt in a jar
The waves rise, the waves fall.
Ninkasi, you are the one who soaks the malt in a jar,
The waves rise, the waves fall.

You are the one who spreads the cooked mash on large reed mats,
Coolness overcomes.
Ninkasi, you are the one who spreads the cooked mash on large reed mats,
Coolness overcomes.

You are the one who holds with both hands the great sweet wort,
Brewing it with honey and wine.
Ninkasi, you are the one who holds with both hands the great sweet wort,
Brewing it with honey and wine.

You [...] the sweet wort to the vessel
Ninkasi, [...] You [...] the sweet wort to the vessel

You place the fermenting vat, which makes a pleasant sound,
Appropriately on top of a large collector vat.
Ninkasi, you place the fermenting vat, which makes a pleasant sound,
Appropriately on top of a large collector vat.

It is you who pour out the filtered beer of the collector vat;
It is like the onrush of the Tigris and the Euphrates.
Ninkasi, it is you who pour out the filtered beer of the collector vat;
It is like the onrush of the Tigris and the Euphrates.

* Bappir is a type of bread made from malted barley.

Carved relief depicting drink offerings to the god Horus, on wall of the Kom Ombo Temple. Horus was sometimes worshipped as the husband of Hathor, goddess of beer.

her the Mistress of Jubilation, the Queen of the Dance, the Mistress of Music, and the Mistress of Inebriety Without End. The worship of Hathor was so popular that more festivals were dedicated to her honor than any other Egyptian deity, and more children were named after this goddess than any other.

Beer is still consumed on the banks of the Nile River, but mostly on tourist cruise ships. Rumor suggests that the odd pot of homebrewed date beer may still be found among Egypt's less fundamentalist rural population. The label on this bottle of beer depicts the step pyramid of King Zoser at Sakkara, in Memphis, Egypt. It is believed to be the first pyramid ever built and the oldest existing stone structure in Egypt, dating from at least 2600 BCE. The Sakkara complex also includes storehouses that were once filled with beer and other funerary offerings.

Juiced Jews and Party Crashers for Christ

The ancient Judeo-Christian tradition also features alcohol prominently in its rituals. On Friday evenings Jews celebrate Shabbat. This practice starts with a family meal that recalls the Jews' exodus from slavery in Egypt. Before the meal begins, a cup of wine is sanctified with the words: "Blessed is the name of the Lord, King of the Universe, who has given us the fruit of the vine," and everyone has a taste. This ancient drinking tradition continues to this very day at Jewish tables around the globe. Though it is wine that currently plays the starring role in this ceremony, beer also has a place in Hebrew tradition.

According to Pete Slosberg, founder of Pete's Brewing Company, makers of the Pete's Wicked line of beers, rabbinical tradition says that Hebrews kept themselves free from leprosy during their captivity in Babylon by drinking "siceram veprium id est, ex lupulis confectam," that is, a strong drink made with herbs. Babylonians were in fact known to make a grain-based alcoholic drink containing myrrh and/or frankincense, coriander, and honey as a tonic for treating or preventing leprosy. Beer is inherently kosher, but Jews also have at least one brewery specifically marketing to their niche, called Shmaltz Brewing, located in New York. Shmaltz produces He'Brew, the Chosen Beer; Genesis Ale, Our First Creation; Messiah Bold, The Beer You've Been Waiting For; and Miraculous Jewbilation, a Most Extreme Chanukah Beer.

Noah and the Brews Cruise

In his book *Noah's Ark and the Ziusudra Epic*, author Robert Best traces the origins of the Noah's Ark flood myth. He claims unambiguously that the ark was actually a commercial barge filled with grain and beer. He also posits that Noah and his family members might have each drunk three quarts of beer per day while living on the boat. This may be a startling revelation for readers who adhere to the Judeo-Christian tradition, but this news is nothing compared to the next surprise regarding the drinking habits of Jesus.

Jesus and the Last Beer Dinner

There has been long and emotional debate about whether Jesus drank alcoholic wine or mere grape juice. This debate is based solely on misconstruing the Aramaic and Greek terms used for various alcoholic beverages. The scientific evidence for Jews, including Jesus, drinking alcoholic beverages is well documented, and is neatly summarized in the book *God Gave Wine*, by Kenneth L. Gentry, Jr.

Though the debate about whether Jesus drank alcohol or not is decidedly closed, another debate is only just beginning, which is whether Jesus' beverage of choice was wine at all, or if it was in fact a grain-based fermentation — that is to say, beer. Jesus probably drank beer at the last supper. In fact, it is possible, even probable, that his very first miracle (or shall we call it a *beericle?*) was to turn water into beer, not wine, as most people think. The debate about what he might have drunk on particular occasions boils down to questions of translation. Just as a few fringe modern translators insist on translating wine as grape juice, ancient translators made mistakes too, both intentional and accidental, i.e. some translators choose words to suit their own agendas.

The central translation issue regarding beer in the Bible is the term "strong drink." Strong drink likely referred to a grain-based fermentation, but in the northern and eastern Mediterranean societies where the Bible underwent its earliest iterations, wine was already considered an upper-class quaff, whereas beer was affordable to commoners. Early Christian Bible translators rendered Aramaic into Greek, and they would have been predisposed to shine the most complimentary of lights on Jesus. Hospitality was highly valued in Mediterranean society, and so they would have wanted to portray Jesus as a generous host. Perhaps they would have presumed to take poetic license and translate "strong drink" as wine rather than beer in cases like the Last Supper and the wedding feast in Canaan. Yet Jesus was a carpenter, a commoner who made a point of associating with ordinary folk like fishermen and prostitutes. He even held forth against the upper crust, reproving the corrupt religious establishment and the wealthy at every turn. As he is quoted in Matthew, "It is easier for a camel to go through the eye of a needle than for a rich man to enter the kingdom of God." Viewed in this light, it seems odd that Jesus would shun beer, the common beverage, and opt for a more expensive and pretentious tipple like wine. Beer was far more commonly consumed at this time, partly because it was inexpensive compared to wine. Might Jesus' "strong drink" have been beer and not wine? Who knows how the debate about the original communion beverage will conclude? In any case, I rather like the image of Jesus as a long-haired, beer-drinking rebel, welcome to crash any party so long as he was willing to conjure a bottomless supply of beer. Rock on, Rock of Ages!

High in the Andes

Not long after Jesus championed the drinking of alcohol as a means of communing with the Supreme Being, another society was also holding beer on high, both literally and spiritually. In the 1990s, Patrick Ryan Williams, archaeologist and curator of anthropology at the Field Museum, began excavating Cerro Baul, a 1,400-year-old city occupied by the Wari Empire, a pre-Incan civilization situated 8,000 feet high in the Peruvian Andes.

"We found what may be the oldest large-scale brewery in the Andes. Our analyses indicate that this specialty brew was a high-class affair. The site was very special to [the Wari]," Williams explains. Donna Nash, an adjunct curator at the Field Museum and part of the study team, claims further that "the brewers were not only women, but elite women." According to Williams,

"The remnants of Cerro Baúl were preserved in a unique way," because the Wari "wanted to make sure the space wasn't used in the same fashion again. Before the Wari abandoned the site, they set it ablaze. After the fire, the Wari placed semiprecious stones and shell-beaded necklaces atop the embers, symbolizing the site's sacredness to their culture." This recent discovery seems to have all the makings of yet another story of divine feminine fermentation.

Drinks Are On the House (of the Lord)

Back in the Mediterranean, we find further proof of the beer-friendly Judeo-Christian god in Isaiah 55:1, where intoxicating beverages are touted as an inalienable human right: "Ho everyone that thirsts, come ye to the waters, and he that has no money; come ye, buy, and eat; yea come, buy wine and milk without money and without price."

> "The selling of bad beer is a crime against Christian love."
> — 13th Century Law, City of Augsburg, Germany

The history of the Catholic Church is soaked in beer. In the early centuries after Christ, brewing became firmly rooted within the Church. As Martyn Cornell explains in *Beer, The Story of the Pint*, "Monastic brewing was universal…. [T]here would not have been a monastery in Britain or Ireland without its brewery to sustain the brothers." In fact, it is believed that the oldest continuously operated brewery in the world is north of Munich at Weihenstephan where this monastery's Christian Brothers were granted brewing rights by the Church in 1040.

Monks and nuns during these times were required to be self-sufficient, which included growing their own brewing ingredients and making their own beer. Governed by principles of charity, these Christian Brothers and Sisters were obliged to be generous with bread, beer, and lodging for pilgrims. Men and women of the cloth were also some of the few educated people of their times. They could read and write and were versed in science, such as it was during the Middle Ages. This combination of circumstances produced remarkable achievements in brewing technology, many of which were recorded in written documents. The most profound development was the utilization of hops cones in beer. St. Hildegard of Bingen, in the twelfth century, was the first to record the results of experimental research on brewing with hops.

Demand for beer from churches grew as pilgrimages became more popular, and eventually monasteries developed strong commercial interests in the beer trade. They were, after all, ideally positioned within the hospitality industry. Their ingredients and labor were free or very cheap, and they were exempt from taxation. Brewing became, in effect, a Church monopoly.

> "Over time, beer's official role in religion diminished, but unofficially it flourished in a ritual performed to ward off evil spirits and ensure good health — the toast."
>
> — Gregg Smith, *Beer Drinker's Bible*

Drunken German Stages Protest, Starts New Religion

One of the great myths of Christianity is that the instigators of the Reformation opposed alcohol use. Both John Calvin and Martin Luther were in fact great drinkers and heartily advocated on behalf of both beer and wine. Martin Luther was an Augustinian monk who nailed his famous 95 Theses to the door of Castle Church, listing his grievances against papal rules. One of his main complaints concerned the restriction against the lay public consuming the Eucharist, i.e., bread and wine in which Jesus Christ was believed to be explicitly present. Pope Leo X wrote Luther off as "a drunken German" who "when sober will change his mind." Leo turned out to be wrong about the latter but right about the former, for if Church corruption was the first thing on Martin Luther's mind, beer was probably the second.

It was beer that sustained him during the two most important days of his life: his excommunication trial, and his wedding. In 1521, Duke Erich I of Brunswick gave Martin a cask of Einbecker beer to help him through his ordeal before the Diet of Worms (I'd be drinking lots of beer too if my diet consisted of worms), the court before which he had to defend his stance against the Pope. Luther was probably buttressed by this very beer on the day this religious court expelled him from the Church. Was Luther drunkenly belligerent, talking trash about the Pope and telling the authorities where to go? Perhaps we'll never know, but his spirited performance did manage to earn him excommunication, and thus kick-started the Reformation.

Four years later, Luther married Katharina of Bora, a brewster and former nun. Knowing his taste in beer, the town of Wittenberg gave him a cask of Einbecker for the occasion. As a nun, Katharina had been trained in brewing at the convent of Nimptschen, near the Saxon town of Grimma. In 1535,

> "But while I sat and drank beer with Philip and Amsdorf, God dealt the papacy a mighty blow."
>
> — Martin Luther

Luther declared, " I much rather drink a tankard of ale against the devil so that I can despise him." As an old man, he wrote, "We old folks have to find our cushions and pillows in our tankards. Strong beer is the milk of the old."

Calvin the Carouser

John Calvin, another key figure in the medieval reformation of the Church, was no less explicit about his feelings toward alcohol and its divine origins. "Nature would certainly be satisfied with water to drink," Calvin wrote in his *Commentary on Psalms*, "and therefore the addition of wine is owing to God's superabundant liberality ... It is permissible to use wine not only for necessity, but also to make us merry." In another work, *Institutes of the Christian Religion*, the reformer noted that, "We are nowhere forbidden to laugh, or to be satisfied with food, or to annex new possessions to those already enjoyed by ourselves or our ancestors, or to be delighted with music, or to drink wine."

Biblical references to the goodness of drink abound. God commanded alcohol to be proffered to Him as a drink offering in Numbers 28:7. God told the Israelites they may drink of "strong drink" during the tithe feast in Deuteronomy 14:22–26. And according to the Gospel of John, Chapter 2, verses 7–11, Jesus' first miracle after the incarnation was to make alcohol.

His apostles followed their leader's example, as alleged in Acts 2:13 when they got drunk from "new wine" on Pentecost. Proverbs 9:1–5, contains this advice: "Wisdom hath kindled her house ... she hath mingled her wine; she hath also furnished her table ... Come, eat of my bread, and drink of the wine which I have mingled. Forsake the foolish and go in the way of understanding." Mingled wine, it should be noted, means mingled with herbs and spices, not with water, and was a practice intended to increase the wine's potency. The line about "understanding" seems to imply that achieving a state of drunkenness draws one nearer to the Divine. An admonishment against diluted wine appears in Isaiah 1:22: "How is the faithful city become an harlot! ... Thy silver is become dross, thy wine mixed with water!"

To this day, Catholics acknowledge the heavenly origin of alcohol every time a priest performs transubstantiation — the conversion of alcohol into the actual blood of Christ, thus directly equating alcohol and God. Although today wine is used in this ceremony, the ritual is based on the Last Supper, which, as discussed earlier, may have in fact been a beer dinner, rather than a wine tasting.

Calvin's attitude toward alcohol was continued in the New World where the Puritan drink ethic is best captured in the words of minister Increase Mather who preached that, "Drink is in itself a good creature of God, and to be received with thankfulness, but the abuse of drink is from Satan." The term "puritanical" has become associated with prohibition, yet Puritanism was an offshoot of the teachings of Luther and Calvin, and Puritans were ardent beer drinkers, not teetotalers. The abstemious among them were a contentious few and were notable precisely because their views on drinking stood in stark contrast to the norm. Believing alcohol to be a gift from God, Puritans drank with both gusto and reverence.

Holy Hooch for Hindus

Some Hindus use alcohol, as well as drugs, to enhance inward spiritual vision. Mead, an alcohol produced by fermenting honey, makes numerous appearances in the holy Rig Veda. Speculation is that the intoxicating drink called soma was in fact mead. Take this verse from the first book of the Rig Veda: "Adored, the strengtheners of Law, unite them, Agni, with their Dames: Make them drink meath, O bright of tongue." Linguists suggest that meath is a variation of the word from which our modern "mead" is derived. It is also mentioned in several places in the Sama Veda, another of the four holy Vedas. The date when these books were compiled is unknown, but it is surmised they came about sometime soon after the Aryans arrived in India around the end of the third millennium BCE. Mead seems to have serious religious significance to the Hindus of that time and given that soma was a drink of their gods, perhaps mead was as well. This verse shows again that mead was found in that ancient culture: "Soma, while thou art cleansed, most dear and watchful in the sheep's long wool, most like to Angiras! thou hast become a sage. Sprinkle our sacrifice with mead!"

Beer for Buddha

Buddhism's fifth moral Precept encourages abstention from intoxicating drink and drugs. However, the emphasis is avoiding intoxication rather than consumption, and an explicit exemption is made for intoxicants taken as healthful medicines. The health benefits of moderate beer-drinking are covered in depth in Chapter 14, but regarding Buddhism, consider a few anecdotal suggestions that moderate beer-drinking may be okay. The classic image of the round-bellied Buddha looks curiously similar to the archetypal image of a German brewmaster, both of which suggest a robust healthful- ness. Prominent Buddhists have openly consumed beer, and Tibetan Buddhists are known for brewing a barley-based beer called *chang*.

> "If you ever reach total enlightenment while you're drinking a beer, I bet it makes beer shoot out your nose."
> — From a "Deep Thoughts" postcard by comedy writer Jack Handey

The most amusing, and per- haps most illustrative of the Buddhist approach, is a story about the Dalai Lama addressing a crowd in England. According to an eye-witness account related to me personally, an audi- ence member asked one of the Dalai Lama's monks how to prac- tice "visualizing god." His response was that one should "imagine whatever is most holy to them. So, Buddhists should imagine the Buddha; Christians, the image of Jesus; and Irish Catholics, the icon of Mary, or else a pint of Guinness, or a pint of Guinness in the shape of Mary."

Ale for Allah

Among the major religions of the world, Islam is unique in its prohibition of alcohol. This is a difficult nut for the beer historian to crack. The fact that Islam emerged from the very bosom of humanity's first beer-drinking civi- lization may hold a clue. Alcohol consumption was pervasive throughout the Middle East and may have reached extreme levels in some cases. Perhaps the Islamic prohibition of alcohol was a radical response to overindulgence, just as America's own prohibition movement grew in response to the increasing instances of alcohol abuse in 19th century industrializing nations. Or perhaps it was a way for the first nomadic, pastoralist Muslims to differentiate them- selves from the "decadent" urbanites with whom they sometimes clashed. Whatever the causes, Islam is a belief system noteworthy for its proscription of alcohol consumption.

American Prohibition misfired when it aimed its sights on alcohol rather than on the social breakdown precipitated by industrialization, west- ern expansionism, and mass migrations. Perhaps there were similar social causes for this Middle Eastern over-reaction to alcohol abuse. Studies of the social and economic root causes of Islamic prohibition are rare. Most accounts simply refer to the prohibitory lines in the Koran, without any in-depth analysis of the factors that may have led to such an extreme position. Sources available on the subject are mostly religious and prone to hyperbole, such as the one written by Dr. Zakir Naik in the March 1999 issue of *Islamic Voice*, which recalls the platitudes of American prohibitionist preachers around the turn of the last century:

> Alcohol has been the scourge of human society since time imme-morial. It continues to cost countless human lives, and causes terrible misery to millions throughout the world. Alcohol is the root cause of several problems facing society. The statistics of soaring crime rates, increasing instances of mental illnesses and millions of broken homes throughout the world bear mute testi-mony to the destructive power of alcohol.

The relevant verses from the Koran show how Islam prohibited alcohol in stages, just like the American Prohibition movement. Alcohol was embraced at first and considered at least partially beneficial. But gradually this turned to temperance and eventually to outright prohibition:

> They ask thee concerning wine and gambling. Say: in them is great sin and some profit for people: But the sin is greater than the profit ... Chapter 2, verse 219.
>
> Oh you who believe! Approach not prayers in a state of intoxication until you can understand all that you say ... Chapter 4, verse 43.
>
> Oh you who believe! Truly intoxicants and gambling and divination by arrows are an abomination, of Satan's doing: avoid it in order that you may be successful. Chapter 5, verse 90.

As reported by al-Bukhari, the Prophet said, "Every intoxicating sub-stance is *haram* (prohibited)." And as narrated by at-Tirmidhi, A'ishah said: "The Messenger of Allah said: 'Every intoxicating substance is *haram*, and whatever intoxicates in large amounts, a handful of it is *haram*.'"

There are notable exceptions within Islam to this prohibition. From the Horn of Africa, through the North and to the West, Africans were among the first people to embrace Islam, and yet many in the region continue the practice of millet-based beer brewing. Muslim and non-Muslim alike, people throughout countries such as Burkina Faso, Mali, and Senegal still brew millet and sorghum beers. Local Muslim leaders are slow to criticize the practice, tending to view it as part of their African heritage rather than as contradictory to Islam.

Ironically, it may have been Arab Muslim alchemists who discovered the art and craft of distillation around 800 CE. These alchemists sought to capture the "spirit" of wine, an ingredient seemingly responsible for inducing a sense of vigor, youth, and buoyant health in the imbiber. A number of them documented their experiments, including Jabir ibn Hayyan, who succeeded in inventing the alembic still, a technology that facilitates easy distillation. According to Chauncy D. Leake in *Alcoholic Beverages in Clinical Medicine*, since the "spirit" of the wine was removed in an invisible state, it was called alcohol, an Arabic word meaning "finely divided spirit," a term which itself invokes the divine.

Beer God Is Dead

Eventually, the control of alcohol shifted to the secular domain. For millennia, stressing the religious aspects of drinking helped to keep drunkenness within accepted social boundaries, especially since the strongest brews were reserved for religious festivals and other events associated with worship. As Gene Ford describes in the *The Benefits of Moderate Drinking*, "The Stone Age civilizations solved the problem of excessive drinking by incorporating alcohol into religious and social practices. They worshipped together and drank together to make alcohol a unifying rather than a divisive element."

Any religion with mandatory beer-drinking rituals would seem to have at least one redeeming characteristic. But European nobility eventually grew to resent the Church's control over beer and brewing and began asserting their own dominion over them. Incidents of struggle for secular control of beer appear as early as 4,000 years ago when the Beaker Folk tried to wrest brewing from their religious heads. The Beaker people were so named because of the beaker-shaped drinking vessels associated with their culture. They were spread widely across Europe and the British Isles and are thought to have reserved beer drinking for a prestigious upper class of cult members.

This transition of alcohol from the sacred to the secular occurred in Mesopotamia during the late Babylonian period, and then again with the

Beaker folk in Western Europe around 2400 BCE. By the end of the first millennium CE, the transition was underway all across Europe and the transfer was nearly complete by the end of the Middle Ages. Thenceforth, the religious trappings of drinking would forever take a back seat to the new dominant forces in society: science, industry, and capitalism. But during this long European period of transition, religious mythos appeared and evolved around the western world linking beer directly with the Divine.

CHAPTER 3

The Beer Pantheon

Ninkasi, the Sumerian beer goddess whose story was presented in the preceding chapter, may be the first beer deity on record, but she certainly was not the last. The history of religion is rife with immortal beer drinkers all the way up until the time brewing was taken over by industrialist fat cats. Mesopotamian deities are routinely and intricately linked with the very creation of human society. Egyptian mythos similarly credits the most powerful supernatural beings with all things related to beer, fertility, and agriculture. Likewise, the roots of Judaism and Christianity — and therefore Islam as well — connect alcohol directly with the Divine. Beer so pervades the human notion of spirituality that modern America is practically unique in its ambivalent, sometimes hostile, attitudes toward beer and alcohol in general. Ancient Western and Middle Eastern religious beer culture eventually fell prey to industrialization, and Americans developed dangerously contradictory views on alcohol. To fix this, we must recover a suitably reverent attitude towards beer. To that end, let us peer back through the canon of the High Powers of Beer. Our chronicle of "sbeerituality" picks up in Egypt, the dominant seat of human civilization as Sumeria and Babylon began their declines.

The Divine Drinking Duo
Isis was first a Nubian earth-fertility goddess, whose name meant Queen of the Flesh. She was later adopted by the Egyptians who called her the Mother of all Goddesses, the Lady of Green Crops and the Lady of Beer. This last name,

according to Egyptian myth, came because she gifted humanity with the art and science of beer making. Her mythology later merged with Hathor's (who is herself thought to have become the Greek goddess Aphrodite), the famous Lady of Drunkenness who would have wiped out the entire human race had it not been for an extended beer-drinking binge — it appears beer not only created civilization, but saved it as well. Isis continues to be praised for her generosity with beer. A statue of her was recently erected at the Cameron Mews housing development in the famous English brewing city of Burton. Perhaps not coincidentally, the development itself is located on the site of the former Heritage Brewery and Goat Maltings.

Osiris was the husband of Isis and is equally credited with providing humans with the divine gift of beer. With a couple of supreme beer deities at the helm of their civilization, it is no wonder beer was included as part of the traditional Egyptian holy offering formula: "O you who give bread and beer to beneficent souls in the house of Osiris …" According to the Book of the Dead, the beer of Osiris was said to make the drinker immortal. In the Pyramid Text of Teta, Osiris Teta "receives thy bread which decayeth not, and thy beer which perisheth not." In the Text of Pepi II, the aspirant prays for "thy bread of eternity, and thy beer of everlastingness."

The term "zythum" or "zythem" was a word for beer commonly attributed to the Egyptians, but it actually has its origin in later Greek beer mythology. Demeter was the Greek goddess of grain and fertility, called the "Barley-mother." Ceres was a similar Roman Earth goddess, whose name provides the root of *Saccharomyces cerevisia*, the scientific name for ale yeast. It is also the root of "cervesa," the Latin word for beer. The term cereal, e.g., barley and wheat, is also derived from Ceres. Demeter was the older sister of Zeus, the Greek uber-god who is credited with the discovery of barley-based beer. Thus the Greeks called beer "zythos," perhaps after the supreme god whom they believed brought it into being.

Dionysus was the son of Zeus, and like most gods had many names. As Oeneus, he was God of the wine press, and as Liknites he was the one who winnowed the grain from the chaff, a reference to brewing technique. In general, he represented the beneficial social attributes of alcohol, as he was also worshipped as the promoter of civilization, law, peace, relaxation, and freedom from worry, and was the patron deity of agriculture and theater. Another form of Dionysus, worshipped by the Phrygians, was Sabazius, a wild, bearded God of fertility, snakes, and ritual ecstasy, whose followers attained union with him by drinking a beer called seba. Romans called him Bacchus and worshipped this party god in secret rites called the Bacchanalia. These rites were drunken festivals that probably began around 200 BCE, and were at first held in secret and attended only by women. Women were responsible for beer brewing at the time so perhaps they were trying to protect the secrets of their craft. Or maybe it was just a formalization of the "girls' night out." Bacchus wore a circlet of leaves around his head, purportedly as a means of preventing hangovers. Some refer to this practice as the beginning of the royal tradition of crown-wearing. Was the royal crown really a symbol of imperial immunity to hangovers?

A color painting depicting beer and food offerings, on the wall of the rock-hewn tomb of a noble, buried on Elephantine Island in Aswan, Egypt, dating to the 23rd century BCE.

Valhalla, Great Mead Hall in the Sky

To explain the creation of mead (more precisely braggot, which is a combination of grain and honey, i.e., a beer-mead cocktail), Norse mythology tells of two races of gods who ended a great war. At the peace conference members of both sides sealed their accord by spitting into a vessel, giving rise to a wise man named Kvasir. Kvasir's knowledge was envied by a race of dwarfs, who murdered him and in an attempt to steal his intelligence collected his blood in an iron kettle. They mixed honey with his blood and produced an intoxicating beverage called the Mead of Poetry.

The Norse paradise, called Valhalla, was no less than a giant mead ale house with 540 doors where the Viking god Woden entertained the dead with war stories over flagons of drink. This ale streamed from the udders of a mythic goat named Heidrun, whose endless bounty of beer kept the divine company in a constant state of bliss.

The ancient Finnish people credited the birth of beer to the efforts of three women preparing for a wedding feast. Osmotar, Kapo and Kalevatar all labored to produce the world's first beer, but their efforts fell flat along with the beer. Only when Kalevatar combined saliva from a bear's mouth with wild honey did the beer foam and the gift of ale come into the world of men. From the Kalevala, the ancient Finnish account of the creation of the world, we can see the importance of ale in human society. In this early tale of the origin of all things, the creation of ale is given twice the narrative space that is devoted to the creation of the world.

May the Beer Saints Be Praised

It was during the decline of the Roman Empire that Jesus of Nazareth made the scene and spawned a prolific Age of Beer Saints. The tour guide at the St. Arnold brewery in Houston, Texas, claims that there are more Christian saints dedicated to drinking than to any other subject. It's difficult to verify this assertion, but there is certainly no shortage of beer-drinking saints.

With a name like Christopher Mark Patrick O'Brien, you might guess that I was raised Catholic. I am named after three saints and one king. The surname O'Brien means I am descended from the Irish clan of Brian Boru. He ruled Ireland just over a thousand years ago, back when being a king was synonymous with being divine. He was most certainly a beer drinker; however, he was never a saint. He did build many fine castles, including one called Bunratty, which stands to this day. St. Christopher was a contemporary of

Jesus and is said to have carried him across a river. Jesus, as we know, was a beer drinker, and is believed by many to be God. Alcohol continues to be consumed in his name and is believed by Catholics to be the very blood of the Almighty. St. Mark probably drank beer with Jesus at the Last Supper and various other parties. According to the Senchus Mor, an ancient book of Irish law, Saint Patrick (438–441 AD) employed a priest by the name of Mescan as his own household brewer. Sadly, however, it appears that although all of my namesakes are saints and kings, and even though they all drank beer, neither the Church nor popular tradition recognizes any of them as official saints of beer.

Saint Luke the Evangelist (1ˢᵗ century CE) is the first beer saint and one of the few to be formally recognized as such by the Church. The funny thing is, no one seems to know why. Perhaps as a physician he understood, like St. Arnold of Metz would five hundred years later, the health benefits of drinking beer. At that time, hundreds of herbal beer elixirs were commonly prescribed for maladies of all kinds. Besides this, no theory would seem to explain why this most eminent and ancient of saints would be sanctioned as the Church's official Patron Saint of Brewing.

Saint Lawrence (died 258) was an archdeacon of the Roman church during the reign of Pope Sixtus II. The cruel way in which he achieved martyrdom has endeared him to roasters of grain and earned him praise as the Patron Saint of Maltsters. For it seems Lawrence himself was slow-roasted over an open fire. According to popular account, once his backside achieved an appropriate level of toastiness, he exclaimed, "Turn me over. I'm done on this side!" Steve Frank and Arnold Meltzer describe in their article *Saints of Suds* how the Bamberg Brewery Museum holds Lawrence as its patron saint and the Bamberg brewers' guild required young brewers to carry his likeness in processions and make donations to the church on his feast day. Saint Dorothy (died 311) of Cappadocia, now part of Turkey, is another patron saint of brewers due to her being tortured in a similar way — she was cooked over flames on a bed of iron.

It might astonish you to know that Saint Nicholas, better known as the gift-giver we call Santa Claus, is also officially listed by the Church as a Patron Saint of Brewing. It was in the early 4ᵗʰ century that St. Nick served as Bishop of Myra, a land located in modern-day Turkey. Nick was a rich man who took great joy in using his wealth for the benefit of others. According to one legend, three young church scholars stopped at an inn for nourishment and lodging. The innkeeper was greedy and evil and slew them for their money. Furthermore, because people in that land were enduring a great famine, the innkeeper sliced the corpses, pickled them in a barrel of brine, and sold their salty flesh as beer snacks. Now jolly old Nick happened by this perilous pub that very same evening. Given the famine, he was surprised when the innkeeper offered a plate of salted meat with his beer. Nick grew suspicious and snuck into the kitchen where he found the three boys floating in the barrel of brine. He wasted no time in miraculously reviving them into whole and healthy lads again. Thus, St. Nicholas earned the honor of Patron Saint of Brewers, Coopers, and Honest Innkeepers.

But that's not all. Nick was patron saint of more than sixty causes, from prostitutes and pawnbrokers, to shoe-shiners and sailors, as well as the nations of Russia and Greece. His feast day is December 6th, and as such, one of the lesser-known, but more important legacies of this affluent do-gooder is the cornucopia of Christmas ales bearing his name. Topping the list is the world-class Samichlaus Bier. Originally brewed in Switzerland, it is now made in Austria and has become one of the rarest and most sought-after beers in the world. It is brewed only once a year, on December 6th, and then matured for ten months before being bottled the following October, by which time it has reached 14 percent alcohol by volume. It is unusual in that it is a lager rather than an

When he comes around as a bottle of Samichlaus beer, Santa is short, dark and strong.

BRAUEREI SCHLOSS EGGENBERG

ale, and at this strength can rightly claim to be one of the strongest bottom-fermented beers in the world. Being so strong, it ages well. Schloss Eggenberg, producer of Samichlaus, describes an aged bottle as becoming "more complex with a creamy warming finish," and suggests serving with "hardy robust dishes and desserts, particularly with chocolates, or as an after-dinner drink by itself — as a companion for meditations at the fireplace." Many fine small breweries offer holiday ales nowadays. They are normally strong and dark, sometimes spiced, and add cheer to holiday celebrations with family and friends — or young church scholars.

Saint Augustine of Hippo (353–430) became a Patron Saint of Brewers for rather different reasons than the rest of our beer seers. Old Augustine was a dedicated partier who eventually reformed and renounced his past life of indulgence, thenceforth committing his life to the Church. Perhaps it was Catholic guilt that inspired him to chronicle his sinful adventures in *The Confessions*. But it must have been a residual sense of beer-induced wit that inspired him to summarize his pre-conversion philosophy with the following phrase: "God, give me chastity and continence — but not just now."

Saint Benedict (480–547) is the father of Church monasticism and an unofficial beer saint. He decreed that monks must be self-supporting in every way. According to early monastic tradition, monks were allowed to imbibe generous amounts of beer on a daily basis. The life of a monk being otherwise quite harsh, this one permitted indulgence naturally led monks to acquire expert brewing skills. Benedictine monks, as was earlier noted, were further required to welcome weary travelers into their monasteries and provide for their nourishment and refreshment. As the monasteries grew, their brews became well known and demand increased. This popularity, combined with the requirement for hospitality, positioned the monks well to become small businessmen. As they began selling their high-quality brews to the public the occurrence of "beer saints" took a dramatic spike upward. The monastic brewing tradition is embodied most superbly in the six remaining Trappist breweries in Belgium.

The Irish Beer Trinity

Saints Brigid, Columban, and Patrick are all buried at Downpatrick, and comprise what I call the Trinity of Beer. Saint Brigid (457–525), aka "the Mary of the Gael," was an Irish nun who founded an abbey at Kildare and dedicated herself to working in a leper colony. Her parents were baptized by none other than St. Patrick himself. One day the lepers ran out of beer, and as the story goes, Brigid miraculously transformed bath water into beer to prevent yet further hardship among these poor souls who suffered so much already. She also is said to have brewed a special Easter ale which she supplied to all the churches in the vicinity. From her humble convent (which was the first in Ireland), it is said that she kept eighteen churches in beer from just one barrel, for the entire fifty-day-long Easter season. One wonders whether the miracle was creating a bottomless keg, or somehow satisfying a large Irish congregation with just one ordinary keg. A poem attributed to Brigid praises beer and God with these words: "I should like a great lake of ale, for the King of Kings. I should like the family of Heaven to be drinking it through time eternal." Amen to that. Water-into-ale miracles and bottomless barrels of beer were par for the course for Brigid, whose legend appears to have melded with that of an earlier pagan goddess of plenty whose cows reputedly gave milk three times a day and caused wells to spring forth where there were previously none.

Saint Columban (c. 543–615) was an Irish missionary working in Germany. In his missionary travels he came upon a group of locals preparing to offer a cask of ale to a heathen god. With a mere puff of breath, Columban destroyed the cask and proceeded to lecture the pagans on the evils of wasting good beer on a heathen god like Woden. The Christian god, he explained, loved beer, and he must be praised for providing it. When the crowd repented, he performed a *beer*acle, replenishing the beer he had destroyed. Columban is said to have declared: "It is my design to die in the brew-house; let ale be placed to my mouth when I am expiring so that when the choir of angels come they may say: 'Be God propitious to this drinker.'"

Medieval English brewers called yeast "Godisgood." They didn't know how it worked, but they did know that adding the thick white stuff from the bottom of the last batch of beer would help ensure that the next batch was good. Since the bubbly action of fermentation was such a mystery they attributed the miraculous nature of this good thing to the beneficence of God.

The Three Saint Arnolds of Beer

Saint Arnold of Metz (580–640), variously referred to as Arnou, Arnuph, Arnoldus, Arnould, and Arnouldus, is widely considered to be the real Patron Saint of Brewing even though he is not recognized as such by the Church. He was known to extol the health virtues of drinking beer instead of water and is supposed to have ended a plague by blessing a kettle of beer with his crucifix, thereby inducing the populace to consume his purified beer instead of the local disease-spreading water supply. He is credited with the famous saying, "From man's sweat and God's love, beer came into the world." Arnold served as bishop to the French city of Metz, where it is no wonder that his congregation loved him well — he is said to have provided them with free beer! There are multiple versions of the tale, with the most common one going something like this: A year after his death, the townspeople received permission to move the Bishop's remains to a location near his first diocese. One of the porters, overcome by heat and exhaustion, pleaded to God for a beer to slake his thirst. No sooner had his request been uttered than a font of beer sprang from the casket, drenching all and quenching their thirst most handily. Another version tells of how the funeral procession stopped in the village of Champigneulles for rest and refreshment. The loyal followers sought comfort in a mug of beer as they recovered from their exertions. Unfortunately, only a single mug-full was to be had in the entire town. But to their astonishment, the mug never ran dry and was passed among the faithful until all were sufficiently fortified. They attributed the miraculous mug to their kindly, deceased bishop.

Another Saint Arnold, this one of Soissons (1040–1087), is considered the patron saint of hop pickers, partly because he preached around the Brabant district in Belgium, a region well-known for its hop growing. As story has it, the roof of Arnold's abbey brewery in Soissons collapsed and damaged the monks' beer supplies. Arnold asked God to multiply the volume of the remaining beer and when his prayer was answered in abundance, the monks and townspeople thought to canonize him on the spot. While Arnold is best known for this miraculous provision of beer, he is also credited with a most practical improvement upon the brewing process. While making bee hives for the abbey's apiary, the abbot realized that the straw cones could be used as a filter to help clarify the brothers' beer. In honor of this practical contribution to the brewer's art, the good saint is often portrayed — as on the certificates of the Belgian Brewers Confederation — in the company of bees, with one hand resting on a hive.

A painting of Saint Arnold, Patron Saint of Brewers, adorns the brewery wall at St. Arnold's in Houston, Texas. Bishop heads embellish the tap handles of the brewery bar.

*A small altar honors the image of Arnold of Metz in the St. Arnold Brewery visitors'
room.*

It is difficult to be certain, but there is perhaps yet a third Saint Arnold.
This one was an 11th century Belgian military man, hailing from Oudenaarde,
who went on to become a Benedictine monk and founded St. Peter's Abbey
in Oudenburg. Both towns are in Flanders, a region still known for its unique
dark red and brown ales. This Arnold, in fact, may be one and the same with
Saint Arnold of Soissons, but dates and stories conflict as much as they over-
lap. In any case, he is said to have been a distinguished brewer and was called
Arnoldus the Strong in recognition of his military service. Legend holds that
Arnoldus sustained a group of weary Flemish troops during a battle by
invoking the power of God to miraculously create copious beer rations. For
this noble provisioning he became the Patron Saint of Belgian Brewers.

While all the Arnolds liked to transform empty mugs into ones brimming with beer, St. Arnold Brewing, the one in Houston mentioned above,
cites their commitment to recycling as the motivation behind a unique
transubstantiation plan of their own. Customers are encouraged to return
their used cardboard six-pack carriers and the brewery will change them into
pint glasses and t-shirts.

Give Us This Day Our Daily Beer

Saint Cuthbert (ca. 634–687) was a Bishop in Scotland who eventually retired to a rocky island hermitage. Unfortunately, his monastic retreat was devoid of potable water and the land was barren. According to a medieval biographer named Bede, Cuthbert entreated the Lord to rectify this most thirsty of predicaments, exclaiming, "Let us dig in the middle of my hut, and, I believe, out of His good pleasure, He will give us drink." I can imagine how his conversation with God might have continued, "Yea, but Lord, what good is water without barley?" And indeed, Cuthbert's next miracle was to produce barley instantly and abundantly where his previous crops had failed. But further disaster struck when flocks of birds came pecking away at his grain. His third miracle was to issue them no more than a word of admonishment, at which they dispersed, never to harass him again. With pure water and plentiful barley one can only guess how he wiled away his cloistered days. It is said that sometime long after his death and burial Cuthbert's body was found in a preserved state, clutching a chalice to the chest. What ever could he have been drinking in his final hours?

Saint Hildegard von Bingen (1098–1179) was a Benedictine nun and Abbess of Rupertsberg, Germany. She was thought to be a prophetess and mystic and was well regarded for her poetry, which remained popular for centuries. As an herbalist and brewster she recorded her experiments with hops in one of her two books on natural medicine. One of them, *Physica Sacra*, contains the earliest known reference to hopped beer, wherein she writes, "[Hops], when put in beer, stops putrification and lends longer durability." Although she was never canonized, she has been beatified and is considered a saint by many. Her confidence in medicine and brewing was surpassed only by her assertiveness within the Church, which led her to become one of the few women to serve as a close papal adviser. Indeed, her use of natural healing, especially through herbal beers, would be considered pioneering even today.

The King of Beer

Gambrinus (1251–1294) is widely worshipped in Europe as the "King of Beer." Beers and breweries around the world are named in honor of this so-called king. Yet Gambrinus was neither king nor saint. The name is believed to be a corruption of either Jan Primus, or Jean Sans Peur (John the Fearless), aka Ganbrivius. Primus was a medieval Belgian duke, depicted in folktales as King of Flanders, Brabant, Louvain, and Antwerp and credited with inventing hopped beer. *The Encyclopedia of Beer* credits him with introducing the custom of the toast. Jan was a carouser and philanderer of note and was eventually killed in a duel by a jealous husband, whose wife Jan had seduced. However, several years before his ignoble death, the Duke participated in a fateful battle outside Cologne, in which local royalty were pitted against the local Bishop. Primus aided his royal allies in seizing the day and, as a result, the region converted to secular rule and transferred control of brewing from the Church to the nobility. Another result of the battle was the founding of Dusseldorf a few miles up the Rhine from Cologne, a city whose famous Kolsch beer would later be rivaled by Dusseldorf's Altbier. Ironically, Primus was made an honorary member of the Cologne brewers' guild in 1288.

According to a medieval scribe named Johannes Turmair (writing under the pseudonym Aventinus, after whom the deliciously sweet and deviously potent Schneider Aventinus Weizenbock is named), Ganbrivius (a.k.a. John the Fearless, 1371–1419) married Isis, the Egyptian beer goddess we met earlier. According to Turmair's tall tale, the couple invented beer together and taught the secrets of brewing to a German tribe called the Gambrivii. Though the Church holds no record of such a saint, Gambrinus continues to be celebrated by beer drinkers everywhere as the Patron Saint of Beer.

St. Francis of Paola (1430s?–1500?) formed an Italian order of monks who created a beer they called Salvator, which means Savior. The style came to be known as dopplebock and ever since, brewers of dopplebocks have named their beers in words ending in '-ator' as a reference to Salvator, the original dopplebock.

Beer Pilgrims

Churches with their own brewhouses have lured Christian pilgrims for well over a millennium. Upon arrival, weary travelers would avail themselves of the beer and food provided by church caretakers. A number of these destinations still exist around the world. The worship of beer goddesses, gods, and saints has petered out significantly as religion has undergone a general decline in the modern age. But the number of beer pilgrims has been on the upswing in the last quarter century.

Steeped in History

Beer has the power to save. The Church Brew Works is located in a former church in Lawrenceville, Pennsylvania, just outside Pittsburgh. Founded around the turn of the 19th century, Lawrenceville originated as a farm named "Good Liquor." The Whiskey Rebellion transpired in this same region when George Washington, a distiller and brewer himself, tried to impose a stiff tax on liquor.

Lawrenceville was named in honor of Captain James Lawrence who is famed for his exhortation during the Revolutionary War: "Don't give up the ship!" Lawrenceville's first houses are superb examples of a Victorian architectural style called Second Empire Italianate. The Irish and Scotch Catholics who filled them needed a place to worship, so in 1878 the Diocese of Pittsburgh constructed St. John the Baptist church. A trio of respected architects were employed to design the church, rectory, school, and convent. Some of the finest craftsmen of the time decorated the church with exquisite detail, like the multicolored Rose window that stands as a kaleidoscopic backdrop for the turn-of-the-century pipe organ in the church's balcony. Handpainted cypress beams in the vaulted ceiling and European-style stained glass windows accentuate the building's heavenly orientation. When built, the bell tower was twice as high as it is now and held a full peal of bells.

When the cornerstone was laid on June 1, 1902, a copper time capsule was placed inside it with a history of the church and copies of pertinent articles from local publications of the time. During the Depression era, St. John's distributed food to needy members of the community. And in 1936, it sheltered unfortunate folks who were ravaged by flood waters from Pittsburgh's three mighty rivers. Beginning in the 1950s, Lawrenceville, like most industrial centers, began its decline, mills closed down and young people sought opportunities elsewhere. The school was shut down about 20 years before the Diocese officially closed St. John's in 1993.

Don't Give Up the Church

The building lay dormant for three years until the Church Brew Works reopened the doors of St. John the Baptist on August 1st, 1996. Painstaking efforts were taken to maintain original features of the church and rectory. Pews were refurbished and adapted to the worship of beer. The bar was built from oak planks salvaged from the pews. The reddish-orange hue of the flooring comes from the original Douglas fir floors, which were meticulously restored after lying hidden underneath plywood for 50 years. The original lanterns in the center bay were refurbished and reinstalled, and now illuminate the detailing of the ceiling.

One of the confessionals remains intact behind the bar and houses the Church Brew Works merchandise display. Bricks salvaged from another confessional were reused for the pillars on the outdoor sign and the facade of the new kitchen. The former rectory courtyard was converted into an outdoor patio called The Hop Garden, from where a delightful view of the bell tower and the stained glass windows is to be had. But by far the most striking element is the brewhouse itself, situated right atop the altar. The ciborium, a large canopy behind the brewhouse, is a design feature of historic buildings that provided protection against falling ceilings. The steel and copper tanks gleam in a celestial blue backdrop, inspiring a sense of reverence for the mystery of brewing, bringing beer drinkers a step or two closer to god.

The Fish, the Ring, and the Brew-Church

Christian monks at Orval have probably been brewing for almost a thousand years, since the time that brewing was commonplace in monasteries throughout Europe. One of only six Trappist monasteries that still brews beer in Belgium, Orval attracts beer pilgrims from around the world. According to legend, the monastery was established when Countess Mathilda of Tuscany lost her wedding ring in a well. When she prayed for its return, a fish appeared bearing the ring in its mouth. Mathilda is said to have declared the site a "val d'or" or valley of gold, and in gratitude to God she built a monastery on the site. The image of a fish bearing a golden ring in its mouth still represents the brewery to this day.

A statue of St. Arnold graces the entrance room of the Trappist monastery where Orval is brewed.

The monastery also has a thriving bread and cheese business and welcomes pilgrims to stay in its chalet.

The Ethiopian Orthodox Monasteries of Lake Tana

Back in the fourth century, Ethiopia became the first country in the world to adopt Christianity as the state religion. And, just like so many European states would later do, Ethiopia established a monastic tradition that included beer brewing as a means of self-sufficiency and hospitality. The tradition continues to this day in the island monasteries of Lake Tana, in Ethiopia's mountainous northern region that serves as a watershed for some ninety percent of the water that eventually flows into the Nile River. Beer brewing in

A church wall mural on one of the island monasteries of Lake Tana, Ethiopia, depicting King Herod and compatriots drinking t'edj (mead) while brandishing a knife that will be used to chop off John the Baptist's head.

the lakeside town of Bahar Dar is highly developed. Each home-based brewster specializes in a particular style, and each style has its own appropriate drinking vessel. Some of the monks on the lake islands are happy to share a taste of their house brews.

CHAPTER 4

Everything You Wanted to Know About Beer But Were Afraid to Ask

Many peoples through the ages have attempted to describe the spiritual nature of beer, but what about its material attributes? What is beer in practical terms? There is a simple, technical definition: fermented grain. But the story of brewing is a complicated love affair between yeast and sugar. However, rather than delve into the scandalous details, let's stick to the basic "yeast-meets-grain, yeast-gets-grain" story line. Loads of great books get very technical and analytical about beer. Interested readers will find a library of brewing information available online. For our purposes, though, I will skip the beer geek-speak and let everyone live happily ever after.

> "Give a man a beer and he'll drink for an hour. Teach a man to brew and he'll drink for a lifetime."
>
> — Anonymous

Makin' It

Beer Is Fermented Grain

In Africa, people use sorghum and millet to make drinks like *changaa, tela,* and *farsi.* In South America, people use corn to brew *chicha.* Brits sometimes use oats and rye in their ales. In Asia, folks ferment sake from rice. Europeans use barley and wheat to make *cerveza, bier,* and *pivo.* But regardless of the grain or the name, all of these drinks are in the beverage family called beer.

The grain-base is what distinguishes beer from wine, which is fermented fruit. Mead, on the other hand, is fermented honey. Spirits — like whiskey, vodka, cognac, and rum — are drinks created by distillation, the process of concentrating alcohol by collecting steam from a boiling alcoholic liquid. Of course, these are modern categorizations, and there is nothing preventing a drink maker from producing beverages that are combinations of the above. Indeed, many of the ancients did just this, and with flair. But in describing contemporary drinks, these are useful categories.

Grains ferment when water converts their starches into sugars and then yeast turns the sugars into alcohol and carbon dioxide (and some other less important things that get dangerously close to beer geek-speak). Yeast needs certain kinds of enzymes to help it eat the sugars contained in grains. Enzymes are kind of like the matchmaker who gets the sparks to fly between two potential lovers.

Sprouting Your Seed

In places where barley grows, it has become the brewer's grain of choice because it has a high sugar content and the right enzymes built right into it. Other grains either don't have these enzymes at all, or have them in lesser quantities. But barley also has a hard outer shell which is both beneficial and problematic for brewing. The shell acts like a chastity belt, protecting the sweet sugars inside the grain from the lecherous yeast. Getting that shell open requires a separate skilled technique, called malting. Malting is the process of preparing barley for use in brewing and simply means sprouting the barley seed and then drying it. Maltsters start by moistening the barley seeds. This causes the seeds to open up or sprout. As soon as the seeds sprout, they are quickly dried by blowing hot air across them. Since the seed grows by feeding on the starches inside it, the maltster allows the seed to grow only enough so that it breaks the shell and then halts the growth with heat. The temperature of the heat, and the length of time it is applied, help to determine many of the taste and color characteristics the malts impart to beers. Once the malt is prepared, it is run through a grinding mill that cracks the malted grains apart from their husks. Variety is the spice of life, so brewers mix and match different types and amounts of malt to make many dozens of different beer styles.

Gimme Some Sugar (But First Put On a Filter)

Now that their shells are opened and the starch inside is fully exposed, the grains are steeped in hot water, a step called mashing, so that the starches inside convert into simple sugars. The next step, lautering, is where hot water is showered down over the grains, washing the sugar out. During lautering, the outer garments of the grains fall to the floor forming a soft bed that filters out the dirty proteins from the sweet sugar. The resulting sugary liquid is called *wort*, and is now poured into a giant hot tub where things soon get too hot to handle.

Getting Hot and Steamy

In the hot tub, called a brew kettle, the wort is boiled to kill off all the nasty bacteria that can cause infections in beer. Nobody likes tasting an infected beer, so this process is important. During the boil, brewers spice things up by adding special flavorings like hops. Hops are the soft, green cones (shaped like a small pine cone) of the hop bine, a hardy vine-like plant that can grow several meters high. More adventurous brewers try all sorts of things other than hops at this point in the brewing process, and have been known to experiment with everything from squashes to chocolate. Hopped beer is like the missionary position of sex. It's a standby that works just fine, but other spicy variations can keep things interesting. Conventional brewers stick with hops, usually adding some at the beginning of the boil to impart bitterness and flavor, and some more at the end to produce delightful aromas. Occasionally, extra hops are added later on during fermentation, a practice called dry-hopping. Hops smell and taste good but they also help prevent spoilage, thus preserving the good taste of beer.

The length of time the wort is boiled matters. A nice long boil makes for the best, most memorable and satisfying beers. Craft brewers, it should be noted, boil longer, at least an hour and sometimes two, while industrial brewers do it for as short as thirty minutes.

Swirlin' and Chillin'

During the boil, more proteins and other chunky stuff collect and fall to the bottom of the hot tub. This process is enhanced after the end of the boil, by swirling the wort around in a circle, creating a whirlpool where the heavy bits collect in the middle and the clear wort is moved away to chill out. Wort is cooled using a variety of methods, but a common one is the heat exchanger. To understand a heat exchanger, imagine a thin pipe running inside a wider pipe. The hot wort flows through the thin pipe while something frigid, like cold water, flows in the opposite direction through the wider pipe. In this way, heat is quickly transferred from the hot wort to the cold water, allowing the temperature of the wort to slip down into something a bit more comfortable for its impending date with the attractive yeast cells. Properly chilled wort is essential for the next and most important step: fermentation.

Eat, Screw, Fart, Sleep

The life of a yeast cell is pretty straightforward, kind of like the lifestyle of some people. It eats, has sex, farts, and falls asleep. But, unlike some people, yeast cells are very particular about when they are willing to do their thing. They want cool temperatures (hence the cooling described above), lots of sugar, air, and then no air. In this ideal situation they will behave the way we want them to, eating the sugar, reproducing, releasing bubbles of carbon dioxide gas, and producing alcohol. When they have had their fill and can eat, screw, and fart no more, they roll over and go to sleep. But in the process, they have given birth to that effervescent, alcoholic grain juice we all love so well, called beer.

Beer Is Blind, It Comes in All Colors and Flavors
Loving Lovibond

The beer color spectrum is vast, ranging from cloudy white to transparent yellow and opaque black, and covering golden, copper, amber, caramel, and burgundy along the way. These colors are measured in units called Lovibond, starting with light lagers at zero and ending with various stouts and other dark black beers that reach into the hundreds. One common myth is that color somehow equates to flavor, that dark beers taste rich and heavy and are high in alcohol. This is a dangerous misperception. At best, color can only partially indicate flavor. For example, lagers, which tend to be crisp and light, are generally pale yellow, but are sometimes dark black. Belgian ales are mostly dark and strong, but many golden-hued strong Belgian ales exist too. Most people think Guinness is a strong, heavy beer, but actually it has a low alcohol content. However, one version of Guinness, called Foreign Extra Stout, is quite high in alcohol and is indeed a rich, heavy beer, but this version is much less common than the highly quaffable Guinness that is normally served on draft in bars. The lesson here is that judging a beer by its color is a fool's errand. The only true color rule is that there is no rule.

The Colors of Beer, a sampler tray at the Half Moon Bay restaurant and brewery in Prinston by the Sea, California.

Put It In Your Mouth, Roll It Around on Your Tongue, and Swallow

Speaking of Guinness, the stout style is useful in illustrating the variety of beer flavors. Some stouts are very sweet, while others are dry. Some have a huge body that is meant to be slowly savored, but others are thin and easy to gulp down, two or three pints in succession. Beer tastes range from innocuous to sublime, syrupy sweet to bitingly bitter. Taste determines, in part, whether a beer is quaffable or quenching, cloying or tart. All of these flavors are the result of a mind-boggling number of factors, including technical things like the type and volume of each grain used; the kinds and quantities of hops and when they are added; the type of yeast employed; and the duration of fermentation and the type of vessel used for it. Other more subjective issues are equally important, like the time of day and the setting in which the beer is consumed. Even the kind of serving glass can affect flavor. The disposition of the drinker herself plays no small part in determining the flavor experience of a beer. Alas, the tastes of beer are infinite, and the best way to learn about them is to liberate oneself from preconceptions, remove boundaries, and experiment. Drink beer with abandon and the rewards will be immeasurable.

Doing It Yourself

Today, America is brimming with thousands of delicious, ravishing, easily available craft beers. Nearly a thousand brewpubs offer an astonishing array of ripe, bubbly young things begging for your lips to be pressed to them. However, some people prefer to satisfy their needs at home, wearing an apron in the kitchen, wielding a brew spoon and employing all manner of exotic contraptions. To each her own. If using your own hands pleases you the most, by all means please enjoy it.

I started homebrewing as a grad student in upstate New York. My reasons for beginning the pursuit were, if not noble, at least practical. I was living the typical meager student lifestyle. Ramen noodles, macaroni and cheese, and cheap beer provided the bulk of my nutritional intake. I quickly realized the pittance I was earning as a coffee barista wasn't enough to make ends meet. So I reviewed my expenses and looked for places to cut costs. To be honest, it wasn't much of a surprise when I discovered that the majority of my discretionary spending went to beer. Beer, like love, is a necessity, so cutting down on it was out of the question. But, like dating, it is awfully expensive. Whatever was a poor student to do?

Woe was indeed me. My nights were sleepless, my pockets empty, and my head in a cloud. I implored the gods, begging them to reveal a solution. And they showed mercy and sent me a sign. Walking home one evening from the Troy Brewpub, I noticed a fancy little shop that had hitherto escaped my attentions. It must have been the curvaceous carboys in the window that caught my eye. Stainless steel brew pots behind them twinkled in the glow of the store lights. I entered impulsively and illicit thoughts of homebrewing immediately filled my head. But, I wondered, would brewing beer all by myself at home be as satisfying as meeting new beers at a brewpub? Doing some quick calculations, I figured I could cut my beer expenses in half by brewing myself. Not only that, but taking the craft into my own hands promised to considerably improve the quality of my quaff. The fact is, I rarely sprang for the good stuff, and instead usually settled for run-of-the-mill industrial beers that actually tasted kind of horrible. Thinking about it now, I can't begin to count the number of nights I took home a bag of whatever cheap cans of beer happened to cross my path. So it was with a gleam in my eye that I bought a pile of recreational brewing gear and some helpful magazines, ran home, and went at it. I have been homebrewing ever since, and this book is proof of the hobby's hold over my life.

Whether you brew it yourself or buy it at the store, a flirt with high quality beer is exhilarating and guaranteed to turn into a lifetime affair.

Part II

The Death of Beer (and Everything Else)

CHAPTER 5

The Great Beer Gender Bender

B rewing is as ancient as the goddesses who first bestowed the gift of fermentation on humankind. But while the genesis of beer may be divine, its earthly incarnation has always come from the hands of women. For millennia, brewing was counted among the many skills required to run a household. In many societies, women maintained an important avenue of social influence through their control of beer. Since beer was one of the factors motivating early peoples to develop agriculture and build urban civilizations, brewing accorded women a considerable degree of power within those societies. In recent centuries, male industrial-capitalists have robbed women of that power and at the same time destroyed many of the best things about beer. If we are to reclaim the many positive attributes of beer, women must take back the pint.

I Am a Femaleist

I am a "femaleist." I think that beer, when at its best, empowers women. It has certainly done so in the past, and has the potential to do so again today. More women brewing and drinking beer would help correct some of our socially constructed gender imbalances. The drinking cultures of industrialized countries like America have suffered great losses since women became disenfranchised from brewing. Western beer-drinking culture is now so dominated by machismo that it has lost all the benefits of the feminine touch it used to so embody. Don't get me wrong — I enjoy drinking beer and

An ironic twist on the inter-woven histories of brewing, women, and industrialization.

watching sports with the guys, occasionally. But when that becomes one of the only socially acceptable circumstances for beer drinking, we have needlessly narrowed our options. Bikinis and sports cars need not be the only images used in beer marketing. Beer and sex do often go hand in hand, but drinking can also be spiritual, healthful, intellectual, poetic, romantic, convivial, and enjoyed in community. Currently it is mostly sold as a testosterone-fueled aggro-zone for boys. Women should return to the brewing craft and share equally in its joys and benefits, be they economic, social, political, or otherwise. Women can help reinvigorate and rebuild a vibrant and beneficial beer-drinking culture by infusing it with feminine qualities that balance the predominantly masculine beer culture we have today. It is time for women of the world to raise up a tulip-shaped beer chalice and toast the unheralded women's history of beer. It is time for women to lift up the mash fork and brew!

To readers unfamiliar with the importance of women in the history of beer, harkening them to the brewers' arms might sound farcical. But it is a serious calling. The recent trend of male-dominated brewing is related to bigger problems with industrial society, the exploitation of women, and the destruction of nature. Before defending these claims, allow me first to exhort wise male readers to study this chapter closely and to pass this book along to a woman in your life. Pick one who doesn't know much about beer or its history, maybe one you would like to see more often. Increase her interest in beer, and perhaps you will be spending more time together. This chapter could be just the extra push needed to make beer, and maybe you too, central in her life.

To the women reading this, allow me to offer congratulations. As a female beer drinker, you obviously don't mind bucking the trend, or for that matter, blazing a trail. You are part of a tradition that was begun by women, and dominated by women for nearly all of history. Furthermore, if you are a woman who brews beer, then you are in the vanguard of a new trend. Women like you are helping to weave a richer beer culture that celebrates community and craft in a world dominated by industrial scale anonymity. I urge you to read this chapter with an eye toward the future of beer and human culture. I hope it may stir in you a desire to brew up a revolutionary new beer world.

His Story of Beer

There is a collective amnesia regarding the historical role of women in brewing. Most people assume beer is male turf and always has been. This is a mistaken notion, but there are understandable reasons for it. The first and most obvious is that for the last several hundred years, European men, and their descendents in the New World, have indeed dominated commercial beer brewing, both within the West as well as around the globe. They began usurping brewing from women most significantly during the Middle Ages, and the transfer of power continued with zeal during the Scientific and Industrial Revolutions. As modern industrial capitalism emerged as the main organizing force in the world, men transformed brewing from a craft to an industry, and from a culture to a commodity. Beer became big business, and big business is the domain of big men. So, the *recent* history of beer in the Western world is, in fact, a story dominated by men.

The second reason we overlook the female history of beer is that until pretty recent times the written word was almost exclusively a male prerogative. Literacy was limited to very few men, but even fewer women. Women generally managed the household, including the kitchen where they made beer. Scholars were usually men and they wrote about politics and religion, occasionally mentioning beer within these contexts. But rarely were beer, or the women who brewed it, the primary subjects of early history.

As a woman's domestic charge, brewing was passed down through the generations by example. Women taught their daughters the skills of homemaking through first-hand experience, not through written documents. Thus the history of brewing, one of our greatest preoccupations as humans, remains largely undocumented. Combined with the fact that brewing residues and artifacts, such as pots and straw mats, are highly degradable, this explains why we know very little about how brewing was first discovered.

We do know at least that beer making and drinking have gone on for a minimum of ten thousand years. We know that they were exalted in religions, that ancient political leaders relied on them for tax revenue, and that women were at the helm of the craft most of that time. We also know that beer provided a crucial nutritional advantage to the people who learned the techniques of brewing. Yet relatively little is known about its associated customs, about the contributions it made to family and community life, to early social organization, and to human health and well-being. It is for these two reasons, the recent European male domination of brewing, and the lack of earlier historical documentation, that most Westerners today think beer is "a guy thing."

A Female History of Beer

Although much about this female craft is unrecorded, there is enough evidence in the archaeological record for us to be sure that brewing was of central importance to human society, and that the practice was dominated by women since earliest known times until quite recently. But it wasn't until greater numbers of European men started brewing during the Middle Ages that abundant documentation of the culture and process of brewing began. "His story of beer" tends to start in earnest with government documents like the famous German *Reinheitsgebot* of 1516, a time when men were gaining momentum in the contest to control the craft, especially through laws like this one mandating the production of hopped beer and outlawing the recipes of women homebrewers. Many beer experts revere the Reinheitsgebot as a quantum leap forward in controlling beer quality, but the motivation for purity laws like this had more to do with the desire to collect taxes. Standardized beer, brewed in mass quantity in centralized locations, is much easier to regulate and tax than tens of thousands of housewives brewing in small batches with unknown ingredients. As men removed beer from ceremonial and household consumption, society moved toward a hierarchical, industrial power structure. Cooperative social structures lost their predominance as men organized powerful, centralized governments that legislated in favor of a few elite males.

Paradoxically, as men took control of brewing and documented it, the diverse cultural functions of beer started slipping by the wayside. As the political value of beer became increasingly linked to its economic value, it slowly lost its vital place in religion and health. The primary significance of beer from this point on is derived from its value as a commodity, a value that exemplifies a mechanical view of the world, as manifested by science, industrial technology, and so-called free-market capitalism. Ultimately, brewing became driven solely by the profit motive and nearly all of the attendant religious, health, and cultural values of beer were discarded. Women, who had developed and safeguarded beer's multifaceted roles in human society for ten millennia or more, were robbed of this tradition as men reduce it to just one thing: money.

The scientific worldview, that fostered industrialization and capitalism, has not been a complete failure. It did kill beer, but at the same time, many women have made strides toward equality in the last few centuries. Some of this progress was made possible by advances in science and industry. Certainly, Western women today have good life choices they did not have even one generation ago. Most women in industrialized societies are no longer restricted to domestic pursuits, and there are laws that at least attempt to create equal justice and opportunity. Overall, maybe industrialization has been good for women, allowing them to get out of the house and follow other dreams. These points are debatable. But one thing is sure: modernization destroyed the female elements infused in beer culture. It is time for women to return to brewing and resurrect beer from the grave of industrial production.

The so-called "rational" approach to production has enabled the large-scale destruction of nature, and induced beer's industrial death. Western society suffered a great loss when men took a mechanical approach to beer. In particular, women lost a key avenue of societal influence when they lost control of brewing, and to regain it they need to get back in the kitchen and brew. Until recent times, brewing was a skill many women were expected to practice. Then the craft was taken over by male industrialists. Very recently, the art of brewing again has become a choice, but not one that many women have chosen. So I implore you modern women not to throw the homebrew out with the wash water as we struggle together to dismantle the patriarchy. Maintaining influence over alcohol consumption is a road to empowerment, allowing women to exert control over the household and the community at large, and ultimately offering a chance to fulfill ones creative potential as a human being.

Powerful Beer

In ancient times, women derived authority from both brewing and drinking beer. Recall that beer was often associated with female deities and was itself considered an extension of the divine. In historical Sumeria, brewing and consuming beer was at times restricted to priestesses because beer represented such a powerful avenue of communion with the gods and goddesses. The mere act of drinking beer was a symbol of female authority.

Later, in societies that embraced cash economies, beer also served a role in the economic empowerment of women. As brewing became a cottage industry throughout Mesopotamia and the Nile river basin, women were the exclusive overseers of beer sales in taverns. This continued through medieval European times. In England, as late as the 1500s, a great number of women brewed and sold beer. Many brewed on an occasional basis, as it suited their schedules and pocketbooks. Besides brewing for domestic consumption, women were motivated to brew because it provided a decent income. It was one of the more lucrative economic endeavors available to women, and it was an easy business to conduct without needing to leave the house where childcare and other domestic responsibilities also demanded attention.

Cornell writes in *Beer: The Story of the Pint:*

> In Anglo-Saxon England, most brewing outside the monasteries was done by women, as it probably always had been ... A study of one small place, Brigstock in Northamptonshire, between 1287 and 1349 listed more than 300 villagers who brewed for retail at least once; of those, nineteen in every twenty were women "brewsters," not male "brewers" ... [Women] would take turns to brew for the local community, using their domestic pots and buckets and fitting the boiling, mashing and fermenting in around their other domestic tasks.

A. Lynn Martin, an historian at Australia's University of Adelaide, argues that brewing, selling, and drinking beer was a way for women to negotiate their power in medieval English society. Her paper, *Deviant Drinking or Deviant Women?*, cites evidence that once men recognized this power, they tried to control female involvement with beer out of a fear that they were a threat to patriarchal rule.

Throughout Africa, economic empowerment continues to play a role with brewsters to this day. Jon Holtzman, an anthropologist at Kalamazoo College, presents this case in a paper titled *The Food of Elders, the "Ration" of Women: Brewing, Gender, and Domestic Processes among the Samburu of Northern Kenya.* Holtzman explains that Samburu women brew beer and liquor for sale to male elders including their own husbands. He views the arrangement as an example of what he calls a "cooperative conflict" approach to politics. The essay examines brewing as part of the economic and cultural positions of men and women within Samburu households and society at large, explaining

Young brewsters still learn the art from their mothers in Ouagadougou, the capital city of Burkina Faso. They are seen here preparing the red sorghum grist for a batch of ramoora at the brewery of Madame Kere.

that each gender controls key resources: food is controlled by women, and cash by men. Women's brewing beer for sale to men is a way they use "cooperative conflict" to negotiate this imbalance. In other words, without resorting to physical domination, women get what they need from men — cash — while men get what they need from women — beer. This is just a complicated way of saying that the female control of beer helps the Samburu maintain a peaceful balance of power between genders.

The Original "Girls Night Out"

In old Europe, alcohol also played a socialization role among women. A common theme in English literature in the late Middle Ages was a group of women gathered at the tavern enjoying each other's company amid pots of ale and food. Judith M. Bennett covers this in *Women in the Medieval English Countryside: Gender and Household in Brigstock Before the Plague*. But beer drinking wasn't just a social affair for women, it also provided daily sustenance.

Richard Valpy French recounts in his *Nineteen Centuries of Drink in England* that the household books for the court of Henry VIII reveal that three ladies-in-waiting shared one gallon of ale each day for breakfast.

Church and State "Get Medieval"

Throughout the reign of Rome and until the end of the Middle Ages, women throughout the world continued to make beer domestically, but the Catholic Church gradually gained a monopoly over brewing in Europe, helping to transform the brewster's home craft into a businessman's industrial pursuit.

Through the male-dominated monasteries, control of brewing was wrangled from the hands of everyday homemakers and consolidated in the prevailing seat of power, that is, the Church. Beer's role as an economic commodity increased as the Catholic Church manipulated control of brewing during its height of power in the Middle Ages. The Church's primary motivation for controlling brewing was not so much its congregation's spiritual health, nor its physical health, but the accumulation of material wealth and political power. Church-brewed beer was no longer sacred — it was for sale. The Church not only managed to dominate brewing by building its own breweries, but also assumed the right to license and tax other brewers through the control of *gruit*, the herbal mix commonly added to beer during that age. The herbs comprising gruit varied depending on regional availability and local taste preferences, but it usually included bog myrtle, a.k.a., sweet gale (Myrica gale), yarrow (Achillea millefolium), and wild rosemary (Rhododendron tomentosum), and often mugwort, a.k.a., wormwood (Artemisia vulgaris), among other plants. As the Church gobbled up power across Medieval Europe, it washed it down with beer, centralizing its power and becoming rich from brewing — a harbinger of the state-controlled brewing industry that would follow, and ultimately foreshadowing the modern corporate-state duopoly on beer.

The design of the St. Gallen monastery in Germany, built in 816–837, neatly summarizes the three concurrent trends in brewing at the time. Gozbert, the abbot in charge, designed the monastery with three breweries. The first provided for the needs of the monastery itself. The second was for the poor and pilgrims. And the third was for commerce. In this design, we observe the continuing practice of homebrewing for sustenance and recreation, i.e., the monks brewed first and foremost out of a need for self-reliance. Secondly, we see the continued role of beer in religion, the monks feeling a spiritual obligation to provide this most basic of needs to the impoverished and to holy pilgrims. But thirdly, and most importantly, the design demonstrates the growing recognition of beer's commercial value.

The state also played a role in centralizing the control of brewing during this period. In the 12th century, most breweries in Bavaria were appropriated by the ruling noble powers. Brewers officially became civil servants. During the Protestant Reformation, the commerce of brewing passed increasingly from the Church into the hands of private merchants, further reducing women's contribution to the brewing equation — an equation which, from this point on, ended emphatically in a dollar sign. During this same period, hops became a popular addition to beer, which Reformists and merchants cleverly championed over gruit, the herbal beer mix that had accompanied the Catholic Church's ascendancy in the brewing trade. Ironically, it was a women, the nun St. Hildegard, whose records provide some of the earliest evidence of hop brewing experiments. Through intense and prolonged political pressures, these merchants and Protestants were eventually able to replace the Church's domination over brewing with private enterprise. Laws like the *Reinheitsgebot* sealed the fate of gruit by legally banning it, furthering consolidating power in the hands of private, for-profit brewers, and outlawing the knowledge of herbal and medicinal brewing accumulated by women over untold centuries.

Judith Bennett covers the transition of brewing from women to men in England during this period, in her book *Ale, Beer, and Brewsters in England: Women's Work in a Changing World, 1300–1600*. After 1350, brewing became so profitable and prestigious that Englishmen slowly moved into the trade. Bennett's book contradicts some of the traditional theories for this change. "One historian in England said ... 'once brewing became large-scale, women couldn't pick up the barrels,'" Bennett recounts. But Bennett claims that her own evidence "shows definitively that biology has nothing to do with women leaving brewing."

Instead, Bennett claims, cultural ideas about women gradually gave brewsters a sleazy reputation. Hatred and distrust of women were rampant at the time. Bennett refers to "a large literature in late medieval and early modern England that depicts brewsters as filthy, disgusting workers, as women who produce polluted ale and cheat their customers. There's no literature like that about male brewers." These stories were undoubtedly intertwined with men's growing political manipulations of the brewing trade. Economics was the dominant factor behind all of these machinations. Not only were men drawn by the allure of wealth, but as brewing expanded in scale, it required more capital, which favored male participation. In sum, women were systematically cheated out of brewing by men who had their designs on the tremendous profits available to those willing and able to invest in larger brewing operations.

Fermenting the Scientific Revolution

The Scientific Revolution began around the end of this period. Sir Isaac Newton's *Philosophiae Naturalis Principia Mathematica* crystallized the emerging scientific view of the world when it was published in 1687. With this momentous publication, he became one of the chief instigators of our modern mechanized world view. His physics of cause and effect, action and reaction, became the dominant way of analyzing the world. In this outlook, life is broken down to its smallest parts in order to be understood. And yet Newton himself had doubts about this approach. He knew it lacked a real explanation for the interconnectedness and interdependencies of life. Scientific analysis could provide insight into the smallest level of things, but it missed "the big picture." He knew that his laws of motion failed to account for an original force necessary to put the universe into motion in the first place. In the end, he was unable to explain the cause of life itself. He suspected that original motion could actually be created through the human will. But interestingly, he also looked to fermentation to explain the origins of life.

Carolyn Merchant, a renowned modern ecological thinker and scientist, explains Newton's fascination with fermentation in her landmark book, *The Death of Nature*:

> The vegetative spirit produced in fermentation is "nature's universal agent, her secret fire, the only ferment and principle of all vegetation." ... The continual source of new life was therefore to be found in fresh fermentation ... [T]he subtle secret workings of nature took place by means of the vegetative spirit produced in fermentation — "an exceeding subtle and unimaginably small portion of matter diffused through the mass, which, if separated, there would remain but a dead and inactive earth."

> Why did Newton attribute such importance to the concept of fermentation? Fermentation had a long and clear historical

connection with motion and activity and could be viewed as a source of violent change. From a political standpoint, a ferment carried the connotation of agitation — the inflaming and fomenting of passions and tumult. A ferment could "work up to foam and threat the government." In alchemy and chemistry, changes in the properties of metals were thought to be produced by a ferment operating within them. The action of yeast on dough and the brewing of beer produced an internal commotion and effervescence. All were examples of new motions generated in both living and nonliving things.

[Fermentation] was responsible for "the beating of the heart by means of respiration," and of "perpetual motion and heat." Without fermentation as an active principle, "all putrefaction, generation, vegetation, and life would cease."

… Newton's answer to the problem of the revitalization of the cosmos was to replenish its motion through … gravity and fer-mentation: "Seeing … the variety of motion we find in the world is always decreasing, there is a necessity of conserving and recruiting it by active principles, such as are the *cause of gravity*, by which planets and comets keep their motions in their orbs, and bodies acquire great motion in falling; and *the cause of fermentation*, by which the heart and blood of animals are kept in perpetual motion and heat … for we meet with very little motion in the world, besides what is owing to these active principles."

… For Newton, fermentation thus furnished an antidote to the "death of nature" implicit in the mechanical universe, a universe founded on passivity and having an inherent tendency towards decay, decline, and eventual death.

Here is the man most responsible for initiating the Renaissance, himself burgeoning with scientific thought, living during a massive societal casting off of ancient religious illusions. Yet Newton, the premier scientist perhaps of all time, was already suspecting the limitations of science, and searching for a supernatural force to explain life. He looked to the very same force worshipped by the ancients: fermentation. In this passage, Merchant gets at the very heart of what is missing in industrial beer: life. And she illustrates Newton's own fear that scientific industrialization could have a catastrophic effect on the human need to connect with nature on a spiritual level. He looked to fermentation as the last refuge of the sacred mystery of life. One could almost say that Newton, just like the Sumerians and Egyptians, worshipped beer.

Newton's description of the earth respiring foreshadows Gaia theory, with its description of the earth as a unified organism, its parts functioning toward the benefit of a whole. This theory is a cornerstone to our understanding of global warming, which is discussed in more detail in Chapter 9.

During the Age of Reason, the transition to modernity was well under way. Until this time, the vast majority of human beings relied directly on agriculture for their well-being. Extended families and small communities formed the basic social units. Homebrewing and cottage beer sales were of an appropriate scale within these settings. As such, brewing was a valuable way for women to maintain a share of power in society. But with the Scientific Revolution pushing man's control over nature, and sparking industrialism and global capitalism, human society took a drastic turn away from the agrarian lifestyles it had always known. What the Church and state had begun with their consolidation of power and control over brewing, corporations were poised to finish — the complete exclusion of small-scale, home-based, female-controlled brewing traditions from the new industrial-scale, beer-marketing companies that placed monetary profit above all other interests.

Brew On, Ladies

This is, however, the gendered story of only the Western brewing tradition. Women continue to brew at home throughout the rest of the world. The practice is common throughout Africa, from Senegal to Ethiopia to South Africa. Similar traditions exist in Central and South America, and across Asia. Unfortunately, these traditions continue to be mostly unnoticed and undervalued by scholars, economists, and politicians both in their own cultures and in the West. Alas, it is Western men who still write most beer history and they write it primarily about the brewing efforts of other Western men. Instead, small scale brewing by women gains undesirable attention from prohibitionist religious fanatics who advocate disingenuously for the abolition of home brewers in the name of such things as "public health" and "sanitation." More significantly, the brewing traditions practiced by millions of women in industrializing countries are under imminent threat from industrialization itself, a process which seems to inevitably debase traditional brewing cultures.

America has already lost its female brewing traditions. Many other countries have not. It is my great hope that some of the pioneering American and European women, as well as men, who are returning to the art and mystery of brewing will redevelop brewing and drinking customs that emphasize feminine qualities, honor the earth, and strengthen the bonds of community. I hope too that interest in existing customs around the world will grow, preventing them from being overcome by industrial brewing and lost forever.

CHAPTER 6

The Revolutionary Beer Party

As the roots of the modern industrial-capitalist brewing companies were forming in Europe, Britain, and America, the early American brewing scene was still dominated by strong cultural interests that moderated consumption and valued the diversity of beer's beneficial attributes. Lender and Martin explain in *Drinking in Early America*, that "Most beer ... was made at home, and no government could dictate a housewife's recipe." And, they continue, "the new American beer rapidly became a highly diverse creature."

As in previous millennia, during America's colonial years brewing was a craft practiced by average folks on a small scale for home and community consumption, or as a small cottage business to supplement farm income. It continued to be associated with spirituality, health, and nutrition. But most of all, beer was highly regarded for its ability to bring people together for important community occasions. Beer played a vital role in building strong communities.

It was also a weapon against British imperialism. In fact, the founding fathers were early protestors against the globalization of beer, boycotting English imports and passing laws throughout the states to subsidize and encourage an increase in local production. Washington and his crew knew that foreign domination of the beer industry was antithetical to America's nascent democracy. Thus, during Colonial and post-Revolutionary times, brewing thrived with its diversity of ingredients and brewing processes, its decentralized production, its small scale, and through its community centeredness.

77

European colonization of the New World fostered the creation of many new communities, as well as the destruction of many established ones. Native North American inhabitants were decimated through genocidal wars, while communities throughout Europe were weakened by the vast human migrations to the New World. As a result of both, though, new Americans established flourishing communities based on shared values and access to abundant natural resources. But from an historical perspective, many of these communities were short-lived, as the industrialization process struck blows against rural society, cities continuously robbed towns and villages of their young and able members, and the frontier lured folks further and further west across the continent.

Pioneers pushed the edges of America ever westward and also began pioneering the mass-production brewing model. But during this process, beer maintained a prominent and positive role in colonial society. It remained an essential asset in building and sustaining strong communities; it fulfilled nutritional needs; and it provided a lever in the War of Independence. Colonial brewsters adapted brewing methods to include locally available ingredients and celebrate local customs. Beer also served as a beverage of moderation compared to the ardent spirits like rum and whiskey which, to the detriment of all, eventually grew to dominate America. But brewing eventually became dominated by just one value: economics.

Just as it did in so many other great societies, beer played a conspicuous role in the founding of America. According to the ship captain's logbook, the puritans landed at Plymouth Rock because of "our victuals being much spent, especially our beer." A brewhouse was among the first common buildings to be erected in the new settlement. Hundreds of roadside taverns soon dotted the countryside, facilitating the expansion of European invaders throughout New England. For a time, beer was the principle beverage of New Englanders, but it was rum that played the most crucial role in establishing American dominance in the hugely profitable global trade economy based on African slaves and New World cotton and rum. However, American beer brewing maintained a distinctly local identity by not relying on international trade. Women continued to brew at home, using whatever ingredients were available

If barley be wanting to make into malt,
we must be content and think it no fault,
For we can make liquor to sweeten our lips,
Of pumpkins, and parsnips, and walnut-tree chips.
— *Poem composed in 1630s, author unknown*

locally. Just like in the old country, special beers marked important occasions like weddings, ordinations, elections, and harvest festivals, like the one that began America's Thanksgiving Day tradition.

Armed and Loaded

The Mothers and Fathers of the American Revolution understood the importance of brewing in establishing local self-reliance and independence. Sam Adams, who ran a malt house as well as a revolutionary newspaper, jabbed at the English with his advertisements for his Old Malt, discouraging Americans from buying English malt or imported English beers. Patrick Henry and other patriots resisted colonial rule through organized boycotts of English beer, encouraging homebrewing as an act of defiance toward George III. When the British redcoats were sent to quell what was thought to be a small ragtag rebellion, they quickly ran out of beer and had to send for emergency rations. When the revolution ended, the slogan "Home Brew'd Is Best" appeared on banners in victory parades, carried by American brewers wearing garlands of hops and mashing oars propped over their shoulders like muskets.

The United States of America owes its political birth to George Washington, but few people realize that he was also responsible for kick-starting the growth of a domestic beer industry. At the heart of the colonists' revolutionary gripes was discontent with Britain's unfair taxation policies. Though they tried conventional diplomacy, the colonists had little success in effecting long-lasting and significant change in the unbalanced trading relationship between England and America. The colonials grew alienated and disgruntled.

Their discontent eventually erupted into acts of civil disobedience. In the early stages, it wasn't so much a desire to break from the British Empire, indeed many considered themselves good ale-drinking Brits; it was that they wanted the same rights as every other good ale-drinking Brit. As relations became increasingly confrontational, and the revolution began to foment, Americans also recognized the need to ferment. But as America's colonial days ground to an abrupt halt, the country was still heavily dependent on imported supplies of ale.

The Ultimate Sacrifice: Boycotting Imported Ale

Washington, whose penchant for English porter is recorded in a number of surviving documents in which he placed orders for large quantities of the drink, made the ultimate sacrifice for his country, in 1774, when he supported the "non-consumption agreement," a bill drafted by fellow patriot Samuel Adams. The agreement encouraged the colonial population to abstain from imported goods such as tea, madeira, and port wine, and likewise encouraged the consumption of American-brewed beer, so as to curtail reliance on imports. Boycotting English imports, including ale, was a promising strategy, if somewhat hard to swallow for beer-drinking colonists like George Washington and his fellow patriots.

Washington's anger over unfair taxes eventually lead to his dismissal from the Virginia House of Burgesses. In a show of solidarity with the Boston patriots, Washington and fellow legislators Patrick Henry, George Mason, and Thomas Jefferson, had declared June 1, 1774, the day the Port Act sealed off Boston in a commercial blockade, to be a day of "fasting, humiliation, and prayer." Irate at this seditious behavior, the Virginia Governor, a loyalist to the crown, promptly responded by dissolving the Assembly.

In due haste, George and his Assembly mates regrouped at the Raleigh Tavern, where over beers they composed a further proclamation declaring that: "An attack on one of our sister colonies, to compel submission to arbitrary taxes, is an attack made on all British America. That we will not hereafter, directly or indirectly import, or cause to be imported, from great Britain, and of the goods hereafter enumerated, either for sale or for our own use ... beer, ale, porter, malt."

Once the American Revolution began in earnest and Washington became commander of the American forces, he made his headquarters in the home of George Emlen, just outside Philadelphia. Given Washington's known predilection for porter, one must wonder whether it was pure coincidence that Emlen was a commercial porter brewer and descendant of one of Philadelphia's earliest brewing families. On the subject of Pennsylvania, it is also worth noting that the colony's founder, William Penn, built a sizable brewhouse on his original estate in this wooded mid-Atlantic keystone state.

A Well-Supped Army

Washington made sure the soldiers under his command were well-supped. According to a 1775 pronouncement, every soldier in the new Continental army would receive a ration of "1 quart of spruce beer or cyder per man per day." After the revolution, Washington made sure he would himself never again be short of porter by supporting the growth of the local brewing industry.

He grew barley on his own farm and harvested ice from his ponds to be used, most likely, for cooling beer. Describing his post-war efforts to boost local brewing, he said: "We have already been too long subject to British Prejudices. I use no porter or cheese in my family, but that which is made in America: both these articles may now be purchased of an excellent quality." According to records, a certain Robert Hare, brewer of porter in Philadelphia, had the good fortune to be Washington's regular beer supplier. Hare had begun brewing porter in 1774 — probably the first ever made in America.

Drinks Are On the House (of Representatives)

Another noteworthy item regarding Washington's relationship with beer appears in *Drinking in America*. The custom of "treating" citizens to drinks at public gatherings was common among America's early politicians. As Lender and Martin explain: "One did not seek office at any level without 'treating' the electorate during the campaign. Polling places themselves were rarely dry: there was only one poll per county and after making the long trek to do his citizen's duty, the voter expected some tangible reward. He usually got it. This meant that to count as a Founding Father, George Washington … must have provided many a drink for the multitude."

Given the dismal voter turnout levels in contemporary American elections, perhaps this strategy ought to be readopted? One ballot, one beer. Imagine the increase in voter participation.

Whiskey Rebels

Unfortunately, at least one spot mars the first president's record on alcohol and taxation: the Whiskey Rebellion. The new American central government found itself in the uncomfortable position of emulating the very same British behavior that sparked the revolution in the first place. The budding American government needed cash to fund its activities. As the British well knew, alcohol was a tax revenue jackpot, and so Washington followed their example and imposed a whiskey tax. Frontiersmen making their new lives across the Appalachian range in places like western Pennsylvania were outraged by what they rightly perceived as an unfair tax by a faraway government. These frontiersmen were grain and whiskey rich, but cash poor, making a cash tax a particular hardship.

Now in addition to his extensive homebrewing operation, Washington was also a voluminous whiskey distiller. It may have been that Washington's private interests in the commercial whiskey market clouded his commitment to public service in this matter. Multitudes of home distillers producing tax-free whiskey could have been competition for Washington's own distillery, not to mention for the many other politician-distillers comprising his first government. Or perhaps it was the same taxation rationale that had motivated Europeans for centuries. Whatever the justification may have been, Washington responded swiftly when Pennsylvanians near Pittsburgh rebelled openly and violently against the new tax; he crushed them with a hastily assembled national army. And so began the American tradition of running illicit moonshine and evading taxes.

Long Live the Revolution

But where beer was concerned, Washington did his best to encourage the domestic industry with tax incentives, and his efforts were quite successful. In 1789, one of the first bills passed by the new House of Representatives was designed by James Madison to keep taxes low on beer production in order to trigger local brewing. As quoted in *The Good Beer Book*, Madison explained, "This low rate will be such an encouragement as to induce brewing in every State in the Union." Less than a hundred years later, in 1873, America could boast 4,131 commercial breweries, plus countless private home breweries. Unfortunately, the country was also on the path toward industrial brewing consolidation and Prohibition, the combined effects of which would eventually reduce America's total number of breweries to fewer than fifty.

Join the Beer Party

These days, beer is in bad need of political reform. The three-tier beer trade — brewing, distribution, and retail — was designed to help dismantle monopolies, but the requisite middle distribution tier now hinders small breweries by curtailing their ability to distribute their own products and sell directly to consumers. Ironically, America's brewing *beer*hemoths, Anheuser-Busch, SABMiller, and Molson-Coors, lobby heavily to maintain this unfair marketing system because it helps exclude competition from the small brewers who struggle to consolidate resources and change laws to create a more even playing field.

We also need new political support to fix the legislation that codifies unhealthy beer-drinking practices. Teenagers can drive cars and buy guns — some states have no minimum age requirement at all for owning a gun. But the legal drinking age in every state is 21. Young people in the military fight wars and die for their country, but cannot legally drink a single beer. Out of the 1,095 pages in the Code of Federal Regulations 27 (parts 1 through 199), over 600 pages are devoted to alcohol and less than 150 cover guns and ammo. Do Americans really believe that a beer is more harmful than a loaded gun in the hands of a teenager? Because of this restriction, many young people learn to drink in what has become a ritualized binge-drinking spree on their 21st birthday. This becomes a pattern for many young drinkers who never learn to drink moderately. Yet brewers are forbidden from including claims of legitimate health benefits on their packaging, for fear that people might use it as an excuse to drink in excess. So the public is intentionally kept ill-informed about the health benefits of beer, and the minimum drinking age

Beer and Politics

Brewing has always been intricately linked with political power and that continues to be the case today. For example, Denver's mayor, John Hickenlooper, is also founder of Wynkoop, the first brewpub in the Rocky Mountain region. After a landslide election victory, Hickenlooper said, "It's like drinking a glass of the finest beer and wanting that taste to linger as long as you can." Hickenlooper is also known for giving others the chance to win a prize worth savoring. Wynkoop sponsors a Beer Drinker of the Year contest; the winner gets free beer for life at its brewpub.

But beer has an ugly political side too. Most of the big corporate brewing companies grease the palms of politicians from both major political parties but they give disproportionately to Republicans. In the 2004 election cycle, Anheuser-Busch was by far the biggest political contributor in the beer industry, giving a whopping $665,973 (the number of the Beer Beast?) to Republicans and only $377,217 to Democrats. Heineken N.V., Molson-Coors, and SABMiller gave a combined total of $234,433 to Republicans and only $71,167 to Democrats. On the other hand, craft brewers eschew Republicans with their political donations. Boston Beer Co. (makers of Sam Adams) and New Belgium Brewing, two of the largest craft brewers, gave a total of $18,650 to Democrats and nothing at all to Republicans. Sierra Nevada, another of the largest craft brewers, chooses the high road by keeping out of political donations altogether.

makes it nearly impossible for young people to learn responsible drinking practices at home with their family.

It is time for a new political party — a Beer Party — to advocate for policies that support the growth of a healthy, convivial, small-scale, family- and community-oriented brewing and beer-drinking culture. To be success- ful, beer drinkers must first shed the Neanderthal image that is so heavily marketed by the corporate male Beeristocracy. Sustainable, craft-brewed beer is patriotic. But what political party will bear the beer banner? It must start with individual beer activists choosing better beers from better companies and drinking them in more sophisticated circumstances than the college "keg- ger" party. In Chapter 17, I've issued the Beer Party platform and called for the Twenty-Four Point Beer Action Plan. Read on and join the Fermenting Revolution.

CHAPTER 7

Fermenting the Industrial Revolution

The Industrial Revolution was the biggest transformation of human society since we built those first beer cities down in Mesopotamia some eight thousand years ago. And just as brewing helped to trigger that big social change, it also helped touch off the Industrial Revolution. Brewers were a vital source of technological innovation and were eager to utilize new instruments that assisted in their quest for increased profits. Brewers helped to develop and were quick to adopt the industrial approach to production. Their centrality to this human social transformation eventually spelled the doom of their own trade with Prohibition, which was partly a result of anti-Industrial society backlash. After Prohibition, beer became a pale, fizzy imitation of its former self. But today breweries are once again at the forefront of a new social transformation, led by a loosely assembled band, broadly called the anti-globalization crowd, but more comprehensively and constructively labeled "the Sustainability Movement."

Tools of the Revolution

Hardware like thermometers, hydrometers, and microscopes, processes like pasteurization and refrigeration, and the use of coke as a new smokeless fuel source all caused significant change within Western brewing culture, and therefore brewing in the rest of the world too. For example, John Richardson's accounts of testing a hydrometer in the 1780s are called crucial in turning the craft of brewing into a science. An important effect of these tools was a vast increase in the scale of beer production and the creation of the social and political structures required to support it. Not only did production far surpass previous levels, but pasteurization and refrigeration allowed brewers to greatly extend the geographic reach of their markets. As the scale of their operations grew exponentially, brewing became far more specialized and complicated than ever before, requiring more equipment, space, and financial capital. Brewers adopted a hierarchical, centralized organizing structure, reliant on legal supports and distribution networks. This combination of factors made it impossible for female brewsters to compete against men who wielded more political power, had greater access to capital, and were therefore excitedly pursuing ever-grander scales of production and accruing ever-greater profits, fostering ever-larger growth. But ultimately, this industrial capitalist movement rang the death knell for the life of beer culture.

In *Beer: The Story of the Pint*, Martyn Cornell cites the transfer of brewing from women to men as the pivotal phenomenon marking the transition to the modern brewing era:

> The disappearance of women from visible involvement with brewing in London is undoubtedly linked with the increased wealth possible to anyone brewing as a regular trade, thanks to the rise in the city's population: men were now willing to make full-time careers out of what had previously been only a way for women to supplement the household income. The masculinization of brewing is also linked with the most important technological change in brewing since the move from beer-bread to ground malt. This was (its importance should be emphasized) the arrival of hops. An era had come to an end: we are now at the start of modern times.

The fact that Cornell refers to brewing as being *only* a way for women to supplement household income, is indicative of the male bias responsible for destroying so much feminine brewing culture. Furthermore, his claim that the introduction of hops was the most important technological change is highly disputable and fits with a masculine interpretation of brewing history. The fact is women brewed occasionally with hops for hundreds of years without brewing becoming industrialized. Changes in the scale of brewing hardware were more central to the change in beer technology than was the introduction of hops.

Male industrial brewers probably still would have gained supremacy over brewing, regardless of whether hops were the prevailing spice. However, hops did assist in their rise to power. The main quality of hops that is attractive to commercial brewers is its effectiveness as a preservative. This helps lengthen beer's

"As far as the brewing industry is concerned, the move to monopoly went so far that, even if it has now slowed down, it caused significant damage to the industry and to the interests of consumers."
— Richard Boston, *Beer and Skittles*

freshness period by preventing spoilage from airborne bacteria. This extended shelf life converged with the other political and technological changes mentioned above to foster commercialization by increasing capacity and geographic reach. Growth into large-scale operations required large amounts of capital which generally excluded women from participating. Likewise, the eventual formation of male-controlled guilds and laws regulating beer commerce worked to the disadvantage of women. Governments could more easily tax a small, controlled base of professional brewers than a large, dispersed population of female homebrewers. Simultaneously, dramatic urbanization offered more concentrated beer markets than ever before, assisting the growth of large-scale breweries. So hops did mark an historical period in which beer took a turn away from home-scale brewsters, but it was just one of several factors occurring during that time, all of which contributed to a relentless march toward male, corporate, industrial mega-brewers.

Porter, a Beer Burning with Efficiency

The development of the porter beer style spurred the growth of gigantic English breweries during the 18th and early 19th centuries, becoming the ultimate symbol of industrial-scale, profit-driven brewing. According to Daniels and Larson, porter was brewed in facilities that "ranked among the largest industrial undertakings in all of Britain ... And with such scale came a scrupulous attention to the economics of the business venture. Any savings realized in the production of the product paid handsome rewards to the owners of these breweries." This kind of commercial orientation is markedly different from the earlier reasons for brewing: family sustenance, spiritual worship, community conviviality, and eventually occasional supplemental income for women as economies became more cash-based.

"Like many good things, its decline was hastened by technology."
— Ray Daniels and Geoffrey Larson,
Smoked Beers

As a style, English porter beers are noted for their ruby-brown color, a malt-accented, medium body, roasty aromas, and chocolaty flavors. The style actually disappeared from Britain for a time and the world's oldest, continuously-brewed porter beer is from America's oldest brewery, Yuengling and Sons, in Pottsville, Pennsylvania, built in 1829. Just as porter's geographic popularity shifted, so did its style parameters evolve. The beer called porter today probably bears little resemblance to the beer called porter when it first emerged in England around the end of the 18th century.

Porter was born partly out of the need to address a shortcoming of London's water. The water was not as acidic as brewers needed for an efficient conversion of starches to sugars during the mashing process. Adding some burnt malt helped to acidify the mash water. These brown malts, that were dried over wood fires, were used to make the original porters. However, these fires would always scorch a small amount of the malt, causing the grains to explode, guaranteeing that a portion of every batch would be rendered useless. This inefficiency and inconsistency was an inherent limitation in the malting process of the time. In 1817, a man named Daniel Wheeler invented a rotating drum that prevented the grains from burning but still allowed them to become black and roasted. Brewers could now achieve a porter with the desired color and flavor using a smaller amount of this "black patent" malt (so-called because Wheeler patented the process) compared to regular brown malt. This increased efficiency also increased profitability. There was a double savings involved: no more losses from combusted brown malt, and less black malt required to achieve an appropriate color and roasty flavor.

A further savings came with the adoption of coke as a fuel source. Coke, a product of coal, burns at a lower and more controlled temperature than wood or hay, and produces little or no smoke. Wood was also becoming more expensive as the British Isles were denuded of forest, so a transition to coal-based fuels allowed industrialization to continue unabated. But barley malted from coke failed to attain the color and bitterness intrinsic to the smoked, brown malts. Likewise, the resulting beers were missing the distinctive colors, aromas, and flavors that had always been associated with beer. That is where the black patent malt came in handy.

The big porter brewing concerns replaced the more expensive brown malts with a combination of two new industrial malts, one pale and one black. The pale malts were more evenly malted, and therefore more efficient in the mashing process, so a smaller volume was required to achieve the same alcoholic result than with brown malts. But pale malts were light in color, and lacked the bitterness of wood-smoked malt. Beer drinkers reacted against these pale-colored, less-bitter porters. Brewers compensated by adding a very small amount of black patent malt for color and bitterness. This combination of pale and black malts was a big savings over brown malt for brewers, especially because taxes were levied based on the amount of grain used in brewing, not the volume of beer produced. Reducing the "grain bill" thus created tremendous tax-savings for brewers.

Some view these innovations as the triumph of technology in helping man achieve better quality with less work and fewer resources. But the truth is, these so-called advances were driven by one consideration only, and it was neither quality nor sound resource use, but profit pure and simple. Drinkers never asked for "un-smoky" beers (just like they never asked for hopped beers), and they were not looking for lighter-colored beers. As porter underwent this transformation in production methods (from wood-fired brown malt to coke-fueled pale malt), drinkers mourned the loss of the beer's former qualities. In *Smoked Beers*, Daniels quotes one John Tuck lamenting that "... the real flavor of porter, as originally drunk, is completely lost ..." This is a classic example of how industrial changes and the pursuit of profit by a few people can trump the interests of the masses. Beer drinkers weren't asking for a non-smoky beer but they were told that it was better. Better for brewery owners, perhaps, but not necessarily for drinkers. Brewers implementing these new techniques were forced to react to a lack of public acceptance by retrofitting the pale beers with some black malt in order to meet beer drinkers' expectations.

Arising from this scientific and technological foundation, porter became the first mass-produced beer. However, these same innovations would be at least partly responsible for the eventual demise of porter in England. As Foster explains in *Porter*:

Porter was an integral part of the Industrial Revolution ... [it] played an important part in ensuring the decline of both the publican brewer and the craft of brewing at home ... About 1830, a variety of competing pressures combined to decrease porter's popularity.

Perhaps the first was technological progress, founded on porter's own success … The steam engine, thermometer, and hydrometer were quickly adopted by English brewers … Porter accelerated the pace of transformation of brewing from domestic craft to profit-driven industry. Upon the sale of Thrale Brewery, a famous producer of porter, Dr. Johnson commented, "Sir, we are not here to sell a parcel of boilers and vats, but the potentiality of growing rich beyond the dreams of avarice …" According to *The London Tradesman*, it was esti-mated that it took more capital to start up as a porter brewer than it did to get into any other trade except for banking … The rise in scale of porter brewing was linked to its ability to be stored in very large wooden vats. In 1795, Meux Brewing Company built a vat so large (it held 860,000 US gallons) that a promotional kick-off event was held at which 200 people dined inside the vat. Disaster followed in 1814, when another brewery's enormous porter vat burst apart, send-ing waves of porter across its neighborhood, smashing down walls and killing eight people. The deaths were attributed to such causes as "drowning, injury, poisoning by porter fumes, or drunkenness."

Porter was also responsible for the growth of the abominable practice of "tying" English beer retailers. A tied house was a pub owned by, or indebted to the brewer, and therefore was required to sell only that brewery's products. Since this was also a time of consolidation and massive increases in scale, more than half the pubs in London became tied to a decreasing number of ever-larger porter producers. This also led to another despicable practice. Large brewers began buying their competitors out, closing their brewing operations, and supplying their tied-houses with their own beer, which reduced diversity for the consumer.

Industrial porter, named (at least so it is claimed) after the very labor-ers that were the backbone of the Industrial Revolution, represented the fully realized ideal of industrial brewing. With porter, brewing had reached a point of no return. Profit, more than any other value, became the sole motivation for brewing. Ever since, brewing has been shedding the roles it once played in promoting community, spirituality, health, and well-being. The mash forks once held by the hands of priestesses and millions of housewives, who brewed in order to celebrate and enhance life, were seized by industrialist barons whose single object was to accumulate tremendous wealth through the cunning marketing of what they had reduced to a mere commodity. The intangible essence of beer was dead. Choices about what and how to brew were made according to potential profits alone, rather than out of any commitment to craft, quality, regional specialty, or cultural tradition. Before beer was commandeered by corporate brewers, it was an inseparable part of the entire cultural milieu, a part that was controlled by women. This control, it should again be noted, provided a considerable degree of influence for women in the realm of alcohol consumption, which helped to regulate drinking and keep it within socially accepted boundaries. Industrialism changed all of this.

Lager and the Rise of the Corporate "Beeristocracy"

"Men can go wrong with wine and women. Shall we then prohibit and abolish women?"

— Martin Luther

Porter may have been the beer that began the Industrial Age, but American lager soon replaced it and has dominated the globe ever since. Refrigeration, cheap fossil fuel-based transportation, and the growing industrial demand for cheap imported laborers were some of the factors behind the popularity of industrial lager beer in America. Many of the immigrants who crossed the Atlantic seeking industrial jobs were German. They brought lager beer with them from Bavaria and Bohemia where it had been developing since the early 1800s. Simultaneously, clear glass was coming into vogue. Sanitation practices and pasteurization (the practice of heating beer to destroy living organisms) also appeared. These factors combined to create a ripe environment for cheap, mass-marketed beer. Many of the same factors leading to consolidation in Europe also played out on the American stage: urbanization, technological advances, the need for a tax base to support central government, and the male takeover of brewing. Eventually — helped along by Prohibition — this led to absolutely massive consolidation in the American industry. By the 1970s, Americans were left with one bland industrial light lager beer style made by a handful of gigantic corporations. Beer completely lost its value as a food craft, and became the alcoholic equivalent of lemonade, slaking the thirst of male industrial laborers, rather than fulfilling the nutritional and spiritual needs of body and soul for all people.

The first American lager was brewed in 1840 in Philadelphia for German immigrant communities. But within ten years it was making inroads

A wall mural in the foyer of the Beach Chalet brewery restaurant in San Francisco depicts a picnic on the beach outside the Beach Chalet. The mural was commissioned by the Work Projects Administration (WPA) in the 1930s.

into the traditional English ale and porter drinking markets. Foster cites the Milwaukee Brewery as a perfect example of lager's ascendancy. The brewery began brewing ale and porter in 1840. By 1867 its rivals had all converted to lager, but the Milwaukee Brewery, whose name had changed to M. W. Powell & Co., continued brewing ales until 1880, at which point they abandoned it "because the brewing of ale was less profitable than that of lager beer."

Lager arrived at a crucial point in the development of America's brewing industry. Male-led industrialization, not Prohibition, should be listed as beer's official cause of death. During industrialization, society underwent the second decisive shift of its history to date. The first was from nomadic life to settled agricultural societies; the second was from an agrarian to an urban-industrial base. Great insecurity and risks accompanied both shifts. Industrializing America experienced great upheavals as populations moved from rural lifestyles to the stress of urban industrial life, upsetting the delicate balance of small rural communities. Urban communities rapidly changed their job base from skilled craftsmen to industrial workers, and were overwhelmed by domestic and foreign immigrants. This dehumanizing process caused feelings of power-lessness, loss of identity, and lack of self-confidence. One symptom of this social trauma was a dramatic increase in destructive drinking practices, which soon became a serious social problem and reached a scale rarely, if ever, seen before in history. In America this transpired gradually, over a number of centuries as migration, urbanization, technological advance, and capitalism co-evolved.

From the early colonial years up to Prohibition, beer's central, positive role in life changed dramatically. America embraced industrialization with vigor and brewing became the quintessential expression of this trend. American brewers zealously pursued the path of corporate industrial hegemony, maximizing profits and lowering quality, and quashing small breweries as mega-brewers exercised their might. Eventually, through Prohibition, beer itself became a victim of industrialization.

Early in colonial America, life was pretty good for a small but growing class of landed gentry. And for those white men who were still working toward success, life was full of promise. When life is good like this, drinking can make it even better. But many of these entitled white men faced dismal prospects in the urban industrial ghettoes after the Civil War, and for them life was bad. From early colonial times all the way to Prohibition, rum and whiskey consistently grew in popularity. Compared to cumbersome barrels of beer, ardent spirits were compact, which made them more convenient for frontier families on the move, but also more potent and easier to abuse. Alcohol abuse as a way out was an obvious dead end choice for people attempting to escape the challenges of colonial, frontier, and industrial America.

The temperance movement preceded prohibitionist rhetoric and advocated for moderation in drinking, encouraging the drinking of beer rather than spirits. It sprang up to oppose the problems being caused by overdrinking, which were largely linked to liquor rather than beer. However, this abuse was symptomatic of the social upheaval caused by modernization; it was not the original illness itself. Yet it became a target for reform as if it was the cause of all the social problems that accompanied the abrupt swing to modernity.

But the more industrialization and urbanization caused poverty, the more alcohol abuse increased, and the more logical the prohibitionist cause seemed. Prohibitionists grew to the peak of their power during the time of industrial urbanization. Anti-drink agitators painted poverty as a direct result of alcohol. The stereotype of the alcoholic skid row bum became a ubiquitous symbol of this claim, even though, according to Lender and Martin no more than three to four percent of alcoholics lived in skid row circumstances. Even Frances Willard, president of the Women's Christian Temperance Union, grew doubtful of alcohol as the root of all social ills. Instead, she finally concluded that the reverse was true: poverty and other social problems were the causes of alcoholism.

Prohibitionists also exhibited more than a hint of xenophobia. In their view, drinking excessively was rooted in the "free and easy drinking customs of Europe," according to one Reverend Dorchester (as cited by Lender and Martin). And furthermore, he insisted, the country's liquor trade was "in the hands of a low class of foreigners." Yet Jews and Italians, who represented a large number of the immigrant masses at the time, brought with them quite temperate and established drinking practices and probably had the lowest rates of alcoholism of all ethnic groups. An overt fear of foreigners was at least partly responsible for provoking the prohibitionists' ire.

Individualistic attitudes grew common during the modernizing period, helping to shake loose the social controls that used to keep drinking in check and from becoming a social ill. Previously, drinking was generally regarded as safe because even extreme drunkenness was contained within the context of tightly-knit communities where the strong social fabric proscribed misbehavior during a period of drunkenness. In fact, much of the excessive drinking occurred at church-sponsored gatherings, where anti-social behavior would have been restrained despite advanced states of inebriation. Similarly, drinking alone in a remote field during the farm workday, which was common, was unlikely to end in a crime spree. More likely, it was just the right fortification needed to get through another few hours of field work.

Will Work for Beer

Industrial workers were often physically endangered by modern technology. Drinking on the job became a health hazard not because of the physical effects of the alcohol itself, but because one false move could send you into a bubbling cauldron of molten steel, or turn an arm or leg into one more cog in a giant grinding gear. While industrialists came to view drinking as a hazard to the smooth functioning of their factories, another view is that their ghastly industrial jobs were a pox on a culture of perfectly civilized drinking practices. Lender and Martin explain: "industrialists feared that an alcoholic employee could play havoc in a complex workplace … the rise of a mass industrial base, reflected in the production of assembly line goods, gave the issue added importance." Likewise, industrialization's most important new product, the automobile, not only threatened the worker's drinking style by preventing the long-established practice of workday drinking breaks, it also threatened the average consumer's tippling habits. As noted in a 1904 medical journal, "inebriate and moderate drinkers are the most incapable of all persons to drive motor wagons." So this fantastic new technology threatened even the "moderate drinkers." Henry Ford, who blamed "the International Jew" for America's drinking problems, once declared that "booze had to go when modern industry and the motor car came in." Alcohol could come back, he said, only if America was "willing to abolish modern industry and the motor car." On that point, the Luddite in me is inclined to agree. Let's begin the Anti-Industrial Revolution by converting all the Hummers and Escapes into tiny little neighborhood bars so families can walk to the corner together in the evening and spend some quality time relaxing and drinking beer with friends.

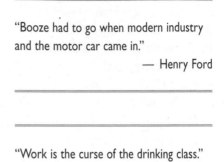

"Booze had to go when modern industry and the motor car came in."
— Henry Ford

"Work is the curse of the drinking class."
— Oscar Wilde

Revolting Women

It was no coincidence that women led the charge for temperance and Prohibition. Brewing had been appropriated from them and changed from a socially regulated part of community life, to a profit-oriented industry controlled by rich, power-hungry men. For a long time, the temperance movement advocated a general return to rural family values, and acknowledged moderate drinking as a wholesome part of that lifestyle. The temperance movement even promoted beer as a healthy drink better suited for family consumption than the much stronger whisky and rum that were gaining popularity. Alcohol itself was not considered the problem, but over-consumption was viewed as linked to the general deterioration of community standards. Alcohol abuse was as much a result as a cause of the many social traumas playing out during industrialization.

Social breakdown was due in large part to the corporate takeover of the means of production. Industrial capitalism created giant rifts in wealth between the growing ranks of laborers and jobless farmers, and the corporate bosses who eventually employed them. Technology played a big part in this process, as indicated earlier. The tools of craft brewing were replaced by outsized machinery, reaching far beyond the human scale. The very process of brewing was no longer a craft of human hands, of mom cooking up some beer in the kitchen, but of the grinding gears of industrial machinery. Simultaneously, the federal government was subsidizing the great westward expansion, promoting the exploitation of natural resources and the growth of the industrial business models that served the urban centers where traditional values were rapidly disintegrating. The unintended effect of these combined processes — industrialization and mass migration — was the undermining of age-old community standards governing drinking practices. Without the safeguards built into small, rural communities, drinking occasionally became a social ill.

The temperance movement, reacting against these processes, spawned modern-day feminism. Women revolted, righteously so, because their control of alcohol, and therefore much of their influence within society, was being stolen by industrialists keen on overturning the very structure of society. Male-dominated corporations valued the individual's right to pursue business unencumbered by law. Women leading the temperance movement, on the other hand, emphasized public welfare, calling for a return to values that held the good of the community above that of the individual. The leadership role of women in the temperance movement cannot be underscored enough. Their very place in society was under siege by modernization. Women were traditionally in charge of the home and of nurturing the family. As such, they were guardians of the family's moral virtue, which itself assured the family's proper status in the community. However, as male roles changed — from farmer and craftsmen to industrial laborers dependent on wages — women's ability to maintain family values was subject to risk, especially if the man failed to earn those wages and turned to alcohol abuse as a means of assuaging the pain of his failure.

But the temperance movement's priority of promoting community welfare changed as the movement converged with the interests of another growing movement: slavery abolitionism. Like industrial capitalism, abolitionism valued individual liberty more highly than community standards. So temperance leaders began seeing the importance of private freedoms, and emphasized abstention from alcohol as a personal choice. The growth of these combined movements set the stage for black Emancipation and women's suffrage and helped to stave off efforts to impose legal restrictions on drinking.

However, industrialization ultimately went too far. It removed alcohol too far from cultural controls and social values, emphasized profit too singularly, and ignored the social problems caused by drinking in a society marred by the breakdown of shared traditional values. Reformers reacted in an equally extreme fashion and eventually full-blown Prohibition made beer illegal, mistakenly targeting alcohol, rather than global corporate industrialization, as the source of America's social ills. Although Prohibition ultimately failed, it did succeed in deeply fracturing American attitudes about drinking. What had once been a celebrated cultural asset became a tolerated commercial interest, further encouraging massive industrial globalization in the brewing industry.

CHAPTER 8

Glob**eer**ization

Beer Dies a Pale, Fizzy Death

After Prohibition, beer was in a precarious position. Some people still considered it a beneficial cultural tradition but they were generally afraid to say so because so many others viewed it simply as an industry, to be tolerated only because Prohibition had failed so extravagantly. This shift in America's view toward alcohol is the root problem with modern American drinking attitudes. The majority of Americans drink, but we do so with guilty pleasure rather than with appreciation, reverence, and joy. This is the worst consequence of Prohibition. Furthermore, Prohibition amplified this splintered drinking mentality by vastly accelerating the pace of corporate consolidation, destroying what little was left of local brewing and drinking traditions and paving the way for the global beer giants that dominate the beer world today. Prohibition tipped the pale remains of what was left of American beer culture right out into the sewer.

Beer's Bloated Corpse

In post-Prohibition America, beer culture's moment of greatest vulnerability, corporate profit-seekers hammered the final nail into the coffin of beer *as a way of life*. Homebrewing was outlawed and the commodification of American beer was complete. At the close of America's Industrial Age the tin-can corpse of beer is found floating down the polluted annals of "scientific progress." The outlook for humanity is decidedly pale. Oversized-industrialization, mega-urbanization, and tyrannical capitalism killed beer dead, destroyed and isolated communities and social structures, and wreaked havoc on nature.

Beer became the ultimate example of a bland, uniform, cheap, and soulless industrial product, its production controlled by a handful of corporate monsters. After 13 years of being knocked unconscious during Prohibition, beer awoke in a zombie-like state.

But could a beverage so integral to the development of human society ever really die forever? Did humans create religious mythologies, devise agriculture, build great cities, form complex centralized governments, advance medicine, develop modern science, and invent powerful technologies, all so that we could be left with just one bland and fizzy excuse for beer called American light lager? Had we reached the Pinnacle of Progress or the Day of Reckoning? Could beer rise again? These questions form the crux of the raging globalization debate today, the outcome of which will shape society for at least the rest of the twenty-first century.

Glo*beer*ization or *Beer*oregionalism?

Our current Age of Globalization is characterized by two simultaneous, yet competing, trends in brewing. Global beer giants bloat into ever-larger corporate behemoths. Meanwhile, thousands of new small breweries are emerging and thriving. "Glo*beer*ization," if you will, represents the triumph of beer-as-commodity while "*beer*oregionalism" marks a turn toward small-scale, local production, with a focus on diversity, craft, community, and tradition. In one model, power concentrates in the hands of a few faceless, distant corporations, while in the other, communities are reining in control and forging regional identities. The efficiency of capital rationalizes an approach to brewing where the ends (profit) justifies the means (crass commercialism); more is believed to be inherently better, and process and context are irrelevant. *Beer*oregionalism, on the other hand, places higher value on the process of brewing and the experience of drinking. Beer is not simply a number of units moving through the supply chain, a data point in the pursuit of profits for a cabal of elites. It is an elixir to be cherished as an integral part of the human experience, one that should be both respected and enjoyed by all. These competing values of corporatism and sustainability are the same ones that frame the broader globalization debate.

To Ale with the WTO

Nothing epitomized these conflicting views on globalization better than the shutdown of the World Trade Organization's ministerial meeting in Seattle, 1999. On this topic, I have a confession to make. I was a turtle.

I hope you haven't forgotten already. The media images were splendid — pictures in the newspapers and footage on TV of hundreds of protestors outfitted in sea turtle costumes marching through Seattle alongside thousands of Teamsters union members. It was a powerful example of labor activists and environmentalists joining forces to strike back against the evil corporate empire. Well over 50,000 citizens stormed the WTO, causing chaos and having great fun in the streets, and introducing the anti-corporate globalization movement to the world.

But that's not my real confession. Nay, I wear that turtle photo as a badge of honor, or at least with guilty pride. Why guilty? Because my real confession is that I spent much of my Seattle protest time in brewpubs. Dodging tear gas is thirsty work. And hey, Seattle is the closest thing to beer nirvana north of Portland, Oregon. What was I going to do, spend all day

The author (far right) dons a sea turtle costume for the protests that shut down the World Trade Organization's 1999 ministerial meeting in Seattle, finding refuge in the city's many brewpubs while dodging tear gas.

performing jail solidarity and miss my chance to savor a pumpkin ale at the Elysian brewpub? Hell No! Let the beer taps flow! To ale with the WTO!

Crafting Community

One of the worst effects of globalization is how it breaks down communities. Sam Calagione is one of America's leading craft brewers. Ironically, his guiding rationale, brewing "off-centered beers for off-centered people," has turned out to be right on the mark. His quixotic "extreme beers" have earned accolades from reviewers as diverse as the New York Times and People Magazine. His willingness to follow a unique vision that throws caution to the wind has made him the envy of the beer industry. But Sam realizes that running his brewery is about more than just making jaw-dropping beers. In his book *Brewing Up a Business*, he states that "the ongoing creation of a community ... is what we are in the business of at Dogfish Head." This sentiment is rooted in American history.

Jim Hightower, "America's Most Popular Populist," is another leading voice in contemporary America. In his many books, he advocates for improving our democracy by leveling the playing field between the haves and have-nots. The fact that Jim has a partiality for beer, reflects his populist views. What kind of populist would he be if he didn't drink the most popular beverage? He also understands how beer helps to build community. In his best-selling book *Thieves in High Places*, Jim comments on the spirit that built America:

"Beer and Benevolence" graces the wall of the brew room at the Dogfish Head brewery.

People came seeking opportunity, for sure. But people came also — came especially — in search of community ... And wherever they landed or moved, they immediately set about building the commons ... including, often, a public alehouse. In [this category] falls the story of Spoetzl Brewery in the little Texas town of Shiner ... One of the first things done by the leaders of the new town, settled by farmers from the old country at the turn of the twentieth century, was to form a beer-making cooperative, called the Shiner Brewery Association. Unfortunately for them, they were much more adept at drinking beer than at making it. Faced with a choice between bad beer and no beer, they did what any group of serious beer drinkers would do: invented a third choice. The leaders met, pondered, pooled their resources, and sent out a search party to find an honest-to-God German brew master willing to relocate to Shiner. They found their man in Kosmos Spoetzl, for whom the brewery was renamed in 1915, and the Shiner brand not only survives today but is the unofficial state beer of Texas — and, I can attest, good stuff, too.

Throughout ancient cultures, and even today in many non-Western societies, brewing is conducted to mark the important occasions of life, and to bind the community in common experiences and a shared understanding of the world. In these instances, money is neither the means nor the motive for beer drinking. The primary importance of beer is in its function as social adhesive, not as financial asset.

Beer for People, Not for Profit

And that is why the emergence of an American brewing renaissance is so relevant to globalization. The brewing field embodies the two conflicting sets of values competing to shape our future. Corporate brewers value economic growth while the new breed of "beer activists" value beer for its culture. On the one hand, corporate consolidation abounds. Three companies control more than 80 percent of the American beer market. On the global scene, corporate beer behemoths are merging to form ultra-mega-brewing conglomerates. Interbrew and AmBev recently formed a company that controls almost one sixth of the world's commercially produced beer and they are preparing to swallow another billion dollar brewing concern as this book goes to press.

Anheuser-Busch (A-B) produces about one in every ten commercial beers worldwide and controls fully one half of the American market. In 2004, its annual sales totaled 17.2 billion US dollars. A-B is expanding rapidly around the world, especially in China where it now has 14 breweries and is part owner of China's largest brewing company.

However, the opposing trend toward small-scale, local brewing is spearheaded by legions of beer activists motivated by many of the same concerns being voiced by the anti-corporate globalization crowd. The American brewing renaissance is a reaction against the principles and products of corporate brewing, but more importantly it is a movement championing beer as cultural capital rather than corporate commodity. If this trend succeeds in altering the entire brewing industry, and beer gets globalization right, then perhaps there is hope for the rest of the anti-corporate globalization movement as well. Add a beery twist to the street protest mantra and one can hear beer radicals chanting: "Beer for People, Not for Profit."

Referring to a similar renaissance in Britain, Richard Boston declared in his book *Beer and Skittles*:

> The consumer revolt against big brewers that has taken place in the last three or four years is unique. I know of no other industry of this size that has been checked in the direction it had taken by the massive resistance of the customers. This is gratifying to beer drinkers, but the achievement is one that is important to others as well. It has demonstrated that we need not be endlessly manipulated by the forces of the state or big business.

Liquid Assets

Beer is especially relevant to globalization in that it is the world's most popular alcoholic drink. According to the Beer Institute, in the US alone, the industry had a total economic output of over US$160 billion, plus an additional US$30 billion in tax revenue, for the year 2004. The industry directly employed nearly one million Americans and another 800,000 were employed indirectly. More than half a million establishments are directly involved in the trade.

Yet beer is far richer in cultural significance than in plain economic value. The history of beer, as detailed in these pages, is indeed the history of human civilization. And if beer helped create civilization, then perhaps it also has a role to play in preventing its collapse.

Beeroregionalism Is Born

Industrial brewing reached its zenith during the mid-seventies, when American brewing culture was hitting its nadir. The better beer revolution was started by people who were fed up with the charade of beer culture being played out by factories marketing industrial light lager. Some of these people visited Europe, where they discovered traces of richer beer cultures. Then they came back to the US and began doing what humans have done since the beginning — they went into the kitchen and made some beer. Real people were using their own hands to make beer again. Other people saw that this was good, and a revolution began to ferment. Then in 1979, President Carter lifted the legal restrictions on homebrewing and the beer drinker rebellion was unleashed. So many people liked this homemade beer that more laws were changed to encourage these people to start small businesses brewing beer and selling it directly to their customers. Some started selling beer out of their basements, garages, and the trunks of their cars. Then, with help from their friends and family, they started small breweries to provide for the growing demand for good beer. Unlike the corporate beer factories that spend millions of dollars on tricky marketing to convince people to buy more of their products, these little home brewers couldn't even keep up with demand. Overnight there were hundreds of small breweries all across America making good beer for their communities.

The ensuing beer renaissance embodied the "anti-corporate globalization" values of localism, diversity, community-mindedness, ecological sustainability, and quality of craft in the face of a dominant corporate culture of quarterly returns. The movement was led by people who love the craft and culture of beer in its own right, rather than by corporations pursuing a fat margin. Beer activists have revived all of the life-enhancing attributes of beer while scorning the profit-oriented approach to industrial beer making.

Globalization zealots try to discredit critics by suggesting that we don't have any better ideas — consider Margaret Thatcher's famous "TINA" slogan: "There Is No Alternative." The success of the better beer movement makes TINA obsolete, proving the anti-corporate globalization movement's claim that "Another World Is Possible." Consider these facts: in 1873 there were 4,131 breweries in the United States. By the 1970s two brewing companies accounted for the majority of the US beer market, and the total number of breweries hit an all time low of 44. But since then the corporate beer monopoly has taken serious blows from the craft-brewing insurgency. Today, US *beero-diversity* is on the climb, topping the 1,500 mark and showing very strong signs of continued growth. These microbreweries, or "craft" breweries, account for less than five percent of total beer sales, but they are the fastest growing segment of the industry overall. In 2005, craft beer production leapt by nine percent, showing faster growth than imported beers, and demonstrating America's return to craft and quality as industrial brewing faces declines. It is a true success story of a citizen-led movement that emphasizes culture rather than money, yet has managed to achieve economic stability as well.

Beer, CAMRA, Action

This trend toward small-scale craft production is paralleled in the United Kingdom where anti-corporate brewing sentiments have been brewing since the early 1970s. The best example is what has been called Britain's most successful civic organization, a beer club with over 75,000 members, called the Campaign for Real Ale (CAMRA). This grassroots beer culture advocacy group is successfully redirecting brewing in the UK away from corporate domination and toward community-based production and consumption and family-friendly local pubs. According to a September 2004 press release:

> Beer lovers are tired of over-hyped national brands and avoid like the plague the bland apologies for lager and the cold, tasteless keg beers produced by the global brewers. Beers with aroma and flavor are back in vogue and smaller brewers are rushing to meet the clamor from consumers. With around 500 micros, 35 family-owned breweries, and several bigger regional producers, there is now greater choice than at any time since the Campaign for Real Ale was founded in 1971. Britain has more micros per head than any country in the world, including the United States.

The Society for Independent Brewers, Britain's trade association of craft beer producers, announced 12 percent growth in sales for the year 2004. Cask beer, aka Real Ale, a traditional specialty of English brewers, which has been in decline for years, is also experiencing a rebound, proving CAMRA's optimistic press release to be more than just wishful thinking.

"Most of all it has become an effective pressure group spearheading a consumer revolt which extends far beyond its membership. Michael Young, chairman of the National Consumer Council, has been quoted as saying that CAMRA is "the most successful consumer organization in Western Europe."

— Richard Boston, *Beer and Skittles*

Homebrewed Rebellion

One of the most interesting beeroregional developments is the return of brewing to the home as a non-commercial endeavor. The American Homebrewers Association estimates there are 250,000 homebrewers in the US. And homebrewers are good at sharing. Just ask anyone who knows one. It's hard to visit a brewer at home without leaving with an armful of homemade beers. We even form clubs to share their brews. About five hundred formal homebrew associations throughout the country celebrate the craft, bringing small groups of friends, family, and neighbors together, using beer as a socializing force. The same resurgence of home-crafting is occurring with wine, cider, soda, and other drinks, not to mention other crafts like soap and candle making and a host of other do-it-yourself hobbies.

Homebrewing is conducted in the heart of the home: the kitchen. As Jim Hightower says, "More good has been launched by more people from kitchen tables than from any other platform in the land ... Many a kitchen table has become the 'official world headquarters' for many a grassroots rebellion." We can count the fermenting revolution as one of these.

Just Beer

Healthy communities do, however, require healthy, sustainable economies. So-called "free market capitalism" has been good at helping a few people become very wealthy. Executives in the macro-brewing companies, and in the advertising industry that feeds them, grow very wealthy indeed. Americans in general are extremely prosperous compared to most of the world. And beer has contributed to this wealth. On the other hand, not everyone is so fortunate.

If you're lucky, two bucks will get you one good beer during happy hour. But for three billion people, mostly farmers, that's the most they'll earn on an average day. And according to the Worldwatch Institute, the ratio of the world's rich to poor is getting worse. Every day fewer people are getting much richer, and more and more people are becoming poor. This disparity between American wealth and the majority of human beings is neither healthy nor sustainable. Clearly, American-style corporate-led globalization isn't working well for everybody. The few, which includes most Americans, get rich at the expense of the many. There is no argument where this is concerned. Leaders of the dominant world powers increasingly recognize the failings of our current economic model. For example, in 2005, the G8 (the so-called Global Eight, the eight nations with the world's most powerful economies) bowed to growing public pressure and vowed to help reduce part of Africa's debt — a debt accrued under the strong-armed influence of the West.

Although corporate beer contributes primarily to economic prosperity for the rich, craft-brewing is helping to build strong local economies, where dollars are kept cycling through regional markets rather than being sucked out by wealthy executives in far-off places. Another promising way that beer, and lots of other products, are spearheading an equitable, sustainable approach to economic development is through "fair trade."

The fair trade movement is best known for the impact it is having on the coffee industry. Fair trade coffee is now available in mainstream chains like McDonalds, Starbucks, and Dunkin Donuts (but make sure you ask specifically for fair trade at these locations or you are liable to be served a brew made from conventionally-traded beans), as well as the growing legion of small, independent roasters and coffee shops that first pioneered the movement. Fair trade is also making inroads with cocoa and chocolate, tea, and fresh fruits like bananas, in addition to a wide variety of handcrafted items from jewelry and furniture to clothing and pottery. Fair trade works within these industries because it benefits small producers and farmers. Conventional global trade in commodities is dominated by strong rich countries buying raw materials from developing countries at meager prices. Value is typically added in the rich country where big profits are made, but the farmers and artisans who provided the main ingredients eke out just enough to survive, or less. Fair trade attempts to make these trading relationships more equitable, so that countries with weak economies can gain clout in trade negotiations for the products they produce.

Corporate Pig-Dogs vs. Enlightened Beer Drinkers

Beer can, and is, helping to change this. But it's a pitched battle between the global macro-brewers and enlightened beer drinkers. On the one hand, bigger and bigger corporate mega-mergers threaten to reduce the world's entire beer culture to one cheap, mass-marketed, barely-noticeable fizz-water. On the other hand, is a vision of a world where homebrewers, small craft breweries and brewpubs create a thriving and diverse beer culture, relying on local ingredients, celebrating local customs, and using profits to enrich the local community. Fair trade is an unusual third way that complements this vision. It applies to beer differently than it does to coffee and bananas because beer is not an internationally traded raw commodity, bought by industrialized countries from developing countries. The main ingredients in most of the world's commercial beers are malted barley, hops, water, and yeast, products not produced for mass export by developing countries. Wheat, rice, corn, and a few other adjuncts contribute a share as well. Millet and sorghum are popular in Africa but are rarely used in industrialized beers and thus don't appear on the global trade scene. Nevertheless, brewers are taking some steps toward fair trade.

In many ways, brewing already lends itself toward being a fairly responsible industry in terms of local self-reliance. Brewing water, the primary ingredient in all beer, is almost always local, and therefore irrelevant as a trade issue. That is likely to change soon though, and in a big way. Many experts expect water to be the cause of the world's next big round of conflicts. But for the moment, brewing water is not a traded commodity as such. Yeast is usually propagated right at the brewery, so again this has little real impact on international trade.

Rich countries don't buy much brewing barley from poor countries. In fact, the reverse is actually true. Europe and North America grow and malt their own brewing barley and export it to developing countries for use by industrial breweries. Hops comprise a fairly small portion of the final product of beer, but these too are grown in Western countries and exported to the global South (although Australia and New Zealand are notable exceptions to this geographic rule). And herein lies a problem.

Does Local Equal Backwards?

The modern brewing industry does not exploit peasant farmers in developing countries by paying low prices for their produce. Instead, industrial brewing replaces indigenous brewing traditions with factories that produce watery light lagers made by international brewing conglomerations, which are often granted monopolies in developing nations. These brewing concerns import raw ingredients from the West, brew them in the market country, and then work hard to eradicate traditional local brewing styles by marketing industrial beer as a symbol of modernity. These industrial beers always cost more than local homebrews but brewing companies rely on the power of marketing to convince locals that drinking industrial brew is a symbol of sophistication and success in the modern world. This powerful marketing, combined with other socio-economic factors, persuades many people that "Western equals better" and "local equals backwards."

But fair trade holds some hope. Current trends in commercial brewing are showing an increase in internationally traded beer. Big and small brewers alike are experiencing an upsurge in export demand. This could be an opportunity for fair trade beers from developing countries to help counteract the contemptible corporate brewing practice of ruining indigenous brewing traditions. As a beer drinker, I look for interesting new products to try, but corporate brewing is doing its best to destroy the world's beerodiversity. Fair trade might provide a strategy for helping to protect and celebrate indigenous beers so that beer drinkers around the world can appreciate them.

Africa: Brewing Tradition

Brewers, beer writers, and beer drinkers ignore Africa. It's understandable to a certain degree. Most of them have never been there. But just because it hasn't received much attention, doesn't mean it is unworthy of our interest. One famous brewer and beer writer (who will remain anonymous since I still want him to give me a personal tour of his brewery someday!) goes so far as to claim in his best-selling book that Belgians have retained more of their ancient brewing culture than any other country. It is true that Belgium is highly revered for its beer diversity and its charming loyalty to tradition. It ranks high in beerodiversity, managing so far to buck the trend of "blandardization" that has overtaken beer in North America. But "more than any other country"? I don't think so.

Africa is brimming with countries that have more ancient brewing traditions than any European country, including Belgium. It is quite possible that brewing originated in Africa. African brewing traditions have withstood the test of time, largely because most brewing continues to be conducted on a small scale at home, by women in rural settings. According to one report, a whopping *four times* more homebrew is consumed in Africa than commercial-industrial brews. The industrial stuff is available, and like everywhere else, it is dominated by the light lager fad. But that is not what most Africans drink.

Throughout Africa, most brewing and drinking still occurs in the home and at community events. Of course, just like Belgian brewing traditions, African beer styles have certainly changed over time. Nothing ever remains completely static. Brewing technology and methods change all the time, everywhere. But some practices retain more of the heart and soul of brewing than others. To oversimplify a bit, beers that are made at home, in small batches, just have more soul. Belgians don't make much beer at home any more, but Belgium's many artisanal breweries are mostly family-owned, and are quite small. They insist on following recipes and using methods that don't follow the logic of industrial production, and as a result their beers have retained lots of soul. And to oversimplify a bit more, the lower tech the brewing method, the more human, and enjoyable, the beers tend to be. The Belgians win high marks in this regard. Their much-vaunted lambics and gueze beers are worth celebrating for their devotion to low-tech spontaneous fermentation methods.

If you think Belgians few scattered examples of funky old-school beers are remarkable, then consider visiting Africa. There are many countries there, like Ethiopia, where virtually *every woman brews beer* (except those who are strictly Muslims). They use proven, sophisticated homebrewing methods. Some are more complicated than others. Many African brewsters make their own malt from grains they grow themselves, and add handpicked herbs and spices. As mentioned, even these "traditional" methods change over time, but in most cases they have maintained the soul of beer. And, despite what you might read in disparaging guidebooks, the homebrewed beers in Africa are damn good!

But what are more important than the methods and the technology are the drinking cultures in Africa. I have yet to find a European beer culture that surpasses that of Ethiopia, for example. Beer is part of everyday Ethiopian life. And life is something shared by all people. So beer drinking doesn't go on behind closed doors, exclusively by men. It is, more often, part of a family or community celebration. Kids get the occasional sip. Grandma and Grandpa get a healthy jug full. Women drink as well as men. In fact, in some places, beer seems to be the beverage of preference for women, while men are relegated to wine or liquor.

But these traditions are under heavy fire from the global industrial beer beasts. As Africa urbanizes and industrializes, gleaming bottles of lager lure men to soulless drinking joints. It is a repeat of pre-Prohibition America, where culture gets a divorce from beer as men get divorced from their communities and head to the grinding poverty of African megalopolises. The result is predictable. Just as men in industrial London headed to the gin joint to get blitzed on cheap rotgut, and American men found solace in whiskey saloons, African men are increasingly chasing the cheap, potent stuff to help them escape their urban misery. This has disastrous effects on traditional drinks. We saw what this trend did to American beer, and now the same trend threatens another entire continent of diverse and valuable drinking cultures. We need to put the breaks on this before Africa heads into a forgetful hangover and its beerodiversity heads into the same pale and fizzy coma that Western beer has endured.

The Potential Is Delicious

Fair trade coffee began with small pioneering companies, and the first fair trade beers are likewise from visionary upstarts. Charles Wells, the UK's largest independent brewery, makes a Banana Bread Beer, riffing on a traditional English bitter by adding the subtle flavor of Britain's best-loved fruit to its best-loved beer. The bananas they use are certified Fair Trade, which means the farmers who grew them were paid fair prices, rather than the rock bottom prices that the so-called free market would normally dictate. In reality, the "free market" is anything but free, since it is highly regulated by complex laws, policies, and governing bodies that are strongly biased in favor of extremely large transnational corporations. Fair trade simply encourages voluntary adoption of trading practices that are accountable and help level the playing field for small-scale farmers.

Mongozo Brewing, based in the Netherlands, is crafting truly unique crossbred African-European brews. In addition to fair trade bananas, Mongozo brews with palm nuts, quinoa and coconuts. These are unusual ingredients for unusual beers. But other fair trade crops are available that are slightly more common ingredients in brewing. Coffee, cocoa (the main ingredient in chocolate), and vanilla are all included in some of today's most exciting and adventurous beers. Coffee and cocoa have grown enough in popularity as brewing ingredients to merit their own category in the World Beer Cup competition.

Innovative leaders in the craft-brewing movement are beginning to popularize beers in these categories. Dogfish Head uses organic coffee in their gold medal-winning Chicory Stout, and Thunderhead Brewing of Kearney, Nebraska, brews a gold medal-winning Black Sheep Espresso Stout. The Boston Beer Company, maker of Sam Adams, brews an award-winning Chocolate Bock. Puget Sound's Vanilla Porter earned accolades from experts in *All About Beer* magazine. Charles Finkel, founder of Pike Brewing Co. and Merchant du Vin, described it as having a "kiss of cocoa and mocha" that is "sensational and seductive."

Unfortunately, none of these beers use the fair trade coffee, chocolate, or vanilla ingredients that are available. When it comes to making the economy more just and sustainable, craft brewing is part of the overall solution, to be sure. But brewers can do even better. If fair trade is going to be embraced in the brewing industry, it isn't going to start with a Chocolate Espresso Stout from Coors Brewing. It's always the little guys, the good guys, who blaze the trail. Here's some encouragement for the craft brewers out there who might be ready to take the fair trade plunge. The fair trade movement is spearheaded by thousands of college student groups across the country. Guess what college kids like to drink? Who will quench their thirst for justice and make America's first fair trade beer?

Mongozo's Mondo Fair Trade Ales

Mongozo beers have some unusual influences: political turmoil, famine, creative fusion, as well as changing gender roles, just to name a few. Their geographic inspirations are equally diverse and remarkable. Henrique Kabia, Mongozo's founder, is ethnically Chokwe, a people who spread across southern Congo, Angola, and Zambia. He fled Angola in 1993 and arrived in the Netherlands as a political refugee. Several years later he was overseeing the brewing of his line of Mongozo beers at the Van Steenberge brewery in Belgium.

Kabia credits his great-great-grandmother with inventing the original Mongozo brew. She lived in what used to be called the Lunda empire. She was married to a brave *shimbiriki*, or porcupine hunter. But, according to the family's oral history, the village experienced a twenty-year period in the 18th century when no wild animals were to be found. Her skill at brewing beer saved the family from disaster. In her small village, brewing was a ritual exclusive to women, handed down from mother to daughter. As Henrique tells it, "My great-great-grandmother bartered beer for agricultural produce and thereby managed to make ends meet each month. Her persistent husband never ceased hunting and each time he returned empty-handed he consoled himself by sitting on a straw mat drinking beer served in a gourd."

Her beer saved the family for 20 years. Her husband kept searching for porcupine, though, and finally he disappeared on a hunt for three months. Lacking any news of him, the family concluded he must have encountered death, and commenced a week of mourning. But on the third day, the sound of xylophones announced his victorious return. He brought porcupine meat with him for all the village to share.

Kabia's great-great-grandmother brewed a special beer to celebrate this triumph. She decided that instead of fermenting palm sap she would use the palm nuts as the base of her brew. She used huge gourds to brew, and the village enjoyed this delicious beer so much that the party lasted three months! The villagers toasted the good times by saying *Mongozo*, which means "to your health."

As Kabia tells it, "The unique taste of the beer was appreciated by the entire village and soon by the whole empire. There was a great demand for it, and so my great-great-grandmother built a small brewery behind her straw hut. A large earthenware jug served as a vat. Her oven consisted of three or four rocks around a few bits of burning wood. This made up most of her equipment."

The Mongozo recipe was passed down through the family's generations of women all the way to Henrique's own mother. But she had no daughters to teach the brewing skill, so she broke with tradition and taught her son instead. "It was a revolutionary step. For the first time, a man — in the Lunda tradition — was allowed to brew Mongozo. Maybe, she wanted me to have something healthy to drink at the University. But, the fact that the whole society was becoming more emancipated in Angola also played a role in my mother's course of action. I brewed the beer during holidays and weekends. You can imagine that I was a very popular guy at the University. Brewing became my favorite pastime," Kabia recounts.

This is fortuitous for Western drinkers who might otherwise never have the chance to taste an African beer style. The Mongozo line includes four different ales, all of which are sold in Europe and are becoming available in North America. The flagship Mongozo Palmnut is brewed with palm nuts just like Henrique's mother taught him. He has adapted his recipes to include some modern techniques as well. For instance, the original Mongozo beer was fermented with wild yeast. While a batch fermented, some was scooped off to be used as a starter for the next batch, but today a controlled yeast strain is used.

After his beer was successfully received at festivals and tastings, he decided to go professional with the product. He formed a relationship with the renowned Van Steenberge brewery in Belgium, brewers of such well-known brands as Piraat and Celis White. Today, Mongozo beers are brewed in partnership with a different world-class Belgian brewery, Huyghe, makers of Delerium Tremens.

Nuts for Fair Trade

Kabia directly controls the import of the palm nuts used in

Mongozo banana beer — "So Fair So Good!"

his ale, as well as the exotic calabashes recommended for drinking it. His direct trading relationship ensures that the African women who grow, cut, and dry the calabashes receive a fair percentage of the sales. He is proud of the fair trade aspect of his endeavor and describes it as "a true example of development aid resulting from a private initiative." The fair trade principles Kabia follows are independently monitored and bear the Max Havelaar Foundation fair trade certification, recognizing the contribution Mongozo beer makes toward improving the lives of low-income farmers.

Like every beer brewed in Belgium, Kabia explains that Mongozo is best enjoyed when served in its own specially designed vessel. "When Mongozo beer is served in a natural calabash it froths extremely well, maintains its freshness longer than it would in a normal glass and moreover, a calabash renders the complete flavor. But," he continues with characteristically African equanimity, "for those of you who are attached to your glass: don't worry, Mongozo tastes wonderful straight out of the bottle too, or in a regular beer glass."

Besides Mongozo Palmnut, Kabia also produces Mongozo Banana, Mongozo Quinoa, and Mongozo Coconut, made with fair trade bananas, quinoa grain, and coconuts. Mongozo Banana is based on a traditional beer of the Maasai people of Kenya, called *mbege*, and the coconut beer is also based on a Kenyan brew. The Quinoa concoction originates from the other side of the globe, based on the traditional Andean *chicha* beer. Sadly, Kabia passed away in an accident in 2003, but his original partner Jan Fleurkens continues to brew and market the beers with growing success.

Fair trade may be only in its baby years as far as brewing goes, but the anti-corporate beer revolution has been underway ever since Carter repealed the homebrewing ban. Brewers around the globe are fermenting a new *beer*oregional revolution. The resurgence of small-scale brewing is growing at a trend setting rate. There is now a large and growing international movement of people who value beer for its own sake, rather than as a tool of commerce.

Corporate brewers are taking notice of these changing public attitudes and have begun emulating the small brewers, evidence that the return to craft and quality is more than a burp on the trend screen. The mega-brewers now have products that attempt to appeal to the same set of values that craft beer attracts: small-scale, local, and uncommercialized.

Even though mainstream, American beer culture may not yet be fully recovered from its post-Prohibition profit hangover, its vital signs are improving, and a reversal of trends is well underway.

Dark Storm Brewin':
The Doom and Gloom Chapter

The new culture of *beeroregionalism* couldn't have arrived at a better time. But before we discover the solutions it offers, it's necessary to grasp the extent of the problems corporate *globeerization* presents. First, I advise you to check your fridge. Is there a nice craft-brewed ale in there? Good, because this is *The Doom and Gloom Chapter*, and liquid reinforcements may be required. If you think the story of the industrial death of beer was depressing, wait until you hear the rest of the news. Beer is just one of many things that has been killed by industrialization. The fact is, all of the living systems on earth are in massive decline.

Some of you are already impatiently thumbing the corner of this page, feeling an urge to skip this chapter. Perhaps you already know all about the pathetic state of the planet. Or maybe you just don't want to know. Either way, let me make one thing clear to you:

Stop that right now!

You need to read this chapter. Even if you do already know it all, it's important to get an occasional reminder that what we are dealing with here is nothing short of the possible mass extinction of life on earth, on a scale not seen since the dinosaurs died of thirst. No one wants a repeat of that, so let's keep ourselves informed, and quenched, while we still can. There's another reason you should read this chapter: many people think beer drinkers are dim-witted commoners. Staying informed about the big trends in the world proves them wrong.

If you are unfamiliar with the Earth's general condition of mass ecological destruction, and the very idea of reading about something so terrible makes you tense up, I have some advice:

Don't Despair. What you are about to read is not an exaggeration. It *is* as bad as it sounds. But that is no reason to get all depressed about it. You'll get through reading the bad news and you'll be okay. Remember, you've got some good beer chilling in the fridge. Hope springs eternal.

Be Glad. Armed with information, you will no longer be in the dark about the state of the world. You will therefore be much better equipped to use your power as a beer activist to make things better.

Rest Assured. The rest of this book is basically a good time, filled with witty beer chatter and humorous anecdotes. This is the only chapter that's really brimming with Doom and Gloom.

And now, Fellow Elbow Benders in Brewpub Gaia, behold the end of the World.

Lowlights from the Apocalypse

The planet is, plain and simple, on the eve of destruction. The oceans, the atmosphere, the soil — they're all sullied almost to the point of no repair. Sea turtles, the Chesapeake Bay, the Amazon rainforest, the air in every major city, they're all on a collision course with ruin. This time it is not a nuclear winter clouding the horizon, although, despite the thawing of the Cold War, recent events do make the nuclear threat increasingly plausible again. Oh, and there is that whole global terrorism thing too. But other than that, this is not the pitched battle between good and evil, like the competing ideologies of capitalism and communism were made out to be. The lines are much harder to draw in this "War to Save the Entire Friggin' Planet." The battles of this war are sometimes painted in terms of human needs versus the environment. Loggers versus spotted owls. Oil independence or drilling in the Arctic National Wildlife Refuge. Our god-given right to drive a Hummer versus global warming. Corporate-dominated globalization or anarchy. Whatever the terms used to describe it, the fact is that in every one of the Earth's natural systems, there is a dark storm a-brewin' — and I don't mean porter or stout. One must first comprehend the ravaged state of the planet in order to understand how our heroes — millions of beer activists — are doing their part to save the world.

"No, I Meant *Poor*"

People are part of the planet, so our happiness is part of the overall well-being of the whole Earth. But, in general, we're not doing so well. The modern world is a place where increasing numbers of people lack the fundamental resources needed to live well.

According to the World Bank, about one quarter of the Earth's more than six billion people live in "absolute" poverty. Food and water shortages are chronic for a growing number of people. Many of these same folks are highly vulnerable to additional misfortunes such as disease and natural disasters, like earthquakes, hurricanes, and floods. A recent example is how the poorest residents of New Orleans suffered in disproportionate numbers as a result of Hurricanes Katrina and Rita.

The World Resources Institute, a non-partisan Washington think tank publishes an annual review called *State of the World*. According to the 2004 edition, the wealthiest 20 percent of the world's people account for 86 percent of total private consumption. Extremes of poverty and wealth both contribute to environmental destruction, but most of the blame lies with the wealthy, particularly since they have greater power to influence resource allocation and consumption. The rich consume more, damage the environment more, and cause economic injustice. For beer to be part of the solution, it must be a beverage of the people, by the people, and for the people — not of the corporations, by the corporations, and for the corporations.

> Woody, the bartender: How are you feeling today, Mr. Peterson?
> Norm: Poor.
> Woody: Oh, I'm sorry to hear that.
> Norm: No, I meant "pour."
> — Dialogue from an episode of the TV show Cheers

Creating a Nice, Warm Atmosphere

Global warming is the number one challenge facing human society today, and probably the biggest problem we have *ever* faced. What's remarkable is that we probably created it ourselves, and we are certainly making it worse. "The debate is over," claims Peter Gleick, president of the Pacific Institute for Studies in Development, Environment, and Security. "No matter what we do to reduce greenhouse gas emissions, we will not be able to avoid some impacts of climate change." Thomas Karl of the US Government's National

Climatic Data Center and Keven Trenberth of the National Center for Atmospheric Research write that "global warming is not only real, but manmade. Climate change may prove to be humanity's greatest challenge."

2005 was the warmest year ever recorded, and 1998, 2002, and 2003 are also in the top five. The world is about 1.3 degrees Fahrenheit warmer today than it was in the late 19th century, and the warmest it has been for at least a thousand years. The UN projects that temperatures will rise between 2.5 and 10.4 degrees Fahrenheit in the next hundred years. Most of this temperature change is attributed to the burning of fossil fuels that release gasses that get trapped in the atmosphere and hold heat inside rather than letting it escape into space. This is called the "greenhouse effect." The implications of this warming are widespread in their devastating impacts and many scientists argue that we are already experiencing them. Yet the US refuses to participate in global agreements on slowing climate change and instead continues to subsidize the burning of fossil fuels through artificially low gas prices and a transportation infrastructure designed to require intensive use of fossil fuels. Trucking beer around from giant regional brewing centers to

A growing number of breweries are choosing wind power as a way to reduce their contribution to climate change. New Belgium Brewing, one of America's largest craft breweries, uses 100 percent wind energy to power its operations, including the brewing of their appropriately named Loft Beer.

distributors, retailers, and homes is just one frivolous way we turn up the global heat.

America is the ultimate rogue nation when it comes to addressing climate change. Under the Kyoto Protocol, 157 countries agreed to cut greenhouse gas emissions, but the US declined to sign the pact. In 2005, the same group of nations pledged to begin negotiations on a new set of emission cuts. Despite the fact that the United States generates one quarter of all the world's greenhouse gases, the Bush administration continues to question the need for even non-binding talks on the subject.

Drastic weather change is one effect we are probably already witnessing. These changes cause disease, wildfires, deaths from exposure, heavy rain and flooding, rising seas that overtake land, droughts that could cause wars for water, and massive refugee migrations. In the year 2005, we witnessed the greatest number of extreme weather events for any year on record. One need only recall the recent tsunami flooding in East Asia, and the rash of record-breaking hurricanes that hit the Gulf of Mexico, one of which turned New Orleans into a ghost town.

Writing in the 2003 State of the World report, researcher Chris Bright had this to say about climate change:

> [O]ur world is in profound geochemical flux. Certain forms of pollution are altering the global chemical cycles that regulate key ecosystem processes. The carbon cycle is the best known of these. A vast quantity of carbon that had been removed from circulation millions of years ago — by being absorbed by plants, which were in turn converted to coal and oil — is now being reinjected into the atmosphere. Annual carbon emissions from fossil fuel combustion reached a record 6.55 billion tons in 2001, driving the atmospheric concentration of carbon dioxide to 370.9 parts per million, the highest level it has reached in at least 420,000 years, and probably in 20 million years. Because carbon dioxide traps heat, its increasing concentration is likely to provoke rapid climate change.

Note his mention of coal and recall that the use of coke (a by-product of coal) as a fuel is responsible for the invention of virtually every modern European beer style, since without it, all beer styles would still be using smoky, brown malts.

it takes all sorts to campaign for real ale

join the **campaign for real ale**
www.camra.org.uk

The Campaign for Real Ale promotes Real Ale, a style of serving favored by beer aficionados but that many Americans consider "warm and flat."

Time for a Tall Warm One?

Can drinking beer help halt climate change? We must investigate Real Ale in order to answer this question.

The English are famous for serving beers in a manner that delivers what has come to be referred to as "Real Ale." These are the beers Americans often describe as warm and flat, because they are served straight from the barrel at cellar temperature, which is actually cool, not warm. This serving style allows drinkers to experience a beer's full range of fresh flavors and aromas. Americans tend to think beer should be extremely fizzy and icy cold. Taste is subjective, and there is certainly no right or wrong opinion about what to like or dislike. However, American brewing corporations have marketed a myth about desirable beer flavor. These corporations tell us that cold, fizzy beer is better. They have been able to convince us that they are right, largely because they have had complete domination of the market for so long that no one in this country remembers what beer used to taste like. British Real Ale drinkers know that extreme low temperatures reduce flavor by inhibiting the release of a beer's aromatics. Carbonation can actually help lift these aromatics from the glass to your nose, but not if the beer is too cold to release them.

To address carbonation specifically: it can be good or bad. English Real Ales are lightly carbonated, which is perfectly suitable for their style. American industrial beers are over-carbonated, which is inappropriate for any style. The right carbonation level not only buoys a beer's nose to a drinker's nose, but it also serves to cleanse the palate, which makes beer a great beverage for pairing with full-flavored foods. High carbonation can be appropriate in very rich beers, especially ones that undergo a secondary fermentation in the bottle or cask. But when the carbonation is too high, and the beer's own flavor and aromatics are too low, the bubbles are nothing but a gassy explosion in the mouth. So it makes sense that American industrial brewers have tried to define beer as cold and fizzy, since if they didn't, their lack of flavor and aroma would be painfully obvious.

I like beer both ways, cool and cooler, very carbonated and lightly carbonated, it all depends on the style. Then again, I've never met a beer I didn't like. Unfortunately, climate change is a pretty compelling reason why people should start getting used to things being a bit warmer than usual. As we've seen, global warming is a well-documented phenomenon. The few remaining opponents of taking action on climate change are the companies most responsible for causing it, petroleum concerns and automobile manufacturers. They unscrupulously fund scientists to make deceitful claims about global warming, but today these frauds have been universally debunked.

Brewing companies are at least partly responsible too, since they played a critical role in fostering the industrial revolution which was the root cause of global warming. So it seems fitting for brewers to help sort out some solutions as well. Beer brewing itself is essentially carbon-neutral. Fermentation releases carbon, but that same amount of carbon is offset by the barley fields grown to produce more beer. However, fermentation is not the only source of CO_2 emissions in a brewery. Like any factory, breweries require energy to operate. That energy comes mostly from fossil fuels. So to be carbon-neutral, breweries need to address their fossil fuel-based energy consumption. Some have already made the leap to renewable energies. New Belgium Brewing, America's tenth largest craft brewery, switched to 100 percent wind power, as did Uinta Brewing in Salt Lake City, Utah, and Brooklyn Brewing Company in New York, not to mention dozens of other smaller companies. Uinta estimates that their customers are helping to prevent the annual release of 335 tons of carbon dioxide — the equivalent of planting 132 acres of trees, or not driving 717,030 miles.

Getting back to Real Ale, it is important to note that carbon dioxide is of fundamental importance to this beer serving style. Real Ales are matured by a secondary fermentation in the keg or bottle and are then served without the use of "forced" carbon dioxide. In other words, the carbon dioxide bubbles in Real Ale come from the natural fermentation process, whereas industrial brewers allow the natural CO_2 from fermentation to dissipate and then, later on, they reintroduce CO_2 by forcing it into the bottle or keg. Bars add yet more CO_2 to the equation by using canisters of it to propel beer through the tap system and into a glass. But Real Ale is served using a device called a "beer engine," or what is also called a hand pump or beer pump. These simple levers allow bartenders to pull beer out of a keg using human power — the downward motion of a hand on the pump handle. Sometimes Real Ale is even served using simple gravity. In this case, a keg is set on its side on top of the bar. There are two holes in the keg, one on the top and one on the side. Both are opened, and the beer simply pours out through a tap placed in the lower hole — no forced carbonation, no hand pump, just gravity doing its thing. In addition, Real Ale is served at a "cellar temperature" of between 50 and 57 degrees Fahrenheit. This temperature permits the release of nuanced aromas. Because of their reduced refrigeration needs, and manual serving styles, Real Ales have lower energy requirements and therefore represent a more climate-friendly choice for drinkers who are interested in tasting the full range of beer flavors. Moreover, they reduce reliance on the dangerous refrigerants that cause ozone depletion. So the answer to our earlier question is yes, drinking beer can help halt climate change.

On a related note, the city of Chicago hosts two important carbon affairs. One is the annual Real Ale Festival, and the other is the Chicago Climate Exchange. The Festival presents America's largest selection of Real Ales in one place. The Exchange is a trading system supported by mega-corporations like Dow Corning, Ford, and IBM that helps companies voluntarily reduce their carbon emissions by rewarding those that meet certain goals, and allowing others to buy extra credits from the ones who surpassed their goals.

Some brewers are already taking steps to prevent climate change, but here is some more incentive for the entire industry to be concerned about global warming. Agricultural crops like barley and hops are highly vulnerable to disasters caused by climate change. Martin Parry makes this point very clear with his statement in *Climate Change and World Agriculture*: "Most agricultural diseases have greater potential to reach severe levels under warmer conditions ... To illustrate, increases in infestations of the ... grain aphid (*sitobian avenae*) could lead to increased incidence of Barley Yellow Dwarf virus in cereals." It is one thing to imperil the future of the human race, but when we threaten the natural resource needed to make beer, things have just gone too far.

Hazy Brew

Air, in general, is becoming unfit for humans to breathe. A two-mile-thick stew of pollutant crud hangs airborne over most of Asia. Scientists say it is several times worse than anything ever seen during America's heady coal-burning, air-pollution days of yore. The cloud consists of industrial pollution, smoke from hearth fires, agricultural burning, and wildfires, as well as all kinds of toxic pollutants it picks up along the way. According to a feature article in *US News and World Report*, the effects of this pollution include reduced sunlight, which reduces crop yield, and as many as 1.4 million deaths annually from pollution-related respiratory illnesses in Southern China and Southeast Asia.

Ozone Alert

One of the worst air pollutants is ozone. There is good ozone and bad ozone. Ozone in the stratosphere is good, but ozone in ground-level air is bad. Unfortunately, humans have created holes the size of North America in the good ozone layer over Antarctica, and another giant hole gapes over the Arctic Circle. Man-made chemicals called chlorofluorocarbons that are used in consumer products for air conditioning and refrigeration created these holes. The ozone layer is important to us because it protects people from ultraviolet sun rays that cause skin cancer. These holes remain in place despite wide scale efforts to address the pollutants that caused them.

Bad ozone is the kind that comprises much of the smog which hangs over cities. This ozone is primarily a product of our burning of fossil fuels. Today, many American cities issue alerts warning citizens not to go outdoors when the air is so filled with ozone that it is unhealthy to breathe. The EPA estimates that between 5 and 20 percent of Americans are especially susceptible to the effects of ozone air pollution. This pollution impairs proper lung function, resulting in symptoms like shortness of breath, coughing, and chest pain. Washington D.C., where I live, calls these "Ozone Alert" days and regularly ratchets up the level to "Red," advising people to "avoid or limit outdoor exertion." Good luck following this advice if you're a construction worker, landscaper, or anyone else whose job requires outdoor exertion, not to mention those of us who simply enjoy being outdoors. But this problem doesn't just affect city folks. People in rural areas are affected too, especially when they have coal-burning power plants nearby. Ozone pollution also damages crops, and is estimated to be reducing China's harvests by as much as 30 percent per year. The only real way to fix the ozone layer, and to reduce ozone pollution, is to curb our consumption of the products that cause the problems, i.e., fossil fuels and ozone-destroying chemicals.

Toxic Brew

Besides global warming and holes in the ozone layer, we face a host of other environmental catastrophes. The world is filling up with toxic chemicals. Global production of hazardous waste is estimated at half a billion tons per year or more. Eventually, all of this is released into nature, whether by incineration, or burial in landfills. Much of it winds up in aquifers, where the pollution becomes effectively irreversible. Many of these pollutants, especially the synthetic ones, are known to be harmful, often in minute quantities. Known effects include cancer, immunodeficiency, hormonal abnormalities, and birth defects in wildlife as well as people. Some of these chemicals are known to "bioaccumulate," meaning they build up in increasingly harmful quantities as they move up the food chain, harming bigger animals (like people) more than smaller ones. To put it simply, we are poisoning ourselves with chemicals.

The Great "Ale-ien" Invasion

Invasive alien species cause tremendous damage and pose threats to the plants on which brewers rely. Alien species are plants, animals, and microbes that cause environmental damage in areas where they are not native but have been introduced. This issue overlaps with global warming, since one effect of climate change is that some species will no longer be fit for survival in their native areas and will invade other areas.

Alien invasions cause cascading ecological disruptions. Here's just one example, a fish coincidentally named the alewife (according to *Etymology Online*, the name stems from the fact that it has a large abdomen). The alewife is a species of ocean shad that began invading the Great Lakes when the Welland Canal opened in 1829. The canal facilitated industrial expansion into the American Midwest, but also opened the door for this alien invasion. Population levels of alewives grew unchecked because their natural predators, lake trout, had already been wiped out by overfishing and by the invasion of another exotic species, the sea lamprey. By the 1950s, the alewife had completely colonized the Great Lakes and through competition and predation caused the decline of many other species native to the area.

Other examples, of particular concern to hopheads, are the pests and diseases that torment hop growers in Europe and North America. Somehow, New Zealand has managed to keep these problematic species from entering its shores. As a result, New Zealand has developed a thriving hop-growing sector, especially renowned for its widespread organic cultivation methods, which are due in part to the fact that it has kept out both pest and pestilence. However, if these species, such as aphids, downy mildew, or spider mites, were to be introduced to New Zealand, they would result in crop failures, higher hops prices for brewers, and potentially higher prices on beer for the average drinker.

West Nile virus and bird flu (Avian Influenza) are examples of a different kind of invasive species currently threatening human populations around the world. At the time of writing, these aliens were expected to invade America imminently.

Birds Perched for Extinction

Speaking of birds, our feathered friends are imperiled all around the globe. In 2000, BirdLife International found that nearly one fifth of the world's bird species are threatened or soon to be threatened with extinction. Many species that are still plentiful are in significant decline. Birds are beautiful and they sing. These are reasons enough for me to be worried about their extinction.

They are also meaningful to us in symbolic ways. Imagine, for instance, an America without bald eagles. But birds also provide services that we can't do without. They spread seeds and pollinate flowers, help keep insect and rodent populations in check, and clean up the messy, disease-spreading remains of dead animals. The disappearance of certain birds warns us of other problems. North American crows, hawks, and owls are dying due to the spread of West Nile virus, for example. But what causes most of these threatened extinctions? We do. We destroy the homes of wildlife as we plunder the rainforests and other habitat. Other species are doing some damage too. Invasive, predatory, and competitive species of plants and animals deny native species their habitat and food. Other contributing factors include illegal hunting, insufficient legal regulations, longline fishing that wipes out food sources, pollution (including pesticides and industrial effluents, oil spills and oil drilling), and now climate change.

Brutul, Inc. produces beer gear like the Lagerhead Black and Tan Turtle, a device used for pouring the perfect black and tan beer. Proceeds go towards the preservation of alligator snapping turtle habitat in Mississippi.

Last Call

Unfortunately, it's not just birds that are threatened with widespread extinction. According to Susan Headden in her article *A Heavy Footprint*, more than 11,000 known species of animals and plants are at risk of extinction, and without protective measures, experts say, as many as half of all species could vanish by the end of the 21st century.

The World Resources Institute summarizes the last call for wildlife:

> By virtually every broad measure, our world is in a state of pervasive ecological decline. Primary tropical forests, in general the most diverse ecosystems on the planet, are disappearing at a rate probably exceeding 140,000 square kilometers per year — an area nearly the size of Nepal. Total global forest cover, which now accounts for about a quarter of the planet's land surface excluding Greenland and Antarctica, may have declined by as much as half since the dawn of agriculture. About 30 percent of surviving forest is seriously fragmented or otherwise degraded, and during the 1990s alone, global forest cover is estimated to have declined by more than four percent. Wetlands, another highly diverse ecosystem type, have been reduced by more than 50 percent over the past century. Coral reefs, the world's most diverse aquatic ecosystems, are suffering the effects of over-fishing, pollution, the spread of epidemic disease, and rising sea surface temperatures that many experts link to climate change. By the end of 2000, 27 percent of the world's coral reefs were thought to be severely damaged, up from just 10 percent in 1992. Throughout the oceans, over-fishing is taking an ever greater toll: some 60 percent of the world's marine fisheries are now being exploited at or beyond capacity — an invitation to extensive ecological disruption. And according to the IUCN-World Conservation Union, about one quarter of the world's mammals are now in danger of extinction, as are 12 percent of the world's birds. Comprehensive figures do not exist for other vertebrate classes, but levels of endangerment were similarly high: 25 percent for reptiles, 21 percent for amphibians, and 30 percent for fish.

A Pot of Ale and Safety

Are non-human animals the only ones at risk? Humans don't seem to think so. In fact, we seem to be less certain of survival than ever before. People are acting more endangered every day. Americans in particular are even more security-conscious. Perhaps that is why the US now accounts for about *half* of world military spending. The United Nations estimates that global military spending has surpassed *one trillion dollars per year*. The Cold War may be over, but the War on Terror has taken its place. The modern world is increasingly a fearful one to most people. We don't feel safe and we don't trust each other. This is probably largely due to the fact that communities everywhere have become victims of industrialization, urbanization, and corporate globalization. Community bonds provide the security of belonging, a feeling without which we become isolated and afraid. The rebirth of strong communities is of paramount importance in addressing the long term problems threatening our common future.

> "I would give all my fame for a pot of ale, and safety."
>
> — Shakespeare's King Henry V

It's Unbeerlievable

So that's the bad news about planet earth. We're killing it as fast as we can. It sounds too apocalyptic to be real. In fact, that's one of the perverse ironies about global doom — those who are most culpable for the destruction tend to be the most insulated from its effects. In a global view, that means you and me, my friend. North Americans, Europeans, and other highly industrialized peoples with great material wealth have a hard time grasping the impacts of these frightening trends because we are largely able to ignore them.

We work hard to insulate ourselves from the consequences of our consumer lifestyles. Everyone wants cars, but no one wants air pollution. We want lots of stuff, but who wants to live next to a landfill or incinerator? We live in gated "communities" and we've built massive militaries to keep the problems far away from our own daily lives. But we can only sequester ourselves for so long. Eventually the chickens come home to roost and the effects of our environmental destruction and social injustice hit us where it hurts the most. Now that we're fighting a full-fledged war for oil, people are realizing that our addiction is killing people, and this time some of them are American soldiers. Even George W. Bush admitted in his 2006 State of the Union address that America is addicted to oil.

And in case you haven't noticed, the world's opinion of America has recently turned decidedly sour. Europeans accuse America of going it alone against the wishes of the world community. The Arab world rightly perceives America as an aggressor. The developing world envies our material success but despises us for our selfishness. We act as if the well-being of people outside America doesn't impact us. American workers don't labor in sweatshops, so why should we worry about the poor people in other countries who do? As long as we reap the benefits of having widely available, cheap consumer goods, what's to motivate us to protect workers outside our borders? Well, try telling that to the tens of thousands of Americans who have lost high-paying manufacturing jobs to foreign sweatshops.

Tell it to the hundreds of thousands of American soldiers risking life and limb in the Middle East in order to defend our right to consume more than anyone else. And, at the risk of sounding "new-agey," tell it to the mountains and the trees and the rivers who don't have representatives speaking for them in governments and corporations. They may not have voices, but they do speak. Quite loudly, in fact. They are telling us to change course or else face our own doom. But we need to listen. We need to realize that global climate change, mass extinctions, and human wars are all results of the choices we make. So, with all this in mind, why not make the simple commitment to choose beers that lighten your impact on nature and help to foster peace and prosperity based on mutual cooperation and the good of all?

The Piece Brewery in Chicago

Part III

The Second Fermentation

CHAPTER 10

Beeroregionalism:
Think Globally, Drink Locally

Toward an Ecology of Beer

Earlier, I promised that despite the sorry state of the planet, this book would be optimistic. Why optimism when we are all headed to hell in a handbasket? Better we were headed to ale in a handcart, no? Well yes, actually. Beer is the wellspring of my hope. It's not that I am simply drunk on the fleeting kind of optimism that comes from imbibing good beer. I am optimistic because the craft-brewing movement is steering society towards sustainability. Brewers are perfecting solutions to the global social and environmental problems we face today. Drinking good beer does contribute to my generally cheerful outlook, but it is the accomplishments of dedicated beer activists that give me hope for an enduring shift to sustainability.

"Sustainability" is a catchword used to encompass everything needed to provide circumstances conducive to life on earth, both now and into the indefinite future. Implementing sustainable practices is the central prerequisite for saving the world from long-term social and environmental catastrophes. The global economy is the dominant force influencing our progress toward sustainability, but unfortunately its current form is underpinned by the decidedly unsustainable principles of over-consumption and infinite growth. Corporations are the foremost operators in the unsustainable global economy, and consumption of a finite supply of fossil fuels is one of their most defining practices. Global brewing corporations, for example, rely on cheap access to petroleum products to produce, package, and transport their industrial beers.

But the new wave of small, local breweries and brewpubs is innovating closed-loop systems that shift society away from wasteful, polluting, oil-dependent business practices. Brewers are using small-scale technologies, developing local markets, reducing packaging and shipping requirements, making use of locally available materials, and radically reducing overall waste. The craft beer movement is, in short, putting into practice a sustainability model called "bioregionalism." Bioregionalism is the idea that we can adjust human activities to be sustainable by adapting our activities to a *bioregion*, a geographically distinct area of land, water, and other natural resources. Beer*oregionalism* is this author's term for how the craft-brewing renaissance is putting this concept into practice.

By definition, small-scale, local brewing is more bioregional than industrial brewing. But craft brewers are also very intentionally innovating sustainable practices and working hard to build strong local communities. Here are just a few of the countless examples. Fish Brewing produces organic beers and works to save salmon runs in the Pacific Northwest. New Belgium Brewing runs entirely on wind power. Crannog Ales closes the loop by integrating brewing operations with on-site farm production. Great Lakes Brewing Company (GLBC) has a stated goal of achieving zero-waste operations, and serves as a good case study of a *beer*oregional brewery.

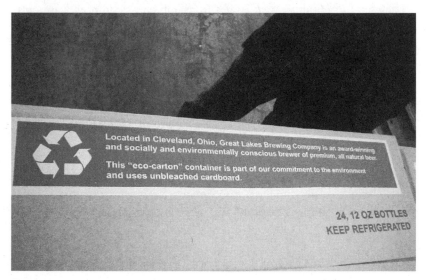

This environmental message appears on the side of every "eco-carton" of Great Lakes beer.

Let's look at their impressive list of achievements. Of course, they have fully covered the easy stuff like recycling. By recycling cardboard, glass, and paper they reduced their trash removal fees by 40 percent. They also purchase recycled products, which is a necessary part of the recycling equation — diverting recyclables from the landfill is one thing, but without a market at the other end of the process, there is no recycling loop. That's why GLBC newsletters, menus, napkins, and promotional items are all printed on 100 percent recycled paper. Six-pack carriers are made of 100 percent recycled fibers, including 50 percent post-consumer waste, and their unbleached "eco-carton" uses 100 percent recycled materials to hold a case of beer.

Although situated in downtown Cleveland, not on a farm, Great Lakes strives to achieve a deeply integrated natural farming-brewing system, turning brewery waste streams into new product lines and making money in the process. It is common for craft brewers to give spent brewing grains to local farmers for cattle feed, and some even make a small profit from the sale. But GLBC takes additional steps to incorporate by-products into value-added

Pat Conway inspects Great Lakes' straw bale, passive solar greenhouse in the urban community garden near his brewery.

cycles. Zoss, a local Swiss baker, uses spent brewery grain to produce cracked barley beer bread and pretzels that appear on the Great Lakes restaurant menu. Another local partner, Killbuck Farms, combines spent brewing grains with sawdust and discarded paper to create a substrate for growing organic shiitake and oyster mushrooms that are featured in the restaurant entrees. Dean McIlvaine, of Twin Parks Organic Farm, raises livestock on spent grain and provides the all-natural beef and pork, and organic cheeses for the restaurant.

Erich Hetzel recycles some of Great Lakes' office paper by feeding it to worms, which produce high quality organic fertilizer that is then used to fertilize the plants, herbs, and vegetables grown in a community garden just a few blocks from the brewery, and which also end up on the menu. At the packaging plant, some bottles accidentally get "low-filled" and can't be sold, so that beer is used in menu items such as salad dressings and Stilton Cheddar Cheese Soup. Nearby Mitchell's Ice Cream uses Great Lakes Porter from some of the "low-fills" for their exclusive Edmund Fitzgerald Porter Chocolate Chunk Ice Cream.

Sustainable brewing practices go hand in hand with great beer. Great Lakes' Dortmunder Gold Lager has won the Great American Beer Festival's gold medal seven times now. Many other small breweries are also implementing innovative, sustainable practices. A guide to choosing the best world-saving beers is included at the end of this book.

Beerodiversity

Diversity is vital to sustainability. *Biodiversity* is the variety of life in all of its manifestations. *Beerodiversity* is a term invented by this author to describe diversity in the beer world, or within a specific *beer*region. The *beerodiversity* of a region can be measured by comparing population density to variety and quantity of different beers available. At the bottom of the *beerodiversity* scale is a place like the state of Mississippi, population 2,902,966, which in June of 2005 was home to a meager two breweries. Mississippi's two breweries are located in Biloxi and Jackson, and since both are brewpubs, they have no distribution, just draft beer at the bar. That means the rest of the state is basically a "*beerological*" dead zone, with nothing but industrial lager which, like a monocrop, actually inhibits diversity. In *beerodiversity* terms, Mississippi is like the Sahara Desert but with humidity and nothing to quench a parched pair of beer activist lips.

At the other end of the spectrum is Portland, Oregon population 533,492. Portland has 26 craft breweries within the city limits and many more within the nearby region. Plus, hundreds of other craft brewery products migrate through Portland, making diverse beers densely available. Portland is like the Amazon Rainforest, except *without* stifling humidity and with lots of refreshing malt beverages. It is akin to what ecologists refer to as a "biological hotspot," where diversity is intense, and that we'll call a "beerological" hotspot, because beer diversity is high.

Take some examples of diversity in nature. In Brazil, only 12 of 32 native pig breeds are left and all are in danger. The genetic diversity of Holstein Friesian cows, the ones with the familiar black and white markings, has been systematically eradicated by selective breeding. According to an article in the *Financial Times*, by John Mason, "The genetic diversity of the world's herd, which totals some 30 million animals, is so limited it equates to a population of under one hundred, had they been left to mate as nature intended." The importance of genetic diversity in livestock becomes painfully obvious when there is a disastrous phenomenon like "mad cow" disease that threatens much of the world's cow population. Diversity helps to limit the damage from outbreaks like this, the same way that financial planners diversify their clients' portfolios to limit the risk of disaster. As Irene Hoffman, the chief of animal production at the Food and Agriculture Organization, says: "Genetic diversity is an insurance against future threats such as famine, drought, and epidemics."

Phony Food Diversity

In a nation so wealthy that food surpluses cause greater social and economic complications than do food shortages, one would expect to find great variety in our available food products. On the surface, this would seem to be true. Yet, upon investigation, exactly the opposite is actually the case. The number of *brands* of food is staggering, but the diversity of the food itself has been on a slow decline. A dwindling pool of ingredients comprise the majority of our actual food products. Marketing creates an illusion of choice, but underneath the packaging, it is all much the same.

> "We now pay more for packaging and advertising than we pay the farmer to produce the food."
> — Cynthia Barstow, *The Eco-Foods Guide*

Save the Ales

Similarly, beer has undergone a horrifying biocidal decline in diversity. This worldwide trend was most acutely felt in the US and Britain when the Industrial Revolution killed beer, as detailed earlier in these pages. When I was growing up in the late 20th century, there was really only one kind of beer, a style technically referred to as American light lager. Brand imagery presented a facade of diversity, but everyone knew that beer had just one flavor: beer. Light lager is the world's dominant beer style, and thus many people assume it is the only style.

But ever since the American beer renaissance began, endangered beer species have been on the comeback. Today, the Beer Judge Certification Program includes over one hundred entries in their list of existing beer styles, all of which are now brewed in America. Unfortunately, this revival was too late for some styles which have been gone so long that no one remembers exactly how they were brewed or how they tasted, and other styles are still just hanging on. Many beer species in the developing world are under heavy fire from industrial lager. But the better beer movement is quickly protecting what it can and has also caused an explosion of brand new beer life forms. Some are new versions of once-endangered styles, while others are unique, new creations.

The Diamond Knot brewpub north of Seattle serves Hemp Ale from a tap handle featuring an illustration of industrial hemp and wrapped with twine, a product which was once commonly made from hemp.

Hempenin' Brews

Take hemp beers for example. Little is known about whether hemp seed has historically been used for brewing, but avant-garde beer crafters are mashing up this grain in experimental brews. Experiments with sterilized hemp seeds began when the Frederick Brewing Company in Frederick, Maryland, first formulated their award-winning Hempen Ale in 1996.

Contributing nutty and spicy flavors to beers, hemp seeds are just one option in the cornucopia of brewing grains. Hops and hemp are both members of the *cannabinacea* plant family, so it seems fitting that another famous hemp beer hales from Humboldt County in northern California, a well-known growing center of hemp's cousin, marijuana, which is also a cannabinoid. Humboldt Hemp Ale was originally brewed in Arcata, California by former Oakland Raiders football star Mario Celotto, and continues to be made today by Firestone Walker, the California company voted mid-size brewery of the year at the 2004 Great American Beer Festival and Champion Brewery and Brewer at the 2004 World Beer Cup. The Lexington Brewing Co. made news in Kentucky when their hemp beer fueled the media buzz about farm advocates pressing for the reintroduction of industrial hemp growing in that state.

Hemp for Victory

What do paper, building products, Mercedes Benz car interiors, pancakes, shampoo, shoes, shower curtains, biodegradable plastic, fuel oil, animal bedding, rope, currency, and burgers all have in common? They can all be made from hemp. Oh yeah, and add beer to that list too.

Hemp is extraordinarily useful as well as eco-friendly. Thousands of products are made from parts of this plant that grows well without herbicides, fungicides, or pesticides.

On the other hand, cotton, which is hemp's main competitor in the marketplace, is the most chemically-intensive crop grown today. Almost half of all the agricultural chemicals used on US crops are applied to cotton, causing severe environmental damage, especially in southern states clinging to the bottom rungs of the economic ladder.

Industrial hemp is the male *cannabis sativa* plant, bred specifically for its long, strong fibers, rather than for THC content, which is the chemical in the buds of the female plant known for the high it give to people who smoke it. Hemp fiber is longer, stronger, more absorbent, more durable, and better insulating than cotton fiber. The bark of the hemp stalk contains fibers called *bast* which are among the Earth's longest natural soft fibers and are also rich in cellulose, the stuff used to make paper and thousands of other pulp products. Long fibers are strong and durable, but short fibers like cotton easily wear out.

Humans may have been using hemp for as long as we've been drinking beer. According to the Columbia History of the World, the oldest relic of human industry is a piece of hemp fabric from approximately 8000 BCE. During Europe's early Dark Ages, Germanic tribes were required to pay tribute to their feudal lords using quantities of both hemp and beer. George Washington, a brewer and distiller of note, as well as many of his contemporaries, were also hemp farmers. In fact, hemp farming remained an important part of America's rural economy all the way up through World War II when the federal government launched the Hemp for Victory campaign to encourage farmers to grow more hemp to be used in military products needed for the war effort.

Unfortunately, American farmers are now stuck in a legal gray zone that prohibits them from growing this useful, eco-friendly, and financially rewarding crop. Meanwhile, cotton-growing chemicals continue to be dumped into the environment and farmers of all kinds struggle to make a living from agricultural commodities that have long since lost value in the marketplace.

Hemp seed is supremely nutritious. It contains more essential fatty acids than any other known source, and is second only to soybeans in complete protein, but is more digestible by humans. It is high in B-vitamins and is 35 percent dietary fiber, which is the stuff that helps keep people "regular." Hemp is not psychoactive and cannot be used as a drug. Its seeds contain barely traceable amounts of THC, the drug that provides the high from smoking marijuana. The American hemp products industry voluntarily regulates itself to guarantee that products contain THC levels lower than what is detectable in drug tests, thus avoiding false positives for consumers of hemp products. These standards ensure THC levels so low that even if a person smoked a hemp joint the size of a telephone pole, the only affect would be an unforgettable headache.

But the Controlled Substances Act of 1970 effectively prevented farmers from ever growing hemp again. Although the Act specifically distinguished industrial hemp from marijuana, and provided an exemption allowing for its continued cultivation, the Drug Enforcement Administration (DEA) has refused to honor that exemption. To the bafflement of many, the regulation of industrial hemp has continued to be under the purview of the DEA — an agency whose job is to ban drugs — rather than the US Department of Agriculture, the body responsible for regulating agricultural crops. Despite this federal drug agency's efforts to keep industrial hemp mired in murky legal waters, 20 states have already passed legislation pressuring the DEA to remove the industrial hemp ban. In 1999, Hawaii planted a small experimental plot, the first legal industrial hemp crop, since the 1950s. At least 30 other countries legally grow hemp, including Canada, Germany, England, France, Spain, Australia, New Zealand, the Russian Federation, China, Thailand, Hungary, and Romania.

So how can brewers make beer with hemp seed if industrial hemp is illegal? Perplexingly, though the *growing* of hemp is banned, products containing it are perfectly legal. And, as mentioned, a huge array of hemp products are indeed available in this country. Besides beer, a growing array of alcoholic hemp beverages are becoming available, including ChanVrin hemp wine, Hemp Cider, and Hemp Vodka. In terms of taste, hemp seeds tend to lend noticeably nutty, earthy, and creamy characteristics to beers. Hemp seeds have a protein content of nearly 33 percent, making hemp seed beers a rich source of protein. So although US-based industrial hemp cultivation remains stuck in a legal quagmire, at least it is still possible to experience the benefit of the many products made from this versatile plant.

California Steam Beer

Probably the most famous American beer style to be saved from extinction is called California steam. Fritz Maytag, great-grandson of the founder of the

This antique sign advertising steam beer for 15 cents decorates the tasting room at the Anchor Brewing Company in San Francisco.

Maytag appliance empire, rescued the very last steam beer brewery in the world. In 1965 Maytag bought the Anchor Brewing Company, preventing its imminent closure and starting the revival of this unique style. In the mid-19th century, "forty-niners" heading West to find their fortunes hankered for the new golden lager beer that had just hit the world beer scene. But lager beer ferments at temperatures lower than California provides, and neither mechanical nor natural refrigeration was available. Thus, a new kind of beer was developed that used lager yeasts, but was fermented at temperatures more suitable for ale yeast. The resulting hybrid was nicknamed "steam" beer. No one knows for sure how the name evolved. One theory maintains it was the rush of steam emitted from the barrels when they were tapped — the steam was a result of storing a quasi-lager beer in warm temperatures. But while we may never know the true origin of the name, thanks to Maytag's Anchor Brewing, we do know how a steam beer tastes, and that's probably more important.

Heather Ale

According to folktales, Picts have been making heather ale since at least 2000 BCE, in the place known today as Scotland. But they were renowned for jealously guarding its secret brewing procedures from covetous invaders, and are thus thought to have caused its demise. A legend recorded by Robert Louis Stevenson tells of a Scots king who set out to destroy the Picts and discover the secret of their heather ale. He slaughtered them ruthlessly until one day when, near a cliff, he came upon the very last chief and his son, whom he immediately set about torturing to gain the secret recipe. The Pictish chief agreed to reveal the mystery but only if the Scots would kill his son first so that he could ensure the death was quick and painless. After the boy's body was thrown from the cliff, the Pictish chief faced the King and said:

> But now in vain is the torture, fire shall never avail.
> Here dies in my bosom the secret of the heather ale.

Then the chief threw himself at the king and they both fell to their death from the cliff. With both the chief and his son dead, the secret was to remain hidden from the Scots conquerors forever. But in fact, the Scots did adopt the heather ale-brewing tradition and continued it until, after centuries of war, Scotland became part of the United Kingdom in 1707. British

Parliament banned Scottish traditions like the wearing of tartan and playing bagpipes. Gaelic was forbidden and clans were persecuted — a whole culture and way of life was virtually destroyed. An act was passed preventing brewers from using any ingredients other than hops and malt, at which point heather ale was once-and-for-all reduced to legend. But in the remote Highlands and Western Isles the brewing of heather ale continued in secrecy.

In 1986, a Gaelic-speaking islander translated an old family recipe for "Leann fraoich" (heather ale) for Bruce Williams, the owner of a homebrew shop in Glasgow. Bruce began a campaign to revive Scotland's brewing heritage and in 1992 he began selling Fraoch (heather) Ale.

Heather Ale's line of beers is brewed without hops and instead uses traditional Scottish brewing spices like heather, pine, elderberry, gooseberry, and seaweed.

Heather ale has since received a "Certificate of Specific Character" protecting the tradition of heather brewing under supervision by the Scottish Office and its successor, the Scotland Office. Today Bruce's enthusiasm yields an entire line of otherwise-extinct traditional ales, including ones brewed with pine, gooseberry, elderberry, and seaweed. His efforts have made a great contribution to the *beer*odiversity of Scotland, and the world, highlighting how

Cultural homogenization kills more than just beer styles. Languages, and the knowledge they contain, are dying too. Nearly a quarter of the human population now speaks English. It is the official language of 75 countries. In just one African country, Ethiopia, at least a dozen languages are threatened with extinction.

the use of local ingredients benefits beer drinkers and helps to ensure the survival of distinctive cultural traditions that were once threatened by imperial obliteration.

Wild Fermentations

Lambic is both a figurative as well as literal example of *beer*odiversity, a veritable poster child for maintaining diversity in brewing. Lambic is a Belgian beer style that relies on a yeast-pitching method (the process of adding yeast to unfermented beer) that is otherwise unused in Western brewing. In fact, the yeast is not actually pitched by the brewer at all. Instead, the fermentation vessels are open-topped, allowing ambient airborne yeast to descend on the wort. It is this "spontaneous fermentation" that has allowed lambic to develop its very own microbial flora endemic only within about a ten-mile radius of Brussels. According to Jean-Xavier Guinard, author of *Lambic*, lambic brewing is the oldest brewing method still in use in the Western world.

Lambic has a number of variations, including gueuze, which is a blend of fresh and aged lambic, and faro, which is a blend of high and low alcohol lambics. According to Guinard, "The microorganisms that are required to successfully complete a lambic fermentation have found a niche perfectly suited to their ecological requirements in lambic breweries. Despite the tremendous amount of research performed at the University of Leuven and elsewhere, the lambic fermentation is not yet completely understood, and lambic beers remain an unsolved scientific issue in many ways." This delicious mystery perfectly symbolizes the value of *beer*odiversity.

Smokin' Beers

Once upon a time, all beers probably tasted a bit smoky, since grains were dried directly over wood fires. Today, as victims of industrialization and cost-cutting, "smoked beers" are quite rare. To be fair, not all smoky flavors are desirable. In England, coal replaced wood as the dominant fuel for drying malts partly because it did not impart unpleasant smoky flavors in the final beer. Indirect heating methods replaced direct fire, further reducing smokiness. As these industrial processes were developed to avoid bad smoke, the good smoke went with it. Today, however, a number of brewers keep the art of brewing smoked beers alive, and produce some exceptional beers.

Smoked beer authorities Ray Daniels and Geoffrey Larson provocatively explain in *Smoked Beers*, "Many brewers live in areas where unique indigenous hardwoods can be found. Use of these woods in the making of smoked malt can lead to a pleasant and enjoyable novelty that might win you awards or even help you launch a brewery." It is inspiring, if somewhat obvious, to be reminded that natural biodiversity creates uniqueness that can spawn business. Brew Moon in Hawaii smokes their malt with Kiawe wood, a hardwood similar to hickory or mesquite. It is indigenous to the Hawaiian Islands and produces a smoked malt that has sweet, fruity overtones, resting on a robust smoky foundation. Alaskan Brewing Company uses indigenous alderwood chips to produce the award-winning flavor of their world-famous Alaskan Smoked Porter. The Otter Creek brewery uses a combination of apple, maple, and hickory woods local to its Vermont home to produce Ipswich Ale.

Barley varieties add diversity to beer too. Maris Otter is a traditional English malt that came close to extinction as large farmers left it behind in favor of higher yielding varieties. Brewers, however, are willing to pay a premium to save this "juiciest, biscuity malting barley," and now small amounts are being grown organically. Distinguished English beer authority Roger Protz has declared it "the finest malting barley grown in Britain." But if the logic of industrial agriculture had taken its full course, this malt would be gone forever.

Xingu: Black Beer from the Amazon

Amazon, Inc. was founded by a group of women who wanted to prevent the extinction of the world's rarest styles of beer. They hired beer historian Alan Eames to research the black beers brewed in the Amazon basin with dark roasted corn and manioc root and fermented spontaneously with wild yeast, just like the famous Belgian lambics mentioned above. The earliest Western account of this beer dates to 1557. The result of Eames's research is Xingu Black Beer, a beer that combines ancient Amazonian tradition with a European lager style to produce a "modern primitive" beer with characteristics of both. The name Xingu (pronounced "shin-goo") refers to a tributary of the Amazon River that is home to a few surviving cultures and many species of native Amazonian wildlife that are threatened by dams, over-development, and forest exploitation.

Speaking of threatened species, Canadian company RJ Brewers (Le Cheval Blanc) produces two beers explicitly devoted to ensuring the survival of species at risk of extinction. Royalties from both beers are donated to Wildlife Habitat Canada to support the recovery of threatened and vulnerable wildlife

RJ BREWERS

Canadian RJ Brewers produces this line of beers dedicated to protecting endangered species, like the copper redhorse depicted on this Rescousse beer label.

in Quebec. Rescousse, a citrusy, golden pilsner, is dedicated to protecting the copper redhorse, a freshwater fish unique to Quebec. A label illustration by artist Ghislain Caron captures the morphological details of Quebec's only endemic vertebrate fish species. Despite all the man-made obstacles in its way, the copper redhorse still manages to return each year to deposit its eggs on the bed of the Richelieu River. The second beer in the line, Escousse, is a schwarzbier-style dark lager dedicated to a different species each year. So far it has helped recovery of the piping plover, the western chorus frog, and the Eastern spiny softshell turtle.

Variety Is the Spice of Beer

As previously mentioned, hops has only recently become the dominant spice in brewing. Throughout history people have undoubtedly experimented with every spice available. Some have proven quite useful, and modern mash magicians are reintroducing the art of brewing with herbal blends. Tomme Arthur's inspired portfolio of herbal infusions at the California-based Pizza Port Brewing Company is hard to match. A sampling of ingredients he has used in creative concoctions includes rose hips, lavender, sweet orange peel, coriander, ginger, black pepper, grains of paradise, chamomile, fried raisins, sour cherries, not to mention at least fifteen varieties of hops.

The Wisconsin-based James Page Brewing Co. proves that even rice, which is normally used as a brewing adjunct by mega-brewers because it is cheap and has little flavor, doesn't *have* to be tasteless. Page brews Boundary Waters Golden Lager with a gourmet manoomin wild rice, grown locally by members of the Ojibwe native American tribe, and thereby pays tribute to genetic diversity in the human population as well as in beer styles.

All of these unique beer styles are part of the *beer*odiversity thriving in small breweries, a diversity that creates a sense of local identity in local communities, and is restoring soul to the spiritless landscapes of industrial society.

CHAPTER 11

Putting Beer in Its Place

Small Is *Brewtiful*

Corporate beer marketing strives to convince customers that drinking a particular beer will induce good times with friends and family. But the social institutions responsible for building real community were largely dismantled after the Second World War, as Americans moved out of towns and cities and the last vestiges of community were cast off in favor of individualistic suburban fortress retreats.

Bioregionalism fosters communities where groups of varied individuals rely on one another for the things that make life both practical and enjoyable. From a *beero*centric standpoint, this suggests the idea of neigh*brew*hoods, small groups of people producing beer locally and consuming it in community. This is where the small scale of brewpubs comes into play.

Human scale is critical in designing lively, supportive, livable communities. Small technologies, be they hardware, like homebrew supplies, or social tools like homebrew clubs and brewpubs, tend to enhance community and diversity, and stimulate innovation and creativity. Case in point, have homebrewers to thank for the contemporary brewing renaissance. People using simple, small tools to make beer at home sparked a revolution that affected the whole beer world. Just 25 short years ago all of America was a *beero*logical waste land, but today, the whole country is a *beero*logical hotspot. Virtually every known style of beer is now being brewed in America and brand new styles are emerging, like the Imperial, or "double" IPA, which just recently appeared when a cadre of over-the-top brewers on both coasts began adding so many hops to their IPAs that beer critics deemed them deserving of their own style name. All of this innovation is being driven by homebrewers and small artisanal breweries. As a result, beer is again acting like a magnet that draws diverse groups of people together into community.

Small breweries may face disadvantages compared to big brewers when it comes to cash flow, capital investment, and prices on small quantities of raw materials. But they are uniquely capable of delivering more valuable experiences along with their services and products, especially when their products are inherently social, like beer. Customer service is more direct, flexible, and friendly. Keeping markets small and sourcing materials locally, brewers can lower their transportation costs, which is increasingly important as we enter an age of oil and water scarcity. Most importantly, small brewers are making beers that more people want and are even willing to pay more to get.

Curbing Sprawl

Sprawl is the dominant development trend today, but it has devastating effects on community. In *Better Not Bigger*, Eben Fodor explains how the majority of Americans now want to put the brakes on the explosive growth of the urban megalopolises that diminish quality of life for so many people. Suburban sprawl depletes natural resources like farms and forests with their soil and trees that serve as natural air and water filters. Instead, sprawl heightens the effects of air pollution and climate change by increasing dependence on cars for transportation. Sprawl also exacerbates and concentrates poverty in cities by transferring resources out of urban areas and into the suburbs.

Fodor explains that people want to control growth in order to preserve quality of life and reduce traffic congestion and he includes walkable neighborhoods in his list of 12 ways to create sustainable communities. Walkable communities would also help to solve an undeniable public health threat associated with beer: drunk driving. According to the Brewers Association, the majority of Americans now live within ten miles of a brewery, which means we're getting close to the day when everyone will be able to walk to the local brewery. But, brewpubs can be part of the problem or the solution when it comes to sprawl. Some are located in the parking lots of suburban strip malls. But many of the new wave of restaurant breweries are located in central, walkable locations, reducing traffic for local residents and customers, reducing drunk driving, and improving the overall quality of life. When brewpubs open in central locations they often serve as anchors, spurring community growth in downtown locations in need of redevelopment, helping to create a sense of centeredness in a town.

The new wave of craft breweries is renewing attractive historic and cultural sites, drawing visitors to revitalized areas, and bringing dollars into local economies that badly need an infusion of renewed interest. These sites help preserve local architectural styles, and generate other new locally-oriented projects. All of this helps to establish the intangible sense of place that is essential for maintaining stable communities.

Beer Builds Beauty

"A bar is the *only* way to kick start new community. The pub is at the heart of every one of our communities."
— Bill Dunster, principal, ZedFactory, ecological building design firm.

If beers are works of art, breweries are works of architecture. Breweries past and present build beauty in the places where we live. In addition to preserving the natural environment, the American brewing renaissance is building creative and beautiful architectural surroundings. Just as cats look for a windowsill to perch and survey their environs, people need beautiful places where they can relax and watch other people. Buildings designed and built with sustainability in mind can be the most inspiring and comforting places to drink beer, enjoy community, and simply watch the world go by.

Where would beautiful beers be without beautiful buildings in which to drink them? Craft breweries are on the cutting edge of the "green building" movement. As the craft-brewing renaissance pioneers radical new beer styles, it is also forging green architectural styles. The new wave of breweries serves as a living tribute to the power beer has to transform our built environments into places of beauty and inspiration in a world overrun by drab cookie-cutter suburban sprawl and depressing urban decay.

Buildings account for a great deal of America's natural resource needs and generate much of our waste. According to the United States Green Building Council, buildings:

+ account for over 65 percent of all US electricity usage
+ generate 30 percent of total US greenhouse gas emissions
+ produce nearly three pounds of waste per American per day

+ use 12 percent of America's potable water
+ account for 40 percent of raw materials use globally.

With numbers like these, it is imperative that we construct buildings that use resources at sustainable rates so we can live in equilibrium with nature. Craft brewers are helping to fit this piece of the sustainability puzzle in place.

What is green building? To paraphrase green building guru Alex Wilson's entry in the *World Encyclopedia of Environmental History*, green buildings adhere to eight guidelines:

- decrease dependence on cars and foster close-knit, neighborly communities where needs are met locally
- protect local ecosystems, including open space
- reduce energy usage
- conserve water
- use green products and materials, reducing the impact of the production and eventual disposal of building materials
- use materials efficiently
- maximize durability and minimize high-impact maintenance requirements
- maintain good indoor environmental quality

Brewing History at Great Lakes

When co-owners and brothers Pat and Dan Conway selected the site for the Great Lakes Brewing Company, it was a lesson in how to achieve commercial and environmental goals in unison. Rather than building from scratch and making a big environmental footprint, Great Lakes decided to renovate an historic site, transforming an abandoned stretch of buildings in the heart of Cleveland's historic brewing neighborhood into a visually attractive magnet for revitalization. Renovating existing structures not only avoided the environmental impacts of new construction, but also allowed them to create a convivial atmosphere with unique architectural elements that emphasize the brewing heritage of Cleveland.

The company's brewpub and restaurant found their home in a century-old Victorian building. The Taproom bar features the city's oldest mahogany bar, where beer has been served to Clevelanders for over 125 years. According to popular legend, the bullet holes visible in the bar came from Eliot Ness himself, the famous Prohibition enforcement officer responsible for taking down Al Capone. As a young attorney, John D. Rockefeller also spent time in an office above the brewpub. Below the Taproom is the Beer Cellar, a charming turn-of-the-century rathskellar-style wooden bar, complete with stone walls and a view of the brewing vessels. Throughout the building, walls are adorned with historic breweriana (that's beer-geek speak for "old beer stuff"), like hundred-year-old Cleveland brewery photographs and serving trays. The brewery and pub contain a number of cabinets displaying antique beer bottles and cans, bottle-openers, and a cornucopia of other beer-related relics. The old two-handled beer pump at the top of the stairway is an antique version of the beer engines used to serve the English-style Real Ales that are appearing in more and more brewpubs today.

The brewery pub combines two buildings, MacClean's Feed and Seed Company, and the Market Tavern, which was established around 1865 and

The Schlather Brewing Company was situated on the lot that now houses Great Lakes' production brewery. The carved stone archway that originally graced the brewery entrance was unearthed during construction and is now on display in the brewery banquet facility, along with photographs of historic breweries in the neighborhood.

became a popular watering hole for Cleveland's legal and civil service workers. Driven by a growing demand for their beers, the company acquired and renovated another adjacent site that once comprised the stables and warehouse facilities of the Schlather Brewing Company. The buildings are undergoing continuous restoration efforts to capture the architectural details of the original brewery, including a gabled roof and the cork walls used to insulate a cold beer storage area. The two-story brewery features full glass walls to provide visitors a view of the gleaming, stainless steel brewing vessels. The brewery tasting room features an antique bar and historic Cleveland brewing memorabilia, including the gigantic, 19th century, carved stone Schlather Brewing Co. archway discovered during excavation of another adjacent building site.

The "tank farm" (where the fermentation vessels reside) and storage cooler allow in natural light, and during the winter months are cooled using outside air. In the brewpub, an air curtain keeps warm air from escaping when patrons enter and exit. All these strategies help to minimize the use of electricity. GLBC received a $150,000 grant from the Ohio Department of Development's Office of Energy Efficiency to develop a cogeneration system that will transform steam and replace the current boiler system with a cleaner, energy-efficient natural gas and biodiesel operation. It will produce heat and electricity and serve as a back-up system in the event of a blackout.

One need not adhere to an environmental creed to appreciate the splendor of such a magnificent site. And yet achieving this brilliant physical setting has allowed the Conways to avoid the considerable waste that would have resulted from a conventional approach to construction. By situating in historic digs, Great Lakes makes the most of its location, celebrating the uniqueness of Cleveland. Entering the Taproom, customers are immediately impressed by the fact that they are in Cleveland and nowhere else. The green building choice maximizes the benefits of that intangible sense of place. It's impossible to quantify the value of this feeling, but without it, people are ungrounded and lost. The security of place and familiarity of surroundings are never so desirable as when people are trying to relax and enjoy a beer in community. With history at hand, place is established. In an atmosphere conducive to a relaxed state of mind, people can focus intently on conversation, or simply on the peacefulness of a solitary moment with a rewarding beer.

Of course, the true test is whether this theory plays out in reality. Do real people consider the Great Lakes pub a place for community? I visited the brewery one day and owner Pat Conway inadvertently answered this question.

As I waited at the bar for Pat to finish another meeting, an older man entered the pub and nodded in my direction as he leaned gently forward against the bar. His appearance elicited a greeting from the hostess and the bartender, who immediately served him a glass of water. When Pat appeared a few minutes later, already running late for our meeting and unaware that I was in the room, he stopped first to chat with the old man, addressing him by name and casually inquiring about his general state of being. Eventually introductions were made all around and Pat explained that Mr. Fox, who works at the cheese counter at the West Side Market across the street, is one of Great Lakes' best customers. Mr. Fox suggested that I try the Dortmunder, which in his opinion, is Great Lakes' best beer. I invited him to have one with us, but he declined, claiming that he just drinks water these days, and further explaining that he comes in here because he just likes the place. Without trying, Pat and Mr. Fox had proven to me beyond a shadow of a doubt that Great Lakes is a true community place — the number one customer is no customer at all, just a member of the community.

If environmental leadership is a sign of a company's care for their community, then Great Lakes is at the head of the pack. Most craft breweries are already using resources like fuel and packaging more efficiently by nature of their small scale and local markets. Serving local markets means reducing the amount of transportation needed, which means reduced reliance on petroleum. Brewpubs, which comprise a majority of the small breweries in America, serve most of their beer from a tap and into a pint glass, eliminating most of the need for packaging like bottles, six-pack carriers, cases, pallets, shrink-wrap and more. Great Lakes Brewery goes a step further in reducing petroleum use by making, using, and marketing their own in-house biodiesel fuel.

The Fatty Wagon is the shuttle bus Great Lakes uses to run customers between Cleveland Indians baseball games and the brewpub. Instead of gas or diesel, the bus runs on vegetable oil. A local business, called Biodiesel Cleveland, takes the used French fry grease from the brewpub and uses the brewery facilities to convert this cooking oil into "biodiesel," a fuel that is gaining in popularity around the country as well as the world and which runs up to 75 percent cleaner than conventional fuels. Thus Great Lakes is able to provide a valuable service to the community by shuttling folks to the home-town game, and also offer some environmental education while reducing their own eco-footprint all at the same time.

The Fatty Wagon runs on used French fry grease to haul customers from the pub to the ball game.

Another way they meet the triple obligations of community, environment, and profit is their involvement with Kentucky Gardens, an urban greenhouse and community garden that produces vegetables for the Brewpub. The Gardens are the site of a passive solar greenhouse pilot project. GLBC partnered with local entrepreneur Mike Stevens on this "SunTrap" greenhouse, which combines the best ideas for using solar energy for winter growing. It takes advantage of the very-low-in-the-sky position of the sun during winter to trap solar energy inside the growing space. The energy conservation techniques incorporated in the greenhouse design allow it to successfully grow organic produce year-round without any supplemental heat or light energy. GLBC also sponsors and receives weekly harvests from Common Ground Garden, a local urban community garden system headed by Cleveland's Summer Sprouts Program.

But the real crown on the bottle is the Burning River Fest. Great Lakes injects their earth-friendly spirit into a large and very successful annual community event. The vision to create Burning River Fest was sparked by a 1969 environmental disaster that left Cleveland's Cuyahoga River in flames. The festival celebrates all that the region has to offer in the performing arts, culinary arts, and environmental activism. As an advocacy vehicle, the Burning River Fest raises public awareness by spotlighting the Cuyahoga River, its neighboring waterways, and other focal points of local environmental efforts. Held every summer in Voinovich Park, which is just behind the world-famous Rock and Roll Hall of Fame, the Fest gathers thousands of locals to do what beer helps us do best: celebrate in community. Organized in partnership with EcoCity Cleveland, the event sets the stage for their annual "Eco-Hero Awards" which are given to worthy citizens and businesses in recognition of their environmental efforts.

Other green groups participating and benefiting from the event include Slow Food, the Northeast Ohio Foodshed, the Chagrin River Land Conservancy, and the Great Lakes Science Center. And of course biodiesel fuel provides some of the energy required to run the operation. A commemorative water ritual also takes place — perhaps this will become a new tradition for breweries. After all, beer is about 95 percent water, a sacred component of every beer!

And what's local beer without local food? The event showcases Ohio-grown ingredients in dishes created at several participating restaurants and taverns. A "floating schoolhouse" schooner boat takes guests on short excursions to teach them facts about Lake Erie. Demonstrations on straw bale building, cardboard furniture-making, and rain barrel construction also take place throughout the day, along with other fun activities for all ages. The local economy benefits from money going directly into the pockets of local businesses, farmers, musicians, artists, and restaurateurs while families and companies learn how to incorporate sustainable and environmentally healthy strategies into daily life and business practices.

In Great Lakes Brewing Company, Pat and Dan Conway have created a masterpiece of brewing art and architecture that gives real cause for community celebration.

Fishing for Sustainability

Great Lakes isn't the only small brewery involved in local environmental protection. Many craft brewers support environmental efforts through education, charitable donations, and staff participation. Take Fish Brewing for example. Each beer in the Fish Tale line benefits an organization working to protect aquatic habitat. Both microbreweries as well as large scale macro-breweries are addressing water consumption issues. On average, small breweries use less water than big brewing companies. But even big companies are finding productive ways to use wastewater, like the Anheuser-Busch factory in Florida that uses it to grow turf.

Breweries adopting ecological architecture, or "eco-tecture," can go in forward and reverse gears. Not only are many of America's hundreds of new breweries located in rehabbed buildings, but old industrial brewery sites are also being converted into new eco-buildings. The Brewery Blocks is an eco-development in Portland, Oregon, converted from the former Blitz-Weinhard brewery.

Beer Party on the Beach

The Beach Chalet is an historic building welcoming beach visitors to Golden Gate Park in San Francisco. The Spanish Colonial-style structure was built by William Polk in 1925, and adorned with murals of everyday San Francisco life by Lucien Labaudi as a project of the depression-era Works Progress

The Dutch windmill that flanks the Beach Chalet.

Administration. The first floor served as a changing room for beach-goers and the upper floor was a restaurant. The building later housed soldiers during World War II and then provided social gathering space for Veterans of Foreign Wars, until it was closed in 1981. Since then, it has undergone several rehabilitations, but languished unoccupied until 1996 when an entrepreneur put together a successful bid to lease the building in a public-private partnership. Today, the first floor is a museum open to the public, and the second floor is a brewpub.

Flanking the Chalet are two more historic sites that help draw visitors in for a pint. The Dutch Windmill and the Murphy Windmill were built in 1903 and 1905 respectively in order to pump well water for irrigation in Golden Gate Park. Today, the majestic "Dutch" is restored to its full glory and

The windmill inspires the brewery's logo.

stands proudly just adjacent to the brewpub, its arms outstretched as if to say: "Welcome, come on in and have a beer."

Sacramento's new Pyramid Alehouse is located in a 1930s-era former department store building along the light rail line on the K Street pedestrian mall. The prominent downtown site continues Pyramid's tradition of locating in interesting older buildings. The new brewpub is a key part of the developing downtown arts and entertainment district. "We want buildings with character," said Martin Kelly of Pyramid's strategy for new locations,

Built in 1878, Coolidge & Bentley Hatters, Clothiers and Outfitters is now the charming two-story home of Glen Falls, New York victuals vendor and watering hole Davidson Brothers Brewery. Kerry Gonyea, general manager, was adding some hops to the brew kettle when I found him in the tiny 217-gallon brewing room.

which generally focuses on occupying interesting properties that create a billboard for the brewery and the beer. "We want to be in a place that has some roots in the community and feels local."

Wood You, Could You, In a Lumber Mill?

The Ellicott Mills Brewing Company shares its name with the town where it is located, as well as the lumber-processing plant that was formerly housed where the restaurant and brewpub are today. The two-story stone building bookends the town's quainter-than-quaint strip of old-timey shops, antique stores, coffee shops, custom furnishing designers, homemade candy shops, and even a comic book store. The town itself is noted historically as the site of the first railroad terminus in the US.

The Little House that Can

Beer-lover John Milkovisch might loosely be included in what is sometimes called "outsider" art, or — perhaps more sympathetically — "visionary" art. He

"John thought beer cured everything," explained Mary, after her husband John, the man responsible for constructing the beer can house, passed away.

attached thousands of beer cans to his Houston house over a 20-year period as an alternative to more traditional home repair. He also made beer can fences and garlands to hang from his roof. The home had become a nationally celebrated folk-art site when the Southern Pacific upholsterer died in 1988 at 75. In 2001, an Orange Show art endowment was secured to fund the home's restoration and open it to public viewing. "The Beer Can House represents the sort of idiosyncratic individualism that Houstonians and Texans pride themselves on," said Emily Todd, the endowment's grant officer.

According to family members, Milkovisch started covering his house with flattened beer cans so he wouldn't have to paint it. He secretly liked the notice his home received but seemed surprised that it was thought of as a work of art. An arch of beer can tops and bottoms once reached across the driveway and there once was a curtain of pop tops on the south side of the home. Can collectors have donated vintage cans to help in the restoration.

Share a Pint

Green buildings can help build community, but a pub's social landscape is just as important as its physical structure. Hospitality is crucial to establishing the social norm of generosity. Nowhere is the tone of a pub more evident than in its bartender's personality. In good bars and brewpubs, the bartenders are quick to share the goods. My common experience in brewpubs and better beer bars is that a quizzical look in the direction of the taps, or a noncommittal inquiry about one of the house beers normally elicits a quickly poured sample for me to taste. Sometimes, as I once experienced at the Jupiter brewpub in Berkeley, this sample sipping can go on through a dozen or more beers without the bartender displaying any semblance of impatience. To the contrary, good brewpub bartenders are happy to encourage a customer's exploration until the proper beer for the moment is discovered.

Hospitality and generosity are traits that are too often overlooked in America. Sharing is under-represented in the media and downright frowned upon by corporate culture. Thankfully, it is a custom that has not yet been completely abandoned, despite the corporate norm of selfishness and greed that dominates so much of the daily experience of most Americans.

One of nature's successful strategies is cooperation, sometimes called co-evolution. It works in the beer world too. For example, Moonlight and Russian River, two breweries in Sonoma County, California, share a hopyard. Cultivating, picking, and the results of the harvest are all shared. Harvest time is a family and friends affair, reviving the community hop-harvest tradition. Rather than viewing each other as competitors, these companies engage in a form of mutual support. They celebrated this new venture by naming the first brew from their own hops "Homegrown Ale," an appropriate toast to the power beer has to build strong local communities.

Sacred Places

Beer is good at building human communities, but as previously discovered, it also facilitates communion with the divine, acting as a bridge between the sacred and secular domains. The best bars and brewpubs are a physical embodiment of that bridge, serving as a crossroads between the holy spirit and the alcoholic spirit. Throughout Asia, it is common to see altars near the bar, where offerings of food and alcohol are made to the deities inhabiting the place. Patron saints of breweries and bars are a related phenomenon. It used to be far more common than it is today, but some bars still serve as threshold between the material and spiritual worlds through a kind of ancestor worship. It's the picture of "Old Joe" hanging behind the bar. "Joe" built the place in nineteen-hundred-and-something-or-other, and now after his death, he offers his blessing or his disapproval to what goes on in his sacred beer-drinking place.

> "The greatest honor of all is to have a pub named after you in your lifetime."
> — Richard Boston, *Beer and Skittles*

Bars like this achieve a status beyond just a community place; they become truly sacred places. A sacred place grounds the believer in a way that silences the cacophony inherent in a confusing and contradictory world. It offers the believer a center from which to view the rest of the world and make sense of it. There is no better manifestation of this sacredness than the classic barroom philosophical ramble — the kind of conversation that often ends with a comment along the lines of: "Now that we have solved all the world's problems, let's get another beer." It's the kind of conversation that creates an ultimate stillness and oneness with everything. At the end, there is nothing left to be said, so the participants can simply sit and enjoy their beer. In this context, the act of drinking becomes a sacred ritual, acknowledging the presence of the divine.

Like the thousands of species of plants and animals nearing extinction at the hands of industrial society, so too are these kinds of sacred bars and pubs

I found this Buddhist altar in a bar-internet café in Hanoi, Vietnam. Notice the prominent position of Tiger beer being offered as a libation.

endangered. Diversity keeps the world interesting, not to mention alive and well. Sacred beer-drinking places help to preserve this diversity by establishing a relationship between humans and the divine universe. Neighborhoods, like the planet, need lots of unique, local creations in order to prosper and be happy. The corner bar or pub, with its house beer on tap, can be the anchor and the kick start that many locales need in order to become vibrant, diverse communities.

What is the Essential Ingredient in a Pub?

"A few pubs are hostile. They are easily spotted and should be avoided. In most it takes only two or three visits to become a regular, the status of full membership being achieved when you can go in and ask for 'the usual.' This enormously comfortable phrase is characteristic of a good pub, which is a place where you should feel welcome, a place for meeting people of all kinds on terms of equality and in an atmosphere of tolerance and conviviality … What is the essential quality that differentiates the old White Horse from the new, or any good pub from any indifferent one? In the end, it is not the difference between an oak beam and a fiberglass one. It's the difference between a place which is the social focus for a community, and one that is merely a commercial enterprise. It's the difference between a pub where for no financial gain someone organizes a competition to guess the weight of a vegetable marrow, and one where it is inconceivable that such a thing could happen. A pub is not just a place for buying and selling food and drink. It is the social and convivial center of a community. This is why the closing of its only pub can kill a village and turn it into an unorganic huddle of dwellings… I would say that more important than any [thing else] is whether or not a pub can pass the vegetable marrow test."

— Richard Boston, *Beer and Skittles*

CHAPTER 12

Make Mine Organic

"Drink organic, think organic, and let us live in harmony with nature."

— Roger Protz, Britain's top beer guru,
and founder of the Campaign for Real Ale

A soup of toxic chemicals is burbling in the world's farmlands, promising a poisonous supper for farmers as well as the land they tend. This lethal chemical gumbo is tainting our food, air, and water, and causing death and destruction to plants and animals. But a hopeful aroma of beer is wafting from a small but growing number of breweries that are part of the promising growth in organic agriculture.

In the 1970s, toxic chemicals became all the rage during what is ironically known as the agricultural "green revolution." Organic farming emerged as a response to this "big ag" and serves as a sustainable approach to food production that works with nature, instead of against it. Organic farming makes use of local, non-toxic farm inputs and natural biological cycles to promote biodiversity and improve soil fertility. It protects people and the planet by preventing toxic chemicals known to cause health problems like asthma and cancer, from ending up in the ground, air, water, and food supply. Because organic agriculture doesn't use toxic and persistent pesticides, choosing organic products is an easy way for consumers to protect themselves while enjoying delicious, nourishing, safe food.

Morgan Wolaver behind the taps at the Otter Creek/Wolaver's tasting room in his Middlebury, Vermont-based brewery. Wolaver's was America's first nationally distributed line of organic beers.

Conventional fertilizers are primarily made from petroleum products that are refined down to the chemicals nitrogen, potash, and phosphorous, which in overabundance kill off helpful soil microorganisms. Organic producers use natural materials and processes instead, like composted manure and crop rotation, to improve soil fertility. As a result, organic practices protect surface and groundwater by preventing the runoff of chemicals known to cause "dead zones" in bodies of water. Organic practices also prohibit the use of hormones, antibiotics, and other drugs for stimulating abnormal growth in livestock. Public health authorities now link the use of antibiotics in livestock to the greater numbers of people contracting infections that resist treatment with the same drugs. For example, microbiologist Rustam Aminov, at the University of Illinois, looked at the soil and water underneath waste lagoons from pigs that were treated with antibiotics. He found that the soil and ground water contained bacteria with genes

"Organic farming is now the fastest growing sector of the world agricultural economy."
— Chris Bright, *State of the World Report* 2003

that were resistant to tetracycline, which is widely used to treat a variety of common infections like strep throat, the flu, and typhus. If the bacteria are resistant to tetracycline it means the treatment will no longer work.

A Household Word

In the US, the term "organic" is now regulated by the Department of Agriculture (USDA) and denotes products made in accordance with the Organic Foods Production Act. In addition to the natural practices described above, food

The all-organic Duke of Cambridge pub in London serves a large range of certified organic Real Ales, including the aptly named Eco Warrior from Pitfield Brewing.

products labeled organic must also be non-genetically modified and cannot be fertilized with sewage sludge — a common practice in conventional farming. From 1997 to the time of this writing in 2006, the US market for certified organic products grew more than 20 percent every year. This growth is expected to increase at even higher rates in coming years. According to *Organic Monitor*, the global organic foods market topped US$23 billion in 2002. It is by far the fastest growing segment of the food market in America. Every food category now has an organic option. And non-food agricultural products are being grown organically too — even cotton, which conventional experts had previously said would be impossible.

Happily, this growth includes an ever-expanding array of organic beers, breweries, and restaurants around the world, particularly in North America and Europe. Restaurant Nora in Washington DC was the first restaurant in America to become certified organic — everything from the tablecloths to the beer is organic. The second US restaurant to become certified organic was Ukiah Brewing Company, a brewpub in California specializing in home-made organic beers, complementing a full organic dining menu, and a fine organic live music scene.

With organic drinks, the barley, hops, grapes, apples, and other ingredients used to make fermented refreshments are spared the application of toxic chemicals. But to fully comprehend the importance of organic beer makers like Wolaver's and Ukiah, it is necessary to bear witness to the fatal chemical mess that is its alternative. Don't be tempted to gloss through this dizzying maze of deadly toxins. By facing the disastrous end that is the logical conclusion of industrial agriculture, the pleasing fruits of the organic brewing revolution will be all the tastier. Fair warning: the end of this chapter is probably a good time for a beer break.

Chemical Weapons

In general, commercial beers are made with just four ingredients: yeast, malted barley, hops, and water. As a living microscopic organism generally cultivated on pure sugar, yeast is not a major concern in any debate about organic brewing. Suffice to say that using organic ingredients sufficiently addresses the issue of organic yeast. Non-organic barley and hops are grown with heaps of horrible chemicals known to be toxic to humans, plants, and animals. Many of them end up polluting the water supply, which in turn ends up killing people and animals. The most dangerous chemicals persist, remaining unchanged and accumulating as they move up through the food chain.

Researchers at Cornell University estimate that at least 67 million birds die each year from pesticides sprayed on US fields. The number of fish killed is conservatively estimated at four to six million. Even more shocking is the evidence cited in Issue 481 of *Rachel's Environment and Health Weekly*, estimating that every year 10,400 people die from cancers caused by exposure to pesticides.

Farmer Friendly

Not only does chemically-intensive farming devastate ecosystems and harm human populations, it also contributes to the crisis in family-owned farms. Chemically-intensive industrial agriculture traps small farmers in debt cycles that run their livelihoods into bankruptcy, forcing them to sell out to corporate ag companies or land developers. Between 1993 and 1997, the number of mid-sized family farms dropped by 74,440. According to Farm Aid, 330 farmers leave their land every week. Less than half of American farmland is controlled by family farmers, and yet a Roper survey shows that 85 percent of American consumers trust family farms more than corporate farms to provide safe and nutritious food.

Organic farming is proving to be both profitable and family-friendly. Farmers like Ron Rosemann, of Harlan, Iowa, say it is a saving grace for family farms. Unlike industrial-scale corporate-owned factory farms, small farmers have a vested interest in their communities, so they are more likely to use sustainable farming techniques to protect natural resources and human health. Organic farmers like Rosemann communicate this commitment to consumers by labeling their food as organic. The result has been a surge in support for small, local, organic family farms.

In addition to sustainable organic production methods, family farms provide jobs to members of their communities, and support local businesses by purchasing goods and services locally. Industrial agriculture operations employ as few workers as possible and, according to William Weida at the Global Resource Action Center for the Environment, they typically purchase supplies, equipment, and building materials from outside the local community. This leaves rural areas with high rates of unemployment and little opportunity for economic growth. As we lose family farms, we also lose diversity in the food supply, and the American diet is increasingly dictated by the interests of a few corporate behemoths.

Franken-Beer-Stein

Genetically modified food products, called "Frankenfoods" by critics like Friends of the Earth, are now common in the American marketplace. Some industrial light lagers probably already include genetically modified (GMO) corn. Aventis corporation produces a GMO corn called StarLink that contains genes from a soil bacterium called Bacillus thuringiensis. The genes enable this "Bt corn" to produce a protein that acts as a natural pesticide. Less insecticide seems like a good thing, right? Unfortunately, in addition to killing the European corn borer, this pesticide also kills desirable bugs like the monarch butterfly. Scarier still is the fact that the insecticidal protein also seems to survive the digestive process intact and enters the human blood stream where it can cause severe allergic reactions. As a result, the EPA banned it from being used in corn meant for human consumption and allowed it only for corn used as animal feed. Unfortunately, corn from StarLink fields get mixed with corn from regular non-GMO fields. Investigations have found at least 300 consumer products that contained Bt corn, including products used by brewers.

Pizza Port, a brewpub in Carlsbad, California, renowned for its high quality beers, reportedly dumped a thirty barrel batch of their Amigo Mexican Lager after being informed by their supplier, Briess Malting, that the corn used in the beer may have contained StarLink GMOs. Briess refunded their payment for the suspected Bt corn, as well as the costs of dumping the batch of beer. Since then Briess began testing to ensure Bt-free corn supplies. Guaranteeing that brewing corn is GMO-free is not a simple test though. Coors Brewing claims that due to the sheer quantities of corn being processed in mills, it is impossible for them to know for sure that the corn that ends up in their beer is GMO-free.

There's Something in the Water

Water accounts for roughly 90 percent or more of most beers. Clean, pure sources are therefore vital to brewers, who constantly monitor water quality, and modify its chemical composition according to the style of beer they want to produce. While conventional farming pollutes water, according to a report by the Food and Agriculture Organization, "Organic farming can help reduce ground and surface water contamination, and can safeguard drinking water supplies in certain areas, thus contributing to food safety in a larger sense and sustainable agriculture."

Conventional practices have led to measurable problems. The 2001 Pew Oceans Commission report "Marine Pollution in the United States: Significant Accomplishments, Future Challenges" found that polluted runoff from farms and cities went largely unabated or actually increased over the previous 30 years. The report notes that many of the nation's coastal environments exhibit symptoms of phosphorous over-enrichment. According to Dr. Donald Boesch, the report's lead reviewer, symptoms include algal blooms, which may be toxic; loss of sea grasses and coral reefs; and serious oxygen depletion. As a result, coastal regions see reduced production of fisheries, threats to biodiversity, and ecosystems less resilient to natural and human influences.

Reinheitsgebot: Pure Beer or Pure Bull?

Renate Kuenast, who served as the German Minister for Agriculture until 2005, vowed to make 20 percent of German agriculture organic by 2010, commenting that Germans must develop the same reverence for their environment as they have always had for their beer. This last remark refers to the German Beer Purity act of 1516, aka the Reinheitsgebot.

This law's enforcement was in effect for nearly 500 years and is believed to be the longest running food hygiene law ever. Since the law forbids the use of anything but barley, hops, and water in the brewing of beer, many modern brewers continue to revere it for protecting beer from adulteration. Others consider it restrictive, saying it stymies creativity by disallowing perfectly safe ingredients like fruits and herbs. In any case, the original intent of the law probably had less to do with quality and more to do with taxes, as covered earlier.

But just as the Reinheitsgebot failed to include yeast as a permissible ingredient in beer (its existence, and therefore its importance to beer, was unknown at the time), neither did it mention the use of toxic chemicals in the growing of brewing ingredients. An effective beer purity law in the modern age, would require such a restriction. Even though craft brewers shun chemical additives and preservatives during brewing, their beers are heavily laden with dangerous chemicals from the dozens of chemical inputs used to grow barley and hops, the primary ingredients in beer.

Healthy Hops

Hops were first planted in the US in 1629 and by the mid-1800s Americans were producing 1.5 million pounds annually, much of it in upstate New York. Due to diseases like powdery mildew, hops production moved westward during the early 1900s. Today, most US hops are grown in the Yakima Valley in Washington state, where disease pressure is lower than in the humid eastern states. Virtually all American hops are grown using conventional agricultural methods, relying heavily on fungicides to control mildews and pesticides to keep hop aphids in check.

An issue of concern to even the most casual observer is the fact that allowable levels and types of pesticide use vary greatly from one country to the next. For example, Germany and the US, two major hop-producing countries, use wildly different regulations on pesticide use for hops. According to Dr. Adrian Forster: "From altogether 80 available hop spraying agents 40 are licensed in Germany at the moment and 11 in the USA. Only six [of these agents] are licensed in both countries. Consequently five agents licensed in the USA may not be used in Germany and 34 sprayings licensed in Germany may not be applied in the USA." Paraquat is a good example. It has been banned or severely restricted in sixteen countries, including most of northern Europe, and is included on the Pesticide Action Network's "Dirty Dozen" list of the worst pesticides, but its use is still allowed in the US.

Endothall is a highly toxic herbicide also allowed on US-grown hops. According to Environmental Defense, it is suspected of causing kidney and blood damage in humans, and is believed to be toxic to fish. Until 1993, the acutely toxic pesticide fosetyl-al was also allowed in US hops production, but was finally banned by the Delaney clause, a landmark directive prohibiting the use of food additives known to induce cancer in humans or animals.

John Barleycorn Gets Blotto

The good news about barley is that much of what is used in American beers is grown and processed right in the US, so at least it's produced relatively locally. The bad news is that loads of toxic chemicals are applied to barley crops. The sheer number and variety employed is enough to give a beer drinker pause, but the nasty health and environmental effects are staggering. Conventional grain production relies heavily on herbicides, particularly to control wild oats and mustards, which are the primary invasive weeds. The following is a mere sampling of the dirty laundry list of toxic chemicals used on barley.

Monsanto's best seller, RoundUp, is perhaps the most famous and probably the worst herbicidal culprit. Glyphosate, the active ingredient in RoundUp, is typical in its range of harmful effects, from making workers sick to contributing to cancer in consumers, and even hurting the plants it is meant to protect. In California, glyphosate exposure was the third-most commonly reported cause of pesticide illness among agricultural workers. For landscape maintenance workers, it ranked highest. What is really frightening is that glyphosate residues are found in food long after their application in the field. Barley planted a year after treatment still contained residues at harvest time. According to a study led by R.L. Tominack that included Monsanto's own toxicologist, ingestion of RoundUp has been shown to cause "irritation of the oral mucous membrane and gastrointestinal tract … pulmonary dysfunction, oliguria, metabolic acidosis, hypotension, leukocytosis and fever." Scary sounding names, but what does it all mean? In plain language, glyphosate causes the worst stomachache imaginable and treatment requires patients to restrict their diets to a very few bland food choices. Glyphosate has also been linked to non-Hodgkin's lymphoma, the worse of the two main forms of lymphoma. Furthermore, tests on pregnant lab rats showed multiple abnormalities in both the mother and the fetus when exposed to glyphosate. RoundUp is also a proven endocrine disruptor, which means it messes with reproductive systems. So if RoundUp is this bad for people and animals, what does it do to plants? Glyphosate application increases the susceptibility of crop plants to a number of diseases. For example, spraying of RoundUp prior to planting barley increased the severity of Rhizoctonia root rot and actually *decreased* barley yield.

Besides malted barley, wheat is another high quality brewing grain. And although these two grains have long been the main ingredients preferred by professional brewers, industrial brewing companies now use a great deal of "adjunct" ingredients like corn and rice, which tend to contribute less body and flavor to beer and are much cheaper. Like barley, these grains are all grown using toxic chemicals.

Dicamba is an herbicide used to kill unwanted broadleaf plants in corn and wheat crops. In humans, exposure to dicamba is associated with the inhibition of the nervous system enzyme acetylcholinesterase and an increased frequency of non-Hodgkin's lymphoma. In laboratory animals, dicamba decreases body weight, causes liver damage, is associated with an increased frequency of fetal loss, and severe, sometimes irreversible, eye damage. Dicamba also causes genetic damage in human blood cells, bacteria, and barley. Because dicamba is mobile in soil, it contaminates waterways, including the groundwater in at least 17 US states. Dicamba evaporates easily and has been known to drift airborne for several miles. It inhibits some of the organisms important in soil nutrient cycling and thus impairs soil fertility and has been associated with an increase in the frequency of some plant diseases, including chromosome aberrations in barley.

Barley Is Better

Organic agriculture can be a lifeline for small farms because it offers an alternative market where sellers can command fair prices for crops. Barley crops can themselves act as good alternatives to chemical inputs. Fred and Paula Smeds come from farming families. With Fred's father Alfred, they grow grapes on their Savage Island Farm in California's San Joaquin Valley. For years they fought pests and weeds with conventional insecticides and herbicides. Then in 1985 Fred got cancer and re-evaluated his farming techniques. "I didn't want to put myself at risk using chemicals that might aggravate my condition," said Smeds. "I didn't want to use any more pesticides than I had to. But I was willing to use what I needed in order to keep my crop free of diseases and pests. It didn't work out at first. I found myself spraying more and more, probably because I had disrupted the natural controls that had once been there."

Then the Smeds tried using a cover crop to reduce pests. The first was a simple mixture of vetch and barley. Fred was amazed to see all the beneficial insects that appeared. "I allowed the vetch and barley to grow well into May. Walking into that waist-high cover was a little spooky — so many things were rustling around in there that I couldn't help wondering what might head up my pants leg," he said. "I've seen the buildup of a whole natural enemy complex as I've converted each block and began mowing the berms instead of spraying them with herbicides. Once the cover crops were established, they provided habitat for the beneficials."

Perhaps the most noticeable beneficial insect population to set up on Savage Island Farm was spiders. Since they can balloon in, spiders are one of the fastest colonizers. "Lady beetles and lacewings are very important as well, but there are so many tiny wasps and flies that we can't even see that are on the job from day one," Fred observed. "If we don't kill them off, then even the first year without spraying can surprise you. Keep in mind that the longer we maintain habitat and go without spraying, the more diverse and resilient the natural enemy complex becomes."

There's Fungus Among Us and Insects Are Inside

Unfortunately, unlike the Smeds, most farmers have yet to switch to organics and still rely heavily on toxic inputs. Triademefon is a fungicide used on grains, fruit trees, vegetables and — wine drinkers take note — grapes. It is a known carcinogen but was long used as a food additive in milled barley and wheat. Imazalil is another fungicide used on barley and wheat. Both of these chemicals were finally regulated out of use in 1985 by the Delaney clause. But many other toxic chemicals have yet to be banned in the US.

Chemical compounds known as organophosphates include some of the most toxic chemicals used in agriculture.

Malicious Malathion Mauls Fish

Malathion is one of the most extensively used organophosphate insecticides around the globe. It is toxic to a wide variety of plants, animals, soil microorganisms, and beneficial insects like snails and worms. One study concluded that malathion is so toxic it should never be used near any natural body of water. Not only does it kill a wide variety of fish, including steelhead trout, striped bass, and starry flounders, it inhibits plant photosynthesis, growth and respiration of wheat seedlings, and causes damage to the chromosomes in pollen cells from barley plants, resulting in chlorophyll mutations.

Based on US Food and Drug Administration residue analyses, malathion is the most commonly detected pesticide in food products. Residues were found in 18 percent of the 936 food items tested. In 1988, EPA estimated that children could be consuming malathion residues 1,133 percent — and adults 507 percent — over the amount currently determined to be unsafe. Malathion residues *increased* with storage time in treated *brewing ingredients* like wheat, barley, and rice.

Ethyl parathion, another organophosphate, is considered to be one of the most toxic pesticides currently in use worldwide and has been shown to be responsible for the deaths of thousands of birds. It has also killed domestic mammals, including humans, in cases where applicators mishandled the chemical. Its toxicity prompted the EPA to restrict its use in 1991 to nine US grown crops, *including* brewing grains like barley, corn, sorghum, and wheat.

Dying from the Ds

Another member of the fine family of organophosphates is 2,4-dichlorophenoxyacetic acid (2,4-D), which is applied to wheat, corn, barley, rice, and oats, and has been proven to be toxic to the eye, thyroid, kidney, adrenals, and ovaries/testes. In a 2003 study of pesticides present in the bodies of US residents, the US Centers for Disease Control and Prevention reported that children

6–11 years of age had significantly higher levels of both 2,4-D and 2,4-dichlorophenol (a breakdown product of 2,4-D and triclosan) than adults and youth aged 12–19 years. Epidemiological studies link 2,4-D to non-Hodgkin's lymphoma (NHL) among farmers. A number of studies also link 2,4-D exposure to childhood cancers including leukemia, NHL, and brain cancers.

While we're on the "Ds" let's cover diazinon too, which includes sulfotepp, an acutely toxic organophosphate. Diazinon has secret ingredients that are supposed to be inert. Though these mystery ingredients are not publicly declared, at least two have been identified as ethylbenzene and xylene, both of which are acutely and chronically toxic. In barley, diazinon exposure caused abnormal cell division in root tip cells, chromosome abnormalities in pollen mother cells, and chlorophyll-deficient mutants. Use of diazinon by farmers in Iowa and Minnesota has been linked to an increased risk of non-Hodgkin's lymphoma and risks of the disease were elevated for farmers who had never even personally handled diazinon. Humans are also exposed to diazinon from a variety of foods, including grains used for brewing. In 1990, the US Food and Drug Administration's Total Diet Study found that diazinon was the eighth most commonly detected pesticide, out of 200 analyzed. Two EPA surveys found diazinon to be the sixth most frequent cause of accidental death due to pesticides and the sixth most frequent cause of pesticide-related hospitalizations. Symptoms of acute poisoning in humans include inhibition of the enzyme acetylcholinesterase, dizziness, muscle twitching, and excessive salivation and urination. Beekeepers and mead drinkers should take note that diazinon is highly toxic to bees.

"Exposure to pesticides can cause a range of ill effects in humans, from relatively mild effects such as headaches, fatigue, and nausea, to more serious effects such as cancer and neurological disorders. In 1999, EPA estimated that nationwide there were at least 10,000 to 20,000 physician-diagnosed pesticide illnesses and injuries per year in farm work. Environmental effects are evident in the findings of the US Geological Survey, which reported in 1999 that more than 90 percent of water and fish samples from streams and about 50 percent of all sampled wells contained one or more pesticides. The concern about pesticides in water is especially acute in agricultural areas, where most pesticides are used." US General Accounting Office, *Agricultural Pesticides: Management Improvements Needed to Further Promote Integrated Pest Management*, August, 2001

Killing with Chlorpyrifos

Chlorpyrifos, yet another organophosphate, is the most widely used insecticide in the US, with pest control in corn crops ranking among its top uses. This pesticide is toxic to a wide variety of beneficial arthropods including bees, ladybugs, and parasitic wasps, and has also been known to poison cats.

As an insecticide, chlorpyrifos is not expected to be toxic to plants, but "surprise, surprise," it is! Of particular concern to beer drinkers, it causes chlorophyll-deficient mutants in barley. If an entire ecosystem is exposed to chlorpyrifos, significant population reductions occur in a number of species. This is well-documented in aquatic ecosystems. Chlorpyrifos products also contain a number of hazardous unidentified inert ingredients like xylene, the same ingredient found in diazinon that causes nausea, vomiting, hearing and memory loss, reduced fertility, and leukemia.

Suffering from Sulfometuron Methyl

Sulfometuron methyl is one compound in a large class of herbicides called sulfonylureas. In addition to their acute and chronic toxicity for humans and many other animals, and being carcinogenic and mutagenic, Oust, which is DuPont's trade name for the herbicide, *kills barley crops by blowing from a* sprayed field to a barley field.

Because tiny amounts of Oust can kill plants, any drift has the potential to cause significant damage. A 1985 incident in Franklin County dramatically illustrates this problem. Located in eastern Washington, Franklin County contains diversified, productive farmland. In April of that year, county and state road maintenance crews applied Oust along 700 miles of roadsides within the county. Almost all of the rainfall in this geographic area occurs during the autumn, so most of the applied Oust remained on top of the very light, sandy soil for several months. The soil blew from the roadsides into agricultural land, causing extensive damage. Corn, barley, and wheat crops, among many others, were all affected, killing many of them outright. Also, because there are no legal residue limits for Oust on food crops (since all of its registered uses are on nonfood crops), processors could not accept crops grown on contaminated acreage. The settlements paid by DuPont, Franklin County, and the Washington State Department of Highways totaled almost a million dollars. Ironically, the Oust used in Franklin County was intended to kill puncturevine, a weed that *according to the product's own label* is not controlled by Oust.

America: World's Leading User of Banned Chemicals

Just as paraquat is banned elsewhere but liberally applied to American-grown hops, barley crops also endure a host of toxic chemicals that are banned in other countries. In September 2002, the EPA approved the re-registration of lindane as a seed treatment for barley, corn, oats, rye, sorghum, and wheat. But in 2004, Canada and Mexico both decided to ban lindane use in agriculture. In fact, the United States is one of the few industrialized countries where lindane is still permitted. At least 18 other countries have completely banned it. The Rotterdam Convention on Prior Informed Consent includes lindane on its list, and the pesticide is restricted under the international protocol on Long-Range Transboundary Air Pollution. Lindane is also considered a potential candidate for addition to the list of chemicals targeted for global elimination under the Stockholm Convention on persistent organophosphates (POPs). Lindane easily meets the POPs criteria of persistence, bioaccumulation, long range transport, and toxicity.

Endosulfan, according to the EPA, is currently registered to control insects and mites on 60 US crops, including barley. Yet many other countries have banned its use out of concern over its health and environmental effects, and they have found and implemented safer alternatives. This neurotoxin is rated by the EPA as a Category I pesticide with extremely high acute toxicity. Health effects of accidental exposure include central nervous system disorders such as dizziness, convulsions, and loss of consciousness. Endosulfan exposure has been linked to dozens of deaths in the US and around the world, and there is strong evidence that it is an endocrine disrupting chemical. According to the EPA's risk assessment, US farm workers face significant health risks from endosulfan exposure. Twelve of the 21 worker exposure scenarios examined found exposure levels "of concern" to the agency.

Clean Dirt

According to a comprehensive European-wide literature review, farm comparisons in Europe have shown nitrate leaching rates on organic farms are 40–57 percent lower per hectare and carbon dioxide emissions are 40–60 percent lower per hectare than conventional systems.

— Stolze, Piorr, Haring and Dabbert, *Environmental and resource use impacts of organic farming in Europe*, 2000

Does Organic Really Work?

Not only does organic farming avoid the problems caused by toxic chemicals, it is also more resource-efficient and economically beneficial for farmers. For example, a 22-year farming study comparing organic and conventional growing practices in corn and other grains, showed that they each produced similar yields, but organic methods used 30 percent less energy, less water, and no pesticides.

David Pimentel, lead author of the study, analyzed the environmental, energy, and economic costs and benefits of growing corn and soybeans organically versus conventionally. Pimental, a Cornell University professor of ecology and agriculture, concluded: "Organic farming offers real advantages for such crops as corn and soybeans ... Organic farming approaches for these crops not only use an average of 30 percent less fossil energy but also conserve more water in the soil, induce less erosion, maintain soil quality, and conserve more biological resources than conventional farming does."

The fact that organic agriculture also absorbs and retains significant amounts of carbon in the soil has implications for global warming, Pimentel noted, pointing out that soil carbon in the organic systems increased by 15 to 28 percent, the equivalent of taking about 3,500 pounds of carbon dioxide per hectare out of the air.

Pimentel also explained that since organic foods command higher prices in the marketplace they make the net economic return per acre either equal to or higher than that of conventionally produced crops, even when including the increased labor costs of organic farming. He specifically concluded that organic farming can compete effectively in growing barley, wheat, and corn.

Cider enthusiasts can celebrate a study of apple farming published in the April 19, 2001 issue of *Nature* which found that organic orchards can be more profitable, produce tastier fruit at similar yields, and be better for the environment. In the six-year study, John Reganold and colleagues at Washington State University farmed three experimental plots of Golden Delicious apples using organic, conventional, and "integrated" growing methods. Although the organic system took longer to reach profitability, by the end of the study it ranked first in environmental sustainability, profitability, and energy efficiency. Integrated farming, reducing the use of chemicals by combining organic and conventional production methods, came in second, with conventional farming bringing up the rear.

Healthy Moms, Dads, and Babies

Growing crops in healthy soils results in food products that offer healthy nutrients. A mounting body of evidence shows that organically grown grains, fruits, and vegetables may offer more of some nutrients, including vitamin C, iron, magnesium, and phosphorus, and less exposure to nitrates and pesticide residues than their counterparts grown using synthetic pesticides and fertilizers. The Organic Center's 2005 *State of Science Review* concluded that organic farming methods have the potential to elevate average antioxidant levels. A report by Charles Benbrook, PhD, reveals that on average, antioxidant levels were about 30 percent higher in organic food compared to conventional food grown under the same conditions. Diets rich in antioxidants and low in calories are known to extend human life spans by as much as 100 percent.

While organics provide health benefits, conventional farming continues to be hazardous to human health. Take these examples where moms and babies are particularly affected. A National Cancer Institute researcher reported that pregnant women living within nine miles of farms where pesticides are sprayed on fields may have increased risk of losing an unborn baby to birth defects. Moreover, the report claims: "Pesticides and other pollutants can interfere with proper sexual differentiation; they can also cause other birth defects and multigenerational health problems, such as allergies, immunotoxicity, neurotoxicity, and cancer in the individual, that individual's offspring, and subsequent generations." A Canadian-US study detected pesticides in the amniotic fluid in one third of human pregnancies.

According to John Aitken, head of biological sciences at the University of Newcastle in Australia, scientists estimate that up to 85 percent of the sperm produced by a healthy human has DNA damage. Scientists suspect a variety of environmental causes, including exposure to pesticides and other industrial chemicals.

Organic Barley Is Better for Beer

British beer guru Roger Protz writes in his *Organic Beer Guide*: "Brewers want the finest malted barley for their brews. The best brewing malts are low in nitrogen, because too much of it can make for a hazy beer. Yet the agro-chemical industry nearly forces farmers to dump nitrogen fertilizers on their fields. This is a very good reason for brewers to choose organic malts."

Ralph Bucca, another beer writer, explained further in a 2002 article in *Mid-Atlantic Brewing News*: "Organic malts have a lower protein content, which produces a clear mash and less haze in the finished product. It has been reported that fast starch conversions and better-than-normal mash efficiencies occur. The health benefits include no chemical residues to interfere with fermentation or leave an unwanted aftertaste in the beer."

But does organic barley cost more? Yes and no. It generally does cost a little more, but the increased price is nominal in the total cost equation of brewing. The slightly higher price is partly a consequence of conventionally grown foods being kept artificially low through externalized costs, like petroleum subsidies, which industrial agriculture relies on to keep its costs low. Organic malts are high quality though, so a small cost premium is easily justified.

Gambrinus Malting in Armstrong, British Columbia, started producing organic malt in 2004, with three 24 metric ton batches to start out. "It's a customer driven item. We'd been approached about certified organic malt for four to five years, but had to wait for critical mass to happen, which did this year," said Robert Leidl, Gambrinus general manager. "It's fantastic. It's plump, has great flavor and yield, and lauters great," says Christian Ettinger of Laurelwood Brewing in Portland, Oregon. Lautering is the part of the brewing process in which sugar is extracted from the grains in a shower of water, so efficiency and reliability are particularly important. "It's really consistent. We've had nothing but luck with it," says Brian MacIsaac of Crannog Ales in Sorrento, BC. "Brewers should try the new malt."

And they are trying it. Oregon brewers were early to embrace the organic brewing trend, organizing the first organic beer festival in 2003, in Portland, Oregon. Thirty organic beers attracted over 1500 festival goers.

Naturally, organic drinks often taste better too. Andy Myers, dining room manager at the all-organic Restaurant Nora, captures the two most important factors driving organic beer sales when he explains: "I recommend organic wines and beers to our customers because of their excellent quality, not just because it's the right thing to do."

CHAPTER 13

Slow Beer

Time for Beer

During the transformational scientific epoch, the concepts of time and space fundamentally changed from malleable, relational ideas to inflexible, measurable units. Previously, distance and time were often a single unified concept, as in "the next village is two days away." Time was related to natural cycles of the sun and moon and social phenomena like births, marriages, and deaths. The rhythm of life was in sync with nature. But then clocks and measurements divided time and space into precise quantities and removed them from the natural pace of the planet. Paradoxically, this quantification demystified time and space, giving us a means of controlling them; but the tables were quickly turned and time soon enslaved us.

These broad concepts, time and space, are central to how we view the world and our place in it. Two popular beer slogans reflect two opposing concepts of time. Coors Light entices drinkers with the promise that "it won't slow you down" as it delivers alcohol to the body in tasteless, watery mouthfuls. The American Homebrewers Association, on the other hand, suggests a different approach to beer drinking: "Relax. Don't worry. Have a homebrew."

Drink Beer and Digress

Modern society insists that faster is better. Growth and progress demand volume and speed. Fast cars. Fast food. Fast Internet connections. Life is fast so you'd better catch up. But with all the speed, there is little time to drink beer

"We do not digress enough in our lives."
— Michael Jackson, the world's foremost beer writer (not the one-gloved wonder)

and digress. Speed has become overwhelming and many people feel that time is always somehow slipping away and we must go ever faster to catch up with it. There are some measurable consequences to our inability to properly rest. According to a study by the US National Commission on Sleep Disorders, drowsiness causes half of all traffic accidents. That's far more than are caused by alcohol. The fact is faster is not always better.

A growing number of people all over the world who care about food and drink now believe that slow is better. And they've started a movement. It's called "Slow Food."

The premise is simple. Food and drink should taste good and enhance well-being. They should be savored and enjoyed as pleasures in their own right. Food is not simply fuel that allows the body to function. Food is an experience. The profit motive drives food and drink companies to develop products that appeal to the lowest common denominator. Low-cost ingredients, fast and convenient preparation, ease of disposal. Companies find ever-more ways of lowering costs, speeding up processes, increasing efficiency. And they are quite efficient indeed, not at making food that is satisfying and makes life better, but at marketing products that reinforce the fast world with instant gratification.

But both of the basic assumptions about fast food are incorrect. It doesn't taste better and it's not cheaper. At first, people do like the taste, but then they quickly tire of a given product and they want something new, a new flavor, a new formula, a new package. If it tasted so good the first time, why didn't it last?

On the other hand, people never want mom's recipe for chicken noodle soup to change. The stock should take hours to boil down. The chicken should baste slowly in its juices. Mom makes it just right and a commercial concentrate or pack of dried ingredients will never be as good. Campbell's is fast fuel. Mom's is slow food.

We have already seen how industrial agriculture is causing wholesale environmental destruction. Chemical pesticides poison the water. Forests are cut to make room for cattle that will be transformed into cheap hamburgers.

The cost of shipping standardized fast food ingredients and products all over the world is subsidized by our reliance on purportedly cheap but nonrenewable petroleum. The real cost of oil has never been as strikingly evident as it is today, with America waging war for it. Ultimately, the result of chemical pesticides, deforestation, war, and other practices needed to make fast food possible, is the loss of life, sometimes the extinction of entire species. The true cost of losing a species is unknowable. Moreover, the human health costs associated with fast food are mammoth and continuing to grow. In addition to fast food being unhealthy in its own right, it has another drawback directly related to the speed with which we eat it. It takes the body about 15 minutes to send a signal to the brain that the stomach is full. We eat fast food so quickly that we easily overeat before our brain has time to tell us to stop. We eat so much fast food that we have caused an illness unique to industrial society — obesity. The health care costs related to this condition are spiraling so far out of control that people are finally waking up to the dangers of fast food and taking what seems like drastic actions, like banning it from schools and getting rid of junk food vending machines.

Slow Food

Manifesto

Our century (the 20th at the time of the manifesto's writing), which began and has developed under the insignia of industrialized civilization, first invented the machine and then took it as its life model.

We are enslaved by speed and have all succumbed to the same insidious virus: Fast Life, which disrupts our habits, pervades the privacy of our homes, and forces us to eat Fast Foods.

To be worthy of the name, Homo sapiens should rid themselves of speed before it reduces them to a species in danger of extinction.

A firm defense of quiet material pleasure is the only way to oppose the universal folly of Fast Life.

May suitable doses of guaranteed sensual pleasure and slow, long-lasting enjoyment preserve us from the contagion of the multitude who mistake frenzy for efficiency.

Appropriately, the Slow Food movement has adopted the snail as its mascot.

Our defense should begin at the table with Slow Food. Let us rediscover the flavors and savors of regional cooking and banish the degrading effects of Fast Food.

In the name of productivity, Fast Life has changed our way of being and threatens our environment and our landscapes. So Slow Food is now the only truly progressive answer.

That is what real culture is about: developing taste rather than demeaning it. And what better way to set about this than an international exchange of experiences, knowledge, products?

Slow Food guarantees a better future. Slow Food is an idea that needs plenty of qualified supporters who can help turn this (slow) motion into an international movement, with the little snail as its symbol.

— Slow Food USA: www.slowfood.com

Slow Is Brewtiful

Where better to begin the Slow Food revolution than with beer, a food that has been central to human civilization since its inception? As a source of subsistence, beer has been good to people. It has provided nutrition, converting raw grains into a delicious, healthful, and pleasurable drink. It has regulated the rhythms of both our social and sacred ceremonial lives; births, coming of age rites, weddings, deaths, and offerings to the goddesses and gods have all revolved around beer, as brewed and disbursed by moms everywhere. If we are to defeat the machine-regulated slavery of time, we must reclaim brewing as a way of life. Homemade beer is a living product. Factory beer is dead, a commodity demeaned by price. Handmade beer, slowly and artfully crafted, is priceless.

Beer-drinking is an experience, a means as well as an end. Experiences range from brief and trifling to protracted and intensely rewarding. Beer stimulates and sustains conviviality, or relieves the fatigued; it strengthens social cohesion and bolsters the spirit. Sometimes a single beer produces euphoric intoxication, while other times a river of beer seems to have no effect. Life circumstances influence the drinking experience. Too often, the price-driven production and consumption of beer emphasize the wrong aspects of drinking. Cheap happy hour specials promote fast consumption of the worst kind of beer. Cheap packaged beer contributes to a preponderance of solitary consumption at home or in drab, lonely bars. Handmade beer, whether made in a brewpub or a home, by its very nature arouses community, enlivens occasions, and heartens the weary in ways that "fast" beer never achieves. As beer is savored in convivial surroundings, the process of drinking it is slow, rewarding in its own right.

The process of brewing beer can also be slow. Slow brewing replaces the monotony and slavery of the wage economy with the sense of satisfaction and exuberance that accompanies the act of creation. People who brew for joy, brew slowly. People who brew for wages, brew as a job. Beers like Budweiser, Coors, and Miller are mass-produced using big machines and computer control systems. Brewing is fast. Quality controls are flawless, but one must wonder what "quality" means. Consistency is valuable sometimes, but surprise can be delightful. Industrial beers are churned out rapidly using the lowest-cost ingredients. Craft beer is made in small batches and with higher-quality ingredients that cost more but also deliver more. More of the process is done by hand; it's more painstaking. Sometimes the results are surprising. The process of brewing becomes its own reward. Brewers who brew for love not only reap the satisfaction of doing something they are passionate about, but they tend to make beers that are more satisfying for the people who drink them.

When Sam Calagione started Dogfish Head in Lewes, Delaware, in 1995 he decided to ignore the industrial rule of time. Industrial breweries view short brewing cycles as efficient, but Sam decided his beers should take as long as possible to brew. That decision resulted in the creation of beers that are unrivaled in their complexity and uniqueness, not to mention their monetary value in the marketplace. It turns out that brewing slowly is not only a more rewarding experience for brewers, and produces a more rewarding product for beer drinkers, but is also more rewarding in the otherwise demeaning sense of market value. In just ten years, Dogfish Head expanded from a barrel glorified homebrewing system to a modern, hundred barrel brewhouse.

All beers used to be slow. In Chapter 7, we saw how the porter beer style in London exemplified the transition from brewing as a process, requiring a long aging period, to brewing for a profit where technological innovation could replace the lengthy aging process. We also saw how pasteurization literally killed beer, destroying and removing yeast cells from the final product. The British grassroots resurgence in cask-conditioned Real Ales is part of the Slow Food movement, demanding a return to process and quality over industrial commodification, holding hand-pumped, cellar-conditioned ales as the pinnacle of fermented achievements.

But beer doesn't have to be "old fashioned" to be slow. Dogfish Head invented Randall the Enamel Animal, "an organoleptic hops transducer module," in

A bartender at Dave Alexander's Regional Food and Drink in Washington DC serves a pint of Dogfish Head 60 Minute IPA through the house hops transducer module.

2000. The device connects to a tap nozzle and allows bartenders to run beer through a cylinder of fresh hops just before it hits the pint glass, thus infusing beer with an over-the-top aroma of hops. A beer served through Randall is to a can of industrial lager what a freshly-shucked oyster is to microwaved fish fingers.

Season-ale

One way brewers are recovering a sense of natural time is by brewing seasonal beers. These are developed and brewed in order to satisfy the rhythmic whimsy of time. Seasonal beers are produced when certain fresh ingredients are available or when tradition recommends. Around Thanksgiving or Christmas a gingerbread beer or pumpkin spice ale reminds us of the rustle of leaves, warm sweaters, and a crispness in the air. Cinnamon and nutmeg may not be seasonally fresh ingredients, but their use in autumnal beers places us in a frame of reference unique to that season. Zest of dried orange peel turns a holiday spice beer into an even more seasonally appropriate quaff, relying on the time-honored tradition of food drying to ward off the winter cold with some vitamin C.

Octoberfest is the quintessential seasonal beer. During the 19th century, Germans and Austrians brewed large volumes of strong beer at the end of spring just before the warm summer months made proper fermentation temperatures difficult to achieve. These March, or Marzen, beers would be laid down in caves packed with ice, where they would stay until the first autumn harvests, at which time they would be consumed with great jubilation and ceremony during a celebration known as Oktoberfest. These beers are malty and sweet, copper to amber in tone, and suitably rewarding and filling after a day of working in the fields.

These days, the craft-brewing renaissance is bursting with seasonal offerings, adding yet another incentive to make regular stops by the local brewpub to be pleasantly surprised by a strawberry lager "lawn-mower" beer in July, a cranberry ale in November, a maple porter in February, or an oyster stout in March.

Slow Beer and Slow Food

For millennia beer was synonymous with food. Pairing exquisite beers with exquisite foods sounds funny to people unaware that exquisite beers exist, and like snobbery to those who assume sophisticated beer must come with an arrogance like that of some oenophiles. But today, adventurous connoisseurs of quaff are rediscovering the joy of beer-food pairing.

Most people, including many educated chefs who really ought to know better, assume wine is the most appropriate beverage for fine dining. But an honest assessment of wine must acknowledge its distinct shortcomings when compared to beer in its suitability for food pairing. Brewer gastronomes like Garrett Oliver are shining light on the darkened corners of the world of haute cuisine, unchaining culinary prisoners from the lead ball of wine and freeing them to navigate the uncharted waters of malt beverages.

Wine experts admit that many foods simply don't go well with wine. In his book, *The Brewmaster's Table*, Oliver questions whether it is possible to find a wine that matches well with Mexican, Chinese, Japanese, Thai, Middle Eastern, Indian, and Cajun cuisine, or American barbecue? His implied suggestion is to not settle for a poorly paired wine with one of these foods when perfectly complementary beers exist for each and every one of them. Wine flavors inhabit a natural territory, outside of which they battle against unfriendly foods. In these outer regions where wine struggles to find balance with rich flavors, the right beer will elevate and add nuance to those same foods. The carbonation in beer helps lift flavors up and across the palate, accentuating similar flavors. The presence of

> "Learn a little bit about the amazing variety and complexity of flavor that traditional beer brings to the table, and in return I *promise* you a better life."
> — Garrett Oliver, Brewmaster, Brooklyn Brewing, and author of *The Brewmaster's Table*

carbonation is the reason wine aficionados recommend Champagne as the wine that goes with more foods than any other. But still, the wonders of wine are delimited by nature.

Consider some examples. Wine with a cheese omelet? Ghastly. But a light, refreshing Belgian-style white beer finds harmony with each gooey, rich morsel of egg and fromage. How about a goblet of wine with a chocolate-covered banana split? Unthinkable. But a chocolaty coffee porter transforms this fruity dairy dessert into a dangerously sensual marvel of mouthwatering delight. Some regions of the beer and food realm are well-worn by millennia of practice — bread and beer, for instance. But other territories remain utterly mysterious and beckon the adventurous to explore.

In these regions of sublime joy, it seems pedestrian to consider something as base as price. And yet, in a cash-based economy, it would be unjust to ignore the implications of cost. On this count, compared to wine, beer rings up as a bargain affordable to all. "The best thing about beer is the cost," says Tomme Arthur, head brewer at Solano Beach Brewing Co. near San Diego. "If you are having a three-course meal and buy a $30 bottle of wine to go with it, it probably won't match well with every course," Arthur says, but "you can buy a different beer to go with each course and spend a lot less money."

In the kitchen, beer can also be used in place of some higher-calorie ingredients, enhancing health and increasing enjoyment. Substitute a stout for some of the oils or sugars in a marinade, maintaining richness while adding beer-inspired nuance. Replacing some sugar, oil, or butter with beer in baked goods adds moistness, but with fewer calories. Instead of oil or syrup, try a slightly sweet bock beer as a glaze during broiling or grilling. Beer is also an excellent tenderizer. Malty beers work wonderfully in soups, sauces, and stews. Drizzle a fruit lambic over fresh fruit for a tart, refreshing dessert. The possibilities are endless.

The Slow Buzz

> "[Industrial lagers] are the 'fast foods' of the beer world."
> — Michael Jackson

Carbonation gives a boost to gourmands pairing beer with food, but it also assists alcohol in entering the bloodstream. This poses a dilemma for those deliberating over which beverage to choose when regulating alcohol intake is the goal. In general, beer is roughly half the strength of wine, yet its carbonation counteracts its low-alcohol level. Enter Real Ale. Naturally low carbonation levels make many Real Ales perfect session beers. But carbonation aside, beer's low alcohol level compared to wine and spirits makes it the natural choice for the moderate daily imbiber. And since regular, moderate alcohol consumption is in fact highly recommended for a healthy lifestyle, the fact that better-tasting beers are now widely available is good news for the health conscious. The topic of beer and health is one that deserves attention. Let's explore this in depth in the next chapter.

CHAPTER 14

The All-Around Wellness Elixir

To Your Health

Jim Hightower is one of my favorite beer-drinking rabble-rousers. He opens his book *Thieves in High Places* with this proclamation: "My double exclamation point (!!) worry is that: 'It'll be discovered that the cause of cancer is: beer!!'"

I would hate to disappoint Jim with double exclamation point bad news. So it's lucky for me (and all us, really) that — now this news could be shocking, so you might want to pour yourself a beer and have a seat — moderate, daily beer consumption is very good for overall health and may even help fight cancer.

I know what you're thinking: "I may be a beer drinker but I'm not an idiot. Everyone knows drinking is bad for your health. You're saying it's actually good for me?"

In a word, "Yep."

Throughout the ages civilizations have recognized, even praised, beer drinking for its healthful effects. The superior nutritional benefits obtained from fermentation helped early urban civilizations to flourish. Even the Bible exhorts believers to use strong drink to treat health conditions. To this day beer is humanity's favorite alcoholic drink. These few facts alone might be evidence enough for some to accept the healthiness of beer. But most people still believe beer, and alcohol in general, is deleterious to health. So let's get down to some of the nitty-gritty health benefits of beer.

Let's start by understanding some background. Contemporary American culture is an historical aberration in its negative stance toward alcohol. Ever since the repeal of Prohibition, Americans have been ambiguous at best, and hostile at worst, toward alcohol consumption. Some powerful, well-organized, and sometimes well-intentioned groups continue to mistakenly target alcohol as the source of modern society's ills. Though their efforts are sometimes heartfelt, they are more often part of the problem than they are the solution.

To begin with, they wrongly targeted moderate alcohol consumption as a problem. Furthermore, their efforts mostly fail. They do have a smattering of laudable achievements, most notably the fact that alcohol-related traffic fatalities are down markedly, although this may be due as much to the educational efforts of the alcohol industry itself as to the work of anti-alcohol watchdog groups. Mothers Against Drunk Driving (MADD) deserves much credit for helping to reduce drunk driving. Unfortunately, they eventually veered from their original mission and have become a virulent anti-alcohol propaganda machine. Their own founder resigned in protest against the organization's prohibitionist misinformation campaigns. Some of the so-called successes of neo-prohibitionist organizations — like raising the legal drinking age to 21 years — are not only damned annoying but also harmful and wrong-headed. Overall, attempts to reduce or eliminate consumption of alcohol have failed abysmally. And for obvious reasons. Alcohol is good for us, we like it, especially beer, and overall it contributes very positively to building a healthy society. Abuse is real and does cause problems, but they are the exceptions, not the rule. Most anti-alcohol groups fail to see the enormous amount of good that alcohol contributes to society. Instead they hold up examples of negative consequences in attempts to implicate all drinking. Why should the bad apples who abuse alcohol spoil it for the vast majority who reap benefits from drinking?

Wisdom about beer's goodness abounds. A German saying has it that "the brewery is the best drug store." In fact, it is not unusual to find a German drinking beer with breakfast. As Adolph Coors Jr. once said, "Americans can be so puritanical. Germans think nothing of giving their children beer."

Okay, I hear you: "Yeah, well sure. People like to drink beer. It makes us feel good. But just because we come up with silly sayings about how good it is doesn't mean that it really *is* good for us."

Actually, taking a holistic view on health, the "feel-good factor" is itself enough to make a strong case for the salubrious nature of beer. Being healthy means, in part, feeling good. And if beer makes you feel good, then it's contributing to a positive state of overall health. Oh sure, you want some proof, right? As if your own intuition and all of history aren't proof enough. Fine, I'll give you some of that stuff they call *scientific* proof.

It's Purified Water

There is a common saying in the development aid crowd: "Don't shit where you eat." Unfortunately, this simple precept is popular for a reason. Many people do not have access to clean water. Every day, due to lack of viable alternatives, millions of people are forced to drink the same water they use for washing and waste disposal.

The primary ingredient in all beer is clean water. The rest is nutritional components from the fermented grain, and alcohol. Throughout the history of settled society, all the way to the present day, people have been plagued by water that is contaminated by human and animal waste and the disease-carrying bacteria that love them, like cholera. Nevertheless, people are clever and develop surprising ways of adapting to the rigors of survival. For ages, brewing beer has been a smart and desirable solution to the water potability problem.

Beer brewing involves a boiling of the unfermented "wort," i.e., the grain-water soup that becomes beer after fermentation. Boiling removes many of the dangers contained in contaminated water. Additionally, the alcohol and natural acidity present in beer kill or reduce the growth of illness-forming bacteria.

We should learn from the wisdom of the ancients. They knew about beer's health benefits. Scientists recently discovered traces of tetracycline in 2,000-year-old human bones found in Sudan. Tetracycline works as an antibacterial medication, and researchers have discovered that it is produced by a bacteria called *streptomycedes*, which has been linked to beer consumption. Scientists think that beer drinking helped keep ancient humans safe from a variety of disorders, ranging from acne to urinary tract infections. George Armelagos of Emory University studied those ancient human bones extensively: "The fact that we didn't find any indication of infection in the bone is an indication that the tetracycline may have been having some effect … Did they know that they had discovered tetracycline? Well, obviously they didn't know it was tetracycline, but I think that they knew that it made them feel better. The alcohol probably had some positive effect, and actually tetracycline works very rapidly, so they may have realized that what they had was making them feel good."

As human populations concentrated into settlements and urban centers, beer became ever-more important. But one thing the ancients didn't seem to realize was the link between sanitation and health. Take, for example, the fact that the famous Coliseum in Rome held 50,000 people but reputedly did not house a single toilet. This was despite the fact that the place was overflowing with food and drink. They reckon 9,000 animals were eaten during one famous celebration in this raucous stadium. What did all these festival-goers do to relieve themselves? Use a pot and toss it over the side? Who knows, but we can be certain that however they discarded of their dirty deeds, it was probably not very sanitary. Their refuse probably ended up right back in the water supply. Therefore, the health benefits of safe, clean beer would have nudged civilization along by helping to combat a dizzying array of public health hazards. The same is certainly true of medieval plague-ravaged Europe. Not a decent drink of clean water anywhere, but beer, that trusty standby, helped those filthy Europeans squeak through to the Renaissance.

Contemporary conflict experts believe that access to clean water will become the driving factor in the world's next series of wars. Perhaps instead of investing in new military wares, we should all be buying good homebrewing equipment. Besides being a source of potable water, beer has other advantages over plain water, clean or otherwise. This brings us to the second major health benefit of beer.

"The association of drinking with any kind of specifically mentioned problems — physical, economic, psychological, social, relational, or other — is rare among cultures throughout both history and the contemporary world."
— D.B. Heath, *A Decade of Development in the Anthropological Study of Alcohol Use: 1970–1980*

Fermenting Nutrition

Since fruit ferments naturally, fermentation precedes human history, but we eventually learned how to control it and use it to our benefit. Given the strong nutritional advantages of this process, fermentation may have been a key tool in assisting the development of human civilization. The earliest evidence of people fermenting beverages is from Babylon around 5000 BCE. Their beverage? Beer, of course. A little later, the Egyptians seem to have caught on.

Mexicans also figured it out pretty early on, around 2000 BCE. And recent evidence shows that the Chinese were brewing almost as early as the Babylonians. In every case, fermentation bestowed a strategic health advantage.

Sandor Ellix Katz wrote his fantastic book, *Wild Fermentations*, while living with AIDS and therefore had a keen interest in investigating the healing properties of fermented foods and drinks. He explains the basic benefit of fermentation like this:

> Fermentation preserves food. Alcohol, a byproduct of fermentation, helps retain nutrients and prevent spoilage. Fermentation not only preserves nutrients, it breaks them down into more easily digestible forms.
>
> According to the UN Food and Agriculture Organization, which actively promotes fermentation as a critical source of nutrients worldwide, "fermentation improves the bioavailability of minerals present in food." Fermentation also creates new nutrients, like the B vitamins folic acid, riboflavin, niacin, thiamin and biotin. Fermentation also removes toxins from food. All grains contain a compound called phytic acid, which can block absorption of zinc, calcium, iron, magnesium, and other minerals and lead to mineral deficiencies. Fermenting grains before cooking neutralizes phytic acid, rendering grain far more nutritious."

Keith Steinkraus, in his *Handbook of Indigenous Fermented Foods*, lists these five main purposes served by fermentation:

1. enrichment of the diet through development of a diversity of food flavors, aromas, and textures
2. preservation of substantial amounts of food through lactic acid, alcoholic, acetic acid, and alkaline fermentations
3. enrichment of food substrates biologically with protein, essential amino acids, essential fatty acids, and vitamins
4. detoxification during food fermentation processing
5. decrease in cooking times and fuel requirements

Additionally, drinking beer with live yeast supplies the digestive tract with living cultures that are essential to breaking down food into nutrients

"In complex societies drink has a role in social jollification by breaking down barriers between persons and groups and by promoting social integration and solidarity; alcohol does this by alleviating anxiety and tension, reducing inhibition, and promoting relaxation."

— Selden D. Bacon,
Alcohol and Complex Society

that are more easy for your body to assimilate. According to Alan Eames, in *the Secret Life of Beer*, "The process of fermentation increases fourfold the vitamin and mineral content of plain seeds or grains. Ambient yeast adds additional and substantial levels of protein and vitamins B and C." Fermentation can also make conditions unsuitable for undesirable microorganisms. For example, in pickling, the acids produced by the dominant bacteria inhibit the growth of all other microorganisms.

The original historic painted billboard on the side of Great Lakes Brewing Company's pub proclaims "Ales and Porters on Draught for Family and Medicinal Purposes.

Relax with a Beer and You'll Feel Much Better

Life is stressful. Traditional nomadic and agricultural lifestyles were marked by anxieties caused by unexpected natural disasters, food scarcity, war, and other equally delightful threats and causes of violent death or dismemberment. Modern life is probably just as stressful or perhaps more so, given the high suicide rates in industrialized societies. According to the Centers for Disease Control and Prevention (CDC), 1.3 percent of all deaths in America in 1997 were by suicide. This compares to 31 percent from heart disease, 23 percent from cancer, and 7 percent from stroke. Suicide is the eighth leading cause of death among the entire population and second among teenagers, among whom it is exceeded only by traffic accidents.

Anti-depressants like Prozac are more common than ever as treatments for stress, depression, and sleep disorders. Beer is much cheaper and has been proven to relieve stress through what is referred to as a stress response dampening effect. This effect is documented in research studies like the one published in 1999 by Michael A. Sayette, a psychologist at the University of Pittsburgh. Admittedly, this issue is complex and the research suggests that alcohol does not always reduce stress, and can even heighten it in some cases. The study found that drinking alcohol can cause more stress in certain people under certain circumstances, but it also clearly showed that for the *vast majority* of drinkers, in *most* situations, alcohol clearly helps to relieve stress, proving what everyone already knows: drinking beer makes you feel good.

Research, in addition to common sense, suggests that the situation in which alcohol is consumed is an important factor in determining the level of stress relief. Reinforcing this theory is research by Dr. Colin Gill at Leeds University which shows that the welcoming atmosphere of the local pub helps men shed the layers of stress caused by modern life and that this relief is vital for their psychological well-being. The report surveyed men on their reasons for going to the pub. More than 40 percent said they went for conversation, with relaxation and a friendly atmosphere being the other most common reasons. Only ten percent listed alcohol as their primary reason. Sayette's research suggests that it is exactly these kinds of situations which enhance the stress relief effect of alcohol. Dr. Gill put it this way: "Pub-time allows men to bond with friends and colleagues. Men need break-out time … and are mentally healthier for it." This research is important in that it emphasizes the importance of communal drinking for people who are depressed, and suggests the possible danger of excessive solitary drinking for people at risk of suffering from depression.

Relieving built-up stress is one thing, but creating a positive state of health is another. In a 1993 National Health Survey of 20,000 Spanish adults, "the results showed that people who drank alcohol, including beer and spirits, were less likely to report ill health than people who abstained altogether," according to a report published in the *Journal of Epidemiology and Community Health.* "Overall, the higher the consumption of total alcohol the lower the levels of subjective ill health." In other words, people who drink alcohol tend to feel better about their own health, which indicates that they actually are healthy.

According to the CDC, more than one in ten Americans visited a doctor's office or hospital in 1997 for "psychological and mental disorders." Nearly one in twenty Americans was treated for depression that year. An equal number were diagnosed with hypertension. More than seven million Americans (2.7 percent of the population) visited a doctor or hospital for "anxiety or nervousness." In all, nearly one in five Americans visited a doctor or hospital for symptoms broadly categorized by the CDC as "mental disorders." This seems like a compelling argument for making communal beer drinking a daily habit.

Brew-Ha-Ha

When people ask me what I do, and I tell them I am a beer writer, the response is always the same: incredulous laughter. Once they realize I am serious, they usually stop laughing and start trying to figure out how they too can successfully base their lifestyle around beer.

Beer is actually no joke, but it does go well with laughter. A common image of beer drinking is the warm room filled with friends striking convivial poses, slapping their knees and laughing. It's no secret that beer loosens the tongue and raises the spirit. It's no coincidence that so many jokes start with "two guys walk into a bar." It is self-evident that drinking induces laughter. And as if it's not already obvious that laughter is a good thing, the experts are finally quantifying its health benefits.

Michael Miller, of the Baltimore-based University of Maryland School of Medicine, led a group of researchers in an effort to determine if laughter could affect health, in particular heart health and mental health. Surprise, surprise, here's what they found: laughter = good; depression = bad.

More specifically, what these researchers found is that laughter helps blood cells expand, improving blood flow, a process called vasodilation. Depression, on the other hand, decreases vasodilation, leading to increased risk of heart attack and stroke. Negative emotions increase the release of hormones like adrenaline and cortisol, which are now thought to have some detrimental effects like suppressing the immune system and constricting blood vessels. Laughter seems to have the opposite effect, causing the body to release other natural chemicals known as endorphins (pleasure-producing agents best known for producing the "runner's high") that may counteract the effects of stress hormones and cause blood vessels to dilate.

> "There's no downside that I know of to laughing. Based on these results, I am happy to recommend laughing to my patients."
> — Michael Miller, University of Maryland School of Medicine, Expert in Hilarity

Lee Berk studies health promotion and education at Loma Linda University in California and is an expert in funny stuff. He has this to say: "Laughter is not dissimilar from exercise. It's not going to cure someone from stage three cancer, but in terms of prevention it does make sense. In a sense, we have our own apothecary on our shoulders. Positive emotions such as laughter affect your biology."

Another hysterical scientist, Robert Provine, at the University of Maryland, commented: "I strongly recommend laughter, based on the fact that a life of laughter is better than one without it. It feels better when you do it."

Backed by the findings of these scientists, I now feel vindicated for every time I have had a couple beers and told stupid jokes.

"Gesundheit! May I Help You?"

Remember the movie *Patch Adams,* in which Robin Williams played a crazy doctor? He wore funny clothes and fell over a lot, making his patients laugh. Well, Patch is a real guy and he believes so strongly in the power of laughter that he started the world's first "free, silly hospital." It's located in West Virginia and is called the Gesundheit! Institute. Their staff answers the phone with this salutation: "Gesundheit! May I Help You?" In his online diary, Patch mentions his son's predilection for wine tasting. Unfortunately, efforts to discover whether Patch is a beer drinker proved fruitless. But can you imagine a conversation like this one?

> Husband to wife: "Hi honey, I'm back from the hospital."
> Wife inquires: "Is it serious? Did they prescribe something?"

Husband responds: "They said my condition was a laughing matter. Then they gave me a six pack and we sat around bullshitting. It was great. I feel much better!"

The Heart of Beer

According to the Centers for Disease Control and Prevention, one out of four Americans has cardiovascular disease, making it the number one cause of death among both genders and all racial groups in the United States. Beer consumption has repeatedly been shown to reduce the risk of coronary heart disease by raising levels of good cholesterol (high-density lipoprotein) and by reducing chances that clots will form and cut off blood flow to the heart and brain.

The amount of evidence for this is overwhelming. A project at the Harvard School of Public Health tracked the health of 38,077 male health professionals across the country while monitoring aspects of their lifestyles. After 12 years, the research found that those who drink one to two drinks, three to seven times a week, had a 32–37 percent lower risk of suffering a heart attack. This effect was independent of age, smoking, exercise habits, diet and family history of heart disease.

The April 18, 2001 issue of the *Journal of the American Medical Association* published a study finding that drinkers also had a lower risk of dying from a heart attack. That is to say, not only does beer *prevent* heart attacks, but it also *reduces the risk of death* in those who do suffer heart attacks. The study, led by Dr. Kenneth J. Mukamal of Beth Israel Deaconess Medical Center in Boston concluded that moderate drinkers had a 32 percent lower risk of dying from a heart attack compared to those who didn't drink alcohol. The findings were similar for men and women.

"What is important is the drinking pattern and not necessarily what the individual is drinking or even the average consumption," said Eric Rimm, associate professor of epidemiology and nutrition at the Harvard School of Public Health, who helped conduct the study. "It's much more beneficial to have about a drink or two a day [than to not drink at all]."

A person could drown in the sea of research results reinforcing the heart-healthy effects of beer. But the media does a good job of hiding this news, so I feel obliged to turn on the taps and let the research findings flow. Here's a study by Dr. Jerome L. Abramson of Emory University. He and his team of researchers studied 2,235 elderly men and women. They found that compared to non-drinkers, those in the group who drank at least 1.5 drinks daily had a 20–50 percent lower chance of developing heart failure.

"The dangers [of moderate] drinking are almost zero, and the benefits are striking. Everybody should be told the facts and let them make up their own minds. If you drink a lot, it's bad for you. If you drink a little, it's good for you."

— R. Curtis Ellison, professor of medicine at
Boston University School of Medicine

Blood-Buddy in a Bottle

In September 2001, Dr. Mukamal reported in *Stroke* magazine that light to moderate alcohol consumption is associated with fewer brain lesions and silent strokes. Mukamal wrote that as a blood thinner, alcohol improves blood circulation in the brain and offers protection from silent strokes caused by tiny blood clots. The results showed that light and moderate drinkers had the fewest white matter lesions and heavy drinkers had the most. (Defining "heavy" is an issue in itself that we'll cover soon.) The fewest signs of silent strokes were suffered by heavy drinkers, who were also more likely to have brain atrophy. "Overall, we found that non-drinkers have the most strokes and white matter disease. Light to moderate drinkers have fewer strokes and the least amount of white matter disease, but somewhat greater atrophy. Moderately heavy drinkers had the fewest strokes but more white matter disease and the most atrophy."

Dutch researchers at the Erasmus University Medical School in Rotterdam believe the effects may be due to ethanol thinning the blood and lowering cholesterol, thereby reducing the chance of vascular dementia, and because alcohol may release acetylcholine in the hippocampus, an area of the brain that facilitates memory.

Vitamin B Is for Beer

Pilsen is the Czech birthplace of the Pilsner beer style. Researchers there conducted a study attributing beer's heart-healthy effects to folate (folic acid, a vitamin in the B complex). Dr. O. Mayer Jr. and his colleagues at the Pilsen-based Center of Preventative Medicine at Charles University published their findings in the July 2001 issue of the *European Journal of Clinical Nutrition*, writing:

"Moderate beer consumption may help to maintain the total homocysteine levels in the normal range due to high folate content. Folate from beer may ... contribute to the protective effect of alcohol consumption on cardiovascular disease in population(s) with generally low folate intake from other nutrients." The study showed that the yeast used to ferment beer gave the beer drinkers the lowest blood levels of homocysteine and the highest levels of folate, compared to non- beer drinkers and those who drank other alcoholic beverages.

Whining about Wine

In the early 1990s people started noticing something funny about the French. They observed that their diet is very high in fat, but that rates of coronary disease are relatively low. This was dubbed the "French paradox."

Initially researchers attributed this effect to the volumes of red wine consumed with the typical fatty French meal. Significant levels of chemical compounds called flavinoids are found in the seeds and skins of red grapes and appear to raise "good" cholesterol levels, lower "bad" cholesterol levels, and reduce clotting. Red wine producers were quick to capitalize on this research and immediately began promoting these positive health effects. In pre-"freedom-fries" America, wine-sipping yuppies were only too eager to associate themselves with something as cultured and refined as French wine, and so the healthy reputation of red wine spread quickly.

Beer drinkers got on the ball but quick. In 2000, Dutch researchers countered the prevailing sentiment that red wine was better for the heart than beer. Dr. Henk Hendriks of the TNO Nutrition and Food Research Institute studied men who drank four glasses of either beer, red wine, spirits, or water with dinner. The results were striking. B6 is a vitamin that prevents the body from building up high levels of homocysteine, which is a chemical linked to an increased risk of heart disease. The men in the study who drank beer showed a 30 percent increase in vitamin B6. Drinkers of red wine and Dutch gin received only one-half that increase in the vitamin. Moreover, homocysteine levels actually rose in those who drank wine or spirits, but did not increase at all in the beer drinkers. In other words, in this aspect of heart health, beer is actually *better* than wine or spirits.

A Danish study further contributed to the wine versus beer debate. "It cannot be proved that there is any health advantage to drinking red wine, for example, rather than beer," according to the study by the Institute of

Beer Is Better

Results from Dr. Denke's 2001 clinical study corroborated the growing body of research showing that moderate consumption of alcohol can considerably decrease the risk of heart disease and stroke. But Dr. Denke goes one step further, asserting that beer is actually more beneficial than other alcoholic drinks because it contains so many more nutrients than wine and spirits.

Nutrition

One average beer contains the following nutritional benefits:

- 11 ounces of pure water
- 14 percent of dietary calories
- 11 percent of dietary protein
- 12 percent of dietary carbohydrates
- 9 percent of dietary phosphorus
- 7 percent of dietary riboflavin
- 5 percent of dietary niacin
- 150 calories
- no fat
- no cholesterol
- no caffeine
- no nitrate
- 1 gram of protein
- significant amounts of magnesium, selenium, potassium, and biotin
- B vitamins including impressive amounts of B3 (niacin), B5 (pantothenic acid), B6 (pyridoxin), and B9 (folate), with smaller amounts of B1 (thiamine), B2 (riboflavin), B12 (inotisol and choline)
- Beer is also considered inherently kosher, conforming to Jewish standards of food purity

Health Benefits

The health benefits of moderate daily beer drinking include:

- 20 percent to 30 percent reduction in death from all causes
- 13 percent reduction in the incidence of all disease in general
- significantly reduced risk of ulcers
- significant (40 percent to 50 percent) reduction in the risk of developing gallstones and kidney stones
- 45 percent reduced incidence of stroke, including among Type II diabetics
- 56 percent lower risk of angina
- 47 percent lower risk of myocardial infarction
- substantially lower risk of carotid arteriosclerosis

Epidemiology and Social Medicine at the University of Muenster. "Studies indicate that light to moderate alcohol consumption from beer, wine or spirits is associated with a reduction in all-cause mortality, owing primarily to a decreased risk of coronary heart disease."

Polyphenols, abundant in red wine, are beneficial for their antioxidant properties that reduce LDL cholesterol (the "bad" cholesterol) oxidation. They were once thought to be an exclusive benefit of wine because, researchers believed, beer did not contain them in sufficient amounts. Dr. Margo A. Denke, a University of Texas professor of medicine, proved them wrong with research that showed beer contains levels of polyphenols similar to red wine (and four to five times greater than white wine). Dr. Denke noted that hops contain several polyphenols that have been shown to reduce test tube growth of human cancer cells. This last insight is a breakthrough that is now being anxiously studied all over the world — more on this later.

Beer for Brains

"Homer no function beer well without." There is truth in these immortal words of Homer Simpson. A study conducted by Dr. Guiseppe Zuccala, of the Catholic University of the Sacred Heart in Rome, found that moderate alcohol use may protect the brain from the mental decline associated with aging. In the report, published in the December 2001 issue of *Alcoholism: Clinical and Experimental Research*, Dr. Zuccala studied the mental abilities and alcohol use of nearly 16,000 elderly Italian men and women, including regular drinkers and non-drinkers. Moderate drinking was associated with a 40 percent lower risk of mental impairment. Dr. Zuccala postulated that the reasons for the difference may be alcohol's beneficial effects on blood pressure and blood flow or perhaps the slowing of arterial disease.

At Indiana University, medical geneticist Dr. Joe Christian observed 4,000 male twins for 20 years to determine if moderate drinking affected the brain. He administered psychological tests to the brothers at ages 66 and 76 and found no harm done from moderate drinking. In fact, brothers who consistently drank in moderation scored higher on mental skills tests than those who drank less than one drink a day or more than two drinks. Moderate drinking was deemed helpful in improving memory, problem solving, and reasoning ability.

Another study disputes the long-held belief that alcohol kills brain cells. Roberta Pentney, former professor of anatomy and cell biology at the

University of Buffalo, and her co-investigator, Cynthia Dlugos, concluded that daily consumption of alcohol does create temporary damage in the connections between brain cells. However, the damage is able to repair itself, a "hopeful note," wrote Pentney in a University of Buffalo press release.

Researchers based at University College London have found that drinking alcohol, even in low amounts, might be associated with higher cognitive ability, particularly for women. The report, published in the *American Journal of Epidemiology*, found that people who consume anywhere from 1 to 30 drinks per week performed better than nondrinkers on a battery of different tests designed to measure their intellectual ability. "Compared with abstainers, persons drinking one or two glasses of alcohol per day had a significantly lower risk of poor cognitive function," the authors wrote. Subjects who drank alcohol occasionally, but who did not drink in the week prior to the tests, also performed better than nondrinkers, but they did not do as well as the people who drank regularly. "In terms of cognitive function, we found that frequent drinking may be more beneficial than drinking only on special occasions," the authors wrote. The fact that this report makes a point of highlighting women prompts the question of whether women have any other special health considerations regarding alcohol consumption.

Alcohol and Women's Health

In addition to the benefits described above that apply to both men and women, there are some extra benefits (and cautions) for women. On the subject of the brain, a paper published by Dr. Meir Stampfer in the *New England Journal of Medicine* in 2001 (as part of the ambitious Nurses' Health Study at Harvard University), determined that moderate drinking of alcohol seemed to preserve the mental abilities of older women. Stampfer collected information about the alcohol intake of over 9,000 elderly women, over a 14-year period, and used 7 tests to measure their mental functions. The results showed that women who drank moderately had significantly better scores on five of the seven tests, as well as better overall scores.

Two studies released in 2002 address women's health issues associated with drinking alcohol. A study published in the *Archives of Internal Medicine* confirmed some benefits. Data collected from more than 70,000 nurses showed that younger women who drink two or three alcoholic beverages a week have a 14 percent lower risk of developing high blood pressure than women who do not drink alcohol.

A study of post-menopausal women found that alcohol helps lower cholesterol levels. Dr. David J. Baer, a research physiologist affiliated with the United States Department of Agriculture's Human Nutrition Research Center, tested women adhering to three different dietary regimens: one with no alcohol, one with one daily drink, and the third with two drinks per day. Dr. Baer's findings showed that the middle group reduced their triglyceride levels by eight milligrams/deciliter and their LDL (bad cholesterol) levels by four milligrams/deciliter. The women who drank two drinks a day increased their HDL (good cholesterol) by three milligrams/deciliter.

Bone Up On Beer

Researchers now think that an ingredient in beer may help prevent osteoporosis, the bone-weakening disease that mostly affects women (though some men get it too). Findings published in 2004 show a striking positive relationship between the intake of dietary silicon and bone mineral density in men and pre-menopausal women. Silicon is found in whole grains such as barley, and is now thought to prevent bone loss and promote bone formation. The use of barley as the main ingredient in most beers, makes beer a readily available source of dietary silicon.

Milking a Myth

Folklore in many societies holds that alcohol consumption boosts milk production in women who are breast feeding their infants. Breweries have even developed special niche products to serve this market, like Malt Nutrine, a low-alcohol beer produced by a major US brewery in 1895 and marketed exclusively in drug stores as a tonic for lactating women. Unfortunately, recent research by Julie Mennella at the Monell Chemical Senses Center in Philadelphia suggests that alcohol actually decreases milk production. This evidence is recent and contradicts traditional beliefs in societies as disparate as contemporary America and rural Africa. Further research seems necessary, but for the time being, it seems that mothers who drink alcohol in order to enhance milk production are doing so to no avail.

A Breath of Fresh Beer

Here's another way that beer is good for health, one that most people don't consider because it requires taking a broader, more holistic approach to well-being than we are trained to consider by our Western medical methods.

Beer that is made and consumed locally can improve the health of an entire region by reducing the amount of fossil fuels burned for transportation. Drinking beer trucked in from across the country adds a lot of pollutants to the air. This is of acute concern to children, who are suffering in record numbers from asthma caused by air pollution. In 2002, 9.1 million children, or 12.5 percent of all kids in the US were diagnosed with asthma. How many of these children would benefit if their parents started homebrewing or supporting the local brewery?

Good News for Jim Hightower

Last but not least, let's get to the good news I already hinted at regarding Jim Hightower's double exclamation point worry that beer might cause cancer. Researchers at the University of Western Ontario found that beer increases plasma antioxidant activity. This helps prevent the oxidization of blood plasma by toxic free radicals, which trigger many aging diseases, such as — you guessed it — cancer. Ditto for diabetes, heart disease, and cataracts.

The researchers explain that "hops have an important role in preventing illness." Humulone and lupulone, constituents in hops, "act as anticarcinogens and antioxidants. These have a beneficial effect on the whole cardiovascular system, as well as on bones and the brain.".

Research at HRI Wye College in Kent, England, indicates that one of the most promising of the hop compounds is xanthohumol. Results from the 2001 hop season showed that the proportion of xanthohumol in the resins can be increased dramatically by selective breeding in new varieties. In Germany, the brewing faculty at the University of Weihenstephan, near Munich, is working closely with local hospitals to research ways hops can fight against cancer. Dr. Denke, from the University of Texas, reported that beer has isoflavinoids, which are a class of so-called phytoestrogens: plant compounds that mimic the activity of the female hormone estrogen. Isoflavinoids have been found to inhibit test-tube growth of prostate, breast, and colon cancers.

Besides fighting cancer, hops are also a natural sleeping aid. In the past, it was common for pillows to be stuffed with hops to help induce a tranquil night's sleep. Given the option of taking a nightly sleeping pill or a nightly beer, I know which one I would choose.

So Jim, don't lose any sleep worrying about beer causing cancer. Pour yourself a cool one and have a good night!

Too Much of a Good Thing

What? All this evidence hasn't convinced you? "It can't be *all* good," you say, "I've seen people get sick from drinking too much beer." And there's the rub: *too much*.

If something so good makes you sick when you have too much, then *don't have too much*. Yes, alcohol in sufficient quantity is, just like carrots and broccoli, toxic to humans. Abraham Lincoln wrote this about alcohol: "It is true that even then it was known and acknowledged that many were greatly injured by it. But none seemed to think the injury arose from the use of a bad thing, but from the abuse of a very good thing."

While studies have shown that daily intake of alcoholic beverages can help reduce the risk of many diseases, biochemistry and kinesiology professor John Trevithick, one of the lead researchers in a University of Western Ontario study and a long-time expert on the role of antioxidants in human health, cautions that larger daily intakes actually increase the risk of these diseases. Another piece of bad news is that some research implicates alcohol in boosting a woman's risk of developing breast cancer.

So what is moderate and what is too much? Moderation is defined differently in different studies, some setting it at one drink a day and others placing it as high as four per day. Interestingly, there seems to be a correlation between the location of the study and the definition of moderate. European studies place the limit higher while Americans place it lower, an obvious reflection of our Prohibitionist fears and a clear demonstration of the social construction of medical science.

Words to Drink By

It boils down to this. Beer can make you feel really good, or it can make you (and others around you) feel damned awful. If you want to drink beer and feel good, then it's worth finding the best ways to a healthy buzz. Drinking in a way that's good for your body takes common sense. Here are some hints.

- Don't be an idiot. As long as you're not an idiot about drinking you can pretty much skip the rest of these hints.

- Water. Drink it. Lots. Alcohol dehydrates your body. Eight cups of water a day is the generally accepted guideline for keeping the body lubricated. Try to drink an extra glass of it for every beer you drink.

- Listen to your body. When it tells you to stop drinking, then call it quits and enjoy the buzz.

+ Food. Eat some before and/or while you are drinking. Food in your stomach helps absorb alcohol and makes your drinking experience smoother on the internal gears.

Hangover Helpers

If you ignored the healthy hints above and woke up with a hammer banging away on your head, or a nauseous feeling in your gut, try these ways for getting yourself back together.

You must have forgotten to drink enough water, so get to it. Stick your head under the faucet and start gulping. Dehydration causes your blood vessels to expand, and that generally makes you feel like crap, all headachy and stiff. You might also consider a cup of coffee or tea — the fully-leaded kind, not decaf. The point is to get some caffeine into your system. Alcohol causes blood vessels to swell, which can make your head feel like an anvil with a nine-pound hammer coming down on it. Caffeine counteracts that, causing blood vessels to contract, providing temporary relief. Since it's also a diuretic, limit yourself to one cup. If that doesn't work, use ibuprofen, but skip aspirin. Aspirin can reduce the pounding in your head, but it can also wreak havoc on a gnarly tummy. Mind you, caffeine is not a cure, it just helps ease the symptoms. The main problem is water, or lack of it, so keep swigging it down.

Get plenty of salt and potassium. Heavy drinking purges the body of these two important electrolytes, which together help transport and distribute nutrients and water throughout your body. To restock these two essentials, try one of the sports drinks that contain ample amounts of both sodium and potassium, or eat a potassium-rich banana or kiwi, or a serving of broth made from salt-rich bouillon cubes.

Fill up on fruit juice. Fruit sugar (fructose) is quickly absorbed into the bloodstream, so any kind of juice will give your energy level a quick boost. In addition, some studies have shown fructose to play a part in speeding up the rate at which the body eliminates toxins, including those from alcohol. Orange and tomato juice are good bets, since both are also rich in nutrients such as vitamin C. Which reminds me, don't forget your B and C vitamins. Supplies of these two are severely depleted when you drink, thanks again to alcohol's diuretic effect, so when you're consuming alcohol, your system needs these vitamins more than ever. There's no time like the morning after a big night out to load up on supplements. Better yet, get your dose naturally in a glass of fresh-squeezed fruit juice.

As mentioned above, brewer's yeast contains lots of B vitamins: B1 (thiamine), B3 (niacin), B12, choline, inositol and B5 (pantothenic acid). So if you're drinking good craft beer you're already replacing some of the Bs that the alcohol is ridding your body of when you urinate. Make sure to drink bottle-conditioned, cask-conditioned, or otherwise unfiltered beers, i.e., beers that contain yeast. If you drink the pasteurized, filtered, industrial stuff they call beer, then consider supplementing your diet with brewer's yeast, it's available at most health food stores.

Stick to light, low-fat foods. Because alcohol can upset your digestive system, it's important to line your stomach with food while you're drinking and on the day after, too. Plus, a balanced meal will help restore your nutrient supply. One thing to keep in mind: fatty and/or fried food is often very tempting on the morning after, but it's usually best to avoid them since they can make your stomach rebel in a rather explosive and unappetizing manner.

Cheers

Now that you are enlightened about the health benefits of beer, go forth, drink beer, and be well.

CHAPTER 15

Brewing Big Solutions

Small, craft breweries are clearly leading the way toward sustainability, but what about the corporate macro-brewers? They dump dollars into sophomoric marketing campaigns, produce beers without flavor or originality, and rely heavily on fossil fuels for massive industrial factories and global shipping. But are they doing anything good? Well, just like other global conglomerates, the big boys of beer still have far to go before achieving long-term ecologically balanced production, but surprisingly the corporate brewing mainstream is actually doing a decent (if less than adequate) job of journeying toward sustainability.

Getting Wasted

Sustainable business guru Paul Hawken, in his seminal book, *The Ecology of Commerce*, offers a simple equation for measuring business sustainability: "Take, Make, Waste." Hawken frames this as an ecological business formula, and makes the obvious but crucial point that ecologically balanced business is synonymous with good business. The basic proposition in any business is to transform raw resources into something of greater value. A business capable of converting a small resource into a big value is on the road to competitive advantage. In other words, take little, waste nothing, make a lot.

The history of business is the history of this efficiency equation and the history of industrial brewing is no exception. Brewing history is filled with efficiency landmarks, inventions, and methodological improvements that reduced inputs and decreased waste. The British "Union system" was a technological invention devised to conserve beer that was lost when fermentation caused it to bubble out of casks. This system was essentially a way to catch that beer, separate out the spent yeast, and return the beer back to the cask. This probably saved about five to ten percent of a cask of beer from being wasted. The yeast, having been separated, was then available for use in the next batch of beer. Wooden barrels are rarely used to store beer anymore and this particular waste issue has long since disappeared, but it is still common practice to save yeast and reuse it from batch to batch.

Industrial brewers, though, have gone much further than simple efficiency and were early to integrate and innovate sustainable practices that are now industry standards. A critical aspect of the "Take, Make, Waste" formula is that waste need not be waste at all, but instead should be the raw material for new products. Waste is food. Whatever comes out of the end of the pipe as "waste" should be used to make something else rather than disposed of as garbage.

In general, brewing has an advantage in the pursuit of ecological efficiency. Brewing ingredients are rapidly renewable. Other industries, like mining, drilling, and industrial forestry rely on the efficient removal of a limited supply of natural resources that are guaranteed to run out before they can be naturally replenished. Brewers rely on energy and the natural process of fermentation to transform water and grain into beer. With these few inputs, along with facilities, packaging, and transportation, brewers have built a global industry that, when compared to many other businesses, has a fairly low impact on the environment.

At its most basic, modern beer making is the blending of water, malted barley, hops, and yeast. Energy, plus the above ingredients, equals beer, wastewater, spent grain, yeast, and some carbon dioxide generated by the fermentation process. On average, industrial breweries use roughly five to six gallons of water to make one gallon of beer and four to five gallons of wastewater. Brewing extracts less than ten percent of the usable material from barley, mostly just the starch, and basically wastes all of the fiber and protein. In other words, the malt sugars are converted into beer, while the rest of the barley is cast off as a by-product. Hops cones are discarded after extracting a minute amount of their potentially useful materials. Yeast volume actually increases during fermentation because the cells reproduce by feeding on the malt sugars. A great deal of energy goes into brewing, some of which is embodied in the beer and eventually metabolized by the person who drinks the beer, but a lot of the energy is spent on making, packaging, and delivering the beer. Considerable natural resources and energy are embodied in brewing equipment and facilities, but much of this is durable metal that is used for many generations and is often recycled at the end of its useful life. So how are breweries transforming their waste into food?

Basic efficiency is the first step. Use less of your raw material to make more of your primary product. Overall, the industry has made big efficiency gains through the usual ways, like preventing water leaks, extracting more sugar from the barley, running factories at full production capacity, and implementing recycling and reuse programs. Water use is down by about 50 percent compared to just a generation ago. But these are the sorts of things most industries are doing at one level or another. In other ways, though, breweries are more advanced in their approach to efficiency. Many breweries now use cogeneration technology to harness the steam emitted by the brewing process and reuse it as a power source. Packaging is highly recycled, with most big breweries reusing their own aluminum, glass, and cardboard several times. More advanced improvements are being used to ensure that wastewater is as clean going out of the brewery as it was coming in and some breweries are even generating energy from their water treatment processes. Between cogeneration and water treatment, big breweries are now generating as much as 20 percent of their energy needs from what was once considered effluent.

After water, spent grain is a brewer's biggest waste product and many are now using this plentiful resource to create new products, from livestock feed to compost and as a substrate for growing mushrooms. And now research is exploring ways to transform spent grain into biofuels that can replace gasoline. Hops, which represent a minor amount of the overall inputs in beer, can also be used to create valuable compost. But the challenge for corporate brewing is to get past simple efficiency measures and move toward zero waste.

About 350 billion 12 ounce servings of commercial beer are brewed worldwide, every year. More than one in five are brewed in the United States. Anheuser-Busch, America's largest brewing company, produces one out of every two beers sold in the US. The Coors brewery in Golden, Colorado is the biggest single brewery in the world,

Since 1989, Miller has reduced its waste sent to landfills by 72 percent, and since 1991, Anheuser-Busch has reduced its landfill waste by 53 percent.

packaging more than 20 million barrels of beer every year. As the world's industrial beer behemoths, these brewers deserve some scrutiny to see if they are doing anything to move toward zero-waste sustainability.

A Coors Course in WasteWi$e Brewing

At roughly half the size of industry leader Anheuser-Busch, Coors may not be the world's largest brewing company, but its environmental story is compelling. The company began small and according to historian Dan Baum, Adolph Coors "was content to sell all the beer he could in an area reachable by horse and wagon." As the company grew, the family was determined to continue focusing on quality and freshness rather than on the meteoric growth that other regional brewers were already experiencing. As part of this commitment they decided not to ship any beer east of the Mississippi. Compared to other large breweries, they spent very little on advertising and had a rule that all ads must focus on the quality of the beer and the purity of its primary ingredient, water. For many years, all Coors ads featured pictures of the source of their famous Colorado spring water. Although Coors has had its share of toxic releases and illegal effluent dumping over the years, one early effort speaks to their focus on pure water as the most important ingredient in their beer. Coors designed and built the first modern wastewater treatment plant in Colorado in 1952, adding a secondary treatment process decades before it was required to do so. Unfortunately, during the 1970s, corporate marketers were able to take control of the company and they made a series of bad decisions that led the company to follow in the corporate expansionism footsteps of the two industry leaders, Anheuser-Busch and Miller. Marketing budgets soared and product compromises produced ever-blander beer. But during this process, a unique environmental tale unfolded.

Bill Coors, grandson of Coors Brewing founder Adolph Coors, credits the jumpstart of his environmental conscience to his meeting two individuals in the 1950s. Beatrice Williard, who then ran the Thorne Ecological Institute in Boulder, Colorado, showed Bill three pictures she had taken in the alpine tundra above the timberline. The first was of a Coors can stuck in the ground. The second was the depression left in the ground after the can had been removed. And the third showed the same depression still visible ten years later. Bill Coors then met David Brower, the Sierra Club's first executive director, whom he had been invited to oppose in a business versus environment debate. He claims he agreed with most of what David had to say and he left feeling enthusiastic about the possibility of pursuing better environmental efforts.

Bill Coors Invents the Recyclable Aluminum Can

Coors, just like everyone else, was packaging their beer in steel cans that required seams between the lid and the body, a design weak point that provided one excuse for the continued use of pasteurization as a means of preventing spoilage. Bill dreamed of the day that Coors could quit this practice and return to the fresh "uncooked" taste on which they had built their empire. The seamless aluminum can was Bill's bright idea.

In *Citizen Coors*, Dan Baum explains that "the very idea of cooking bottles of beer in hot water would have made Adolph Coors shudder. To him, beer was a living thing ... [I]deally beer should be drunk as fresh as possible ... He was content to sell all the beer he could in an area reachable by horse and wagon. To a craftsman like Adolph Coors, drinking a Missouri beer in Colorado was like steeping a cup of tea in St. Louis to drink in Denver. Adolphus Busch, founder of the company that became Anheuser-Busch, introduced his first pasteurized beer in 1876, dealing a knock-out blow to beer from which it has taken more than a century to begin recovery."

After five years of research and development and more than $10 million dollars in investments, Coors produced the first seamless recyclable aluminum beverage can in 1959. The steel can industry erupted in a collective laugh, thinking Coors had wasted his money on a useless technology. Funnier still, they thought, was Coors' intention to ask people to return the cans for recycling. Coors didn't think it was funny and went forward with his plan to offer a penny per returned can. It worked marvelously, kicking off the highly successful "Pitch In" campaign that mainstreamed the anti-litter movement nationwide and eventually spawned the curbside recycling movement. Aluminum recycling not only reduces litter, it is highly energy efficient. Recycling an aluminum can requires just five percent of the energy needed to produce aluminum from raw materials. In other words, each time a can is recycled, it offers 95 percent energy savings. Recycling one can saves enough energy to power a TV for 3 hours.

Today, all major brewers use cans made from recycled aluminum. But let's examine brewers' other packaging of choice, the commonplace keg. Kegs are an everyday, yet ingenious, way of reducing packaging in the brewing industry. Few industries rely as heavily as brewing does on bulk dispensing

containers at the retail level. Beer is one of the few commodities still distributed in and consumed in bulk packaging. Consider all the benefits.
Restaurant and bar owners are relieved of the burden of the packaging waste
associated with individually canned or bottled beers. Business owners order
the kegs they want, pour them until they are gone and then distributors pick
up the empties for reuse. In today's age of disappearing landfill space and increasing waste hauling costs, this packaging take-back system reduces landfill
garbage and curtails waste removal fees for small business owners. Consider
the alternative: 165 individual bottles or cans (nearly seven cases) per standard half barrel keg. This kind of product life cycle management, long used
by the brewing industry, is the envy of other industries rushing to create standards and systems for product take-back schemes before regulation imposes
requirements. Expired computers and cell phones, for example, simply get
dumped. Product life cycle plans in the electronics industry are in their infan-
cy, and yet their waste is toxic and increasing in volume exponentially.

Biodegradable Plastic Made from Spent Beer Grains

The Akita Research Institute of Food and Brewing in Japan has developed biodegradable
plastic from spent brewing grains. The Institute produced an experimental batch of 150
kilograms of L-lactic acid, a biodegradable plastic material, from 1,000 kilograms of spent
grains. The technology is expected to lead to a drastic reduction in the cost of producing
this environmentally-friendly plastic that can replace plastic made from petroleum. The
new technology, which they plan to use on other food waste by-products as well, is expected to help reduce Japan's solid waste problem. In Akita Prefecture, one of Japan's major
agricultural areas, most food-processing waste is incinerated or discarded in landfills.

In addition to can recycling and keg use, Coors addresses packaging
impacts by reducing packaging weight, increasing recycled content and
improving recyclability. Postconsumer recycled content of glass bottles manu-
factured by Coors grew from 9 percent in 1989 to about 35 percent today.
Recycled content of both aluminum and corrugated cardboard used by
Coors is over 70 percent. Most of Coors' paper packaging, which a few years
ago could not be recycled, is now 90 percent recyclable.

But packaging is not the whole story. Since its beginning Coors has
focused on water quality; because of this commitment to clean water Coors

maintains one of America's only organic golf courses. This public course is located near Golden so the company decided to eliminate chemicals from the grounds maintenance in order to protect the brewing water that lies beneath the course. They have also made remarkable strides in energy efficiency. Joseph Romm describes this in his book *Cool Companies:* "Coors Brewing Company has a 60 percent efficient cogeneration system at its Golden, Colorado plant, which is the largest single brewing site in the world. The system, run by Trigen, *saves 250,000 tons of carbon dioxide annually* (emphasis in original)." Trigen's energy system also provides steam energy to some microbreweries like River Market Brewing Company in Kansas City, and Commonwealth Brewery and Brew Moon Restaurant and Brewery in Boston.

Brewing an Energy Solution

Ethanol is an alcohol-based fuel that can be fermented from agricultural waste products. As a domestic product, it can help localize America's fuel supply, support farmers, and reduce pollution. Merrick, a Colorado-based company, transforms beer waste from Coors into ethanol. Ethanol is mixed with gasoline in Colorado during winter months to cut down on pollution. According to Steve Wagner at Coors, "There's a whole bunch of wasted beer that's being dropped on the floor." A plant at Coors turns the extra beer into ethanol. Wagner said the company is so successful it is opening up a second plant that will allow Merrick to make up to three million gallons of ethanol a year. Ethanol can also make gas cheaper at the pump.

Ironically, Henry Ford, who was virulently opposed to the drinking of alcohol, planned for it to be the fuel in his vehicles. His first Model T Ford ran on hemp oil. In an interview with the New York Times in 1925, Ford said: "There is fuel in every bit of vegetable matter that can be fermented. There's enough alcohol in one year's yield of an acre of potatoes to drive the machinery necessary to cultivate the fields for a hundred years." Although it has taken nearly a hundred years since then, America's vehicle fleet is finally filling up on alcohol derived from the cellulose of plants securing some of our energy needs through renewable, local production.

Other Coors accomplishments include slashing their annual generation of hazardous waste by more than 90 percent since 1992. And in 1995 Coors established the largest industrial composting operation in Colorado, each year composting approximately 11 million gallons of biosolids and 68,000 cubic yards of scrap wood and other solid waste. Coors' environmental efforts have been widely acknowledged with honors such as the Environmental Protection Agency's WasteWi$e award in recognition of their sustained leadership in incorporating waste prevention into their core operations.

Some of the things Bill Coors says sound more aligned with the anti-corporate crowd than with fellow industry executives. For example, he openly declares his disdain for fossil fuels. In fact, in an attempt to wean his corporations off the stuff, he claims to have developed a biodegradable, starch-based polymer to replace the petroleum-based plastics they used, but alleges that an industry conspiracy foiled the project. Perhaps his boldest assertion is that the corporate focus on the quarterly return is "an ill in our system." Or that, "If I were the czar of American industry, you know the first thing I would do? I would make stock options illegal." He dislikes the "myopic" view executives acquire when they focus on these short-term returns. Perhaps his long-term vision is linked to the fact that Coors Brewing has been family-run since Adolph Coors founded the company in 1876. The Iroquois, a Native American tribe, had a great law that required all their chiefs to consider the impact of their decisions on the seventh generation to follow them. Given his apparent environmental conscience and Coors' generations of family management, perhaps Bill Coors is trying to practice this precept.

A-Beer

A-B — Anheuser Busch — comes first in the alphabet of beer. Since 1957 Anheuser-Busch has dominated the American brewing market, and for decades has been the world's largest brewer by volume, though they have recently been surpassed by InBev and SABMiller. In 2004, A-B had over 31,000 employees at over 100 facilities and annual gross sales of over US$17 billion. The impact of this mammoth brewing company is monstrous, so their waste reduction numbers are worth considering.

Through a host of conservation efforts since 1991, the company has actually reduced its water usage even as it has increased its revenues through expansion. In other words, they make more beer, but use less water. Through all of their recycling and reuse efforts, A-B has reduced solid waste they send to landfills by 53 percent or 117.6 million pounds.

As a global brewing goliath, they take packaging pretty seriously. Today, the A-B Recycling Corporation is the world's largest aluminum can recycler — recycling more beer cans than they ship worldwide, which is about twenty billion every year. In 2003, the amount of energy saved from recycling aluminum cans was equivalent to 15 million barrels of oil. With all this recycled aluminum, it stands to reason that A-B is also one of the nation's largest purchasers of recycled-content products, purchasing more than one billion pounds of post-consumer content products in 1999.

As the potential of conventional conservation efforts maxed out, the company continued to decrease its resource usage by innovating new technologies, like its Bio-Energy Recovery System (BERS), their version of cogeneration. This system turns wastewater into energy and reduces the quantity of waste solids for disposal by 50 percent. By the year 2000, this system was saving A-B about $40 million per year, while reducing grid electricity usage by 75 percent and reducing carbon dioxide emissions by 80 percent. The system uses bacteria to clean brewery wastewater, producing methane as they clean the water. The methane is used as fuel and the cleaned water reduces the downstream wastewater treatment facilities' energy consumption

In 2004, Anheuser-Busch recycled a whopping 97 percent of its solid waste, including:

- 35,000 metric tons of glass
- 75,000 metric tons of aluminum
- 1.7 million metric tons of spent grains
- 6,400 metric tons of diatomaceous earth into compost or cement
- 5,400 metric tons of beechwood chips into compost
- 24,000 metric tons of cardboard
- 270,000 metric tons of farm materials into compost
- 2,500 metric tons of animal pen and landscape waste into compost
- 1,500 metric tons of plastic strapping
- 2,300 metric tons of office paper and industrial scrap paper
- 4,100 metric tons of scrap metal
- 28,000 metric tons of construction waste
- 24,000 metric tons of miscellaneous materials
- 3.526 billion pounds of spent grains

by 75 percent. By 2000, the BERS system was producing about 15 percent of each brewery's fuel needs.

Compost Happens

A-B breweries compost millions of pounds of wastewater sludge and hundreds of millions of pounds of farm wastes. Busch Gardens in Tampa Bay, Florida, composts millions of pounds of yard and animal waste. The finished compost is reused in the park for landscaping projects. Another by-product of their oil brewing process is used beechwood chips, the bits of wood behind their "beechwood-aged" claim that appears in all their marketing. In 1999, A-B recycled 12.7 million pounds of beechwood chips into compost and mulch. Diatomaceous earth is the medium used to filter A-B's products. A-B now recycles million of pounds of this by selling it as an input for cement products. A-B is a founding member of the EPA's Performance Track, a program which streamlines regulations for companies with top-performing Environmental Management Systems.

Corporate Wildlife

Since 1979, A-B's Jacksonville brewery has piped wastewater to turf farms where sod is grown for stadiums, golf courses, and real estate. Runoff from the turf farms is drained off and collected in retention ponds where aquatic vegetation eats up the water's remaining nutrients. These ponds control the flow of water into wetland habitat where native and migratory birds thrive. This program was certified as Corporate Wildlife Habitat in 1997 by the Wildlife Habitat Council, which also certified six other A-B sites. This system recycles 600 million gallons of water annually, and saves the local wastewater treatment plant 90 percent of the energy — 70,000,000 kilowatt-hours per year — that would have been required to treat the wastewater.

SABMiller

According to their 2004 Corporate Accountability Report, the vast majority of the beer from the world's second-largest brewing concern is dispensed from reusable kegs. Of the remaining beer, most is sold in bottles, over half of which are also returnable and reusable, and the rest are in cans, many of which are recycled. Incredibly, for such a large global corporation, SABMiller can truthfully claim that the vast majority of their beer packaging is reused or recycled. Nearly 90 percent of their solid waste is spent grains and spent yeast, almost all of which are fed to livestock. SABMiller recycles roughly 85 percent of the waste from their global beer production. In 1989, Miller, SABMiller's largest subsidiary, set the ambitious goal of eliminating nearly all waste shipments to landfills by 1995. As a result, they now recycle over 95 percent of their waste.

To reach their waste reduction goal, Miller implemented a combination of reuse and by-product resale programs that, as of 2004, had succeeded in reducing their landfill shipments by 72 percent. A box reuse program reduced their need for corrugated cardboard by 75 percent, diverting more than 9.5 million pounds of waste cardboard in 1 year alone. Brewer's yeast and spent grains are sold to farmers and commercial bakeries for use in soups and frozen entrees. Since 1961, Miller has reduced the amount of aluminum in its cans by 45 percent, creating a savings of more than 100 million pounds of aluminum each year. Nearly all of Miller's aluminum cans are now made from recycled materials. The weight of their glass bottles has been reduced by over 20 percent since 1986 and the bottles now contain more than 30 percent recycled glass, saving more than 8,400 tons of glass each month. In 2000, Miller began using recycled resins for some of its plastic bottles and committed to buy back used bottles.

By the way, the letters in the acronym stand for South African Breweries, and in their home country of South Africa they have some equally impressive percentages, but of a different kind. SABMiller controls 98 percent of the commercial beer market in their national home, making them what can only be called an egregious monopoly.

InBev

When Brazil's AmBev and Belgium's Interbrew merged a few years ago, they took over the number one spot in the biggest brewer rankings. They produce a staggering one out of every seven commercial beers sold worldwide. In Brazil, they control almost 70 percent of the market. As of November 2005, the company had 77,000 employees. Globally, this oversized brewing monster has reached a solid waste recycling rate of 96 percent. A few of their breweries have reached an amazing 99 percent recycling rate. In just two years, from

According to the American Solar Energy Society, it takes 10 fossil fuel calories to produce one food calorie in the average American diet. That means 930 gallons of gasoline are required to grow, process, package and deliver the annual food needs for a family of four.

2002 to 2004, InBev reduced its water to beer ratio by nearly a gallon, from just under 6.5 gallons to just over 5.5 gallons of water used per gallon of beer produced. The fact that it is an obnoxiously huge mega-corporation is partially offset by the fact that they produce a handful of good Belgian beers, including their Belle-Vue line of lambics, the classic Hoegaarden white beer, and the Leffe line of abbey-style beers.

Small Is Still Brewtiful

As a global industry, brewing is highly efficient compared to many other corporate enterprises and it is continuing to move toward zero waste in its operations, serving as a model for other industries. But with the Earth's natural systems in crisis, the goal of industry has to be to move beyond efficiency and toward restorative production. A brewery's net impact on the environment should be positive rather than net-zero. But as the big boys of beer stampede forth into ever greater monopolies, they will never make it all the way down the path of sustainability. Scale itself is a major factor in the sustainability equation, and mondo brewers by definition are out of whack with the ideal. By their global nature, these brewers will always rely heavily on subsidized fossil fuel-based shipping. As a food source, beer that is shipped great distances fails to meet the basic criterion of sustainability. It is a net waste of resources. On average, it takes more energy to ship industrial beers than the beer provides in the form of food energy to the drinker. In theory, converting raw grain into beer should be a process of unlocking stored energy for human consumption, creating a net gain of energy useful to humans. Beer brewed and consumed locally can meet this criterion, but not beers that are shipped long distances using fossil fuels.

A plane uses 15,839 kilojoules of energy per metric ton of goods transported per kilometer. Trains use 677, boats 423, and trucks 2,890.

Even with all the impressive statistics of these mega-brewers, the overall lesson is simple: small is still *brewtiful*.

CHAPTER 16

Putting the Ale Back in Female

"In truth, beer is the most democratic and most feminine of all beverages."

— Alan Eames, *The Secret Life of Beer*

Clearly modern beer drinkers have a great deal to celebrate. Corporate brewers are mashing up industrial eco-efficiency. Craft brewers have ignited a revolution in the brewing industry, producing a dizzying array of beer styles both old and new, experimenting with local, seasonal ingredients, reasserting variety in the land of uniform mass production and building small, local businesses. Growing numbers of people are brewing at home again and using beer to build community. Beer has its soul back. But one thing is still missing, something that was integral to brewing and drinking for the thousands of years of human civilization prior to the machine age. Women remain remarkably absent in the modern world of beer.

Slaves to the Market

In the classic works, *Gender* and *Shadow Work*, philosopher Ivan Illich contends that industrialization robbed Western civilization of creative work and replaced it with meaningless drudgery and shopping. Prior to industrialization, he explains, women and men worked to create the necessities of life as well as the luxuries of mirth. Women, for example, brewed beer for both nourishment and merriment. As a creative process, brewing was a rewarding undertaking for women everywhere. Men engaged in similarly rewarding creative work, including complementary trades such as barrel-making, as well as the many other productive efforts required to contribute to the care of family, tribe, and society. But industrialization changed this, replacing human craft with machine construction.

To oversimplify only slightly, the industrial age enlisted men in repetitive industrial jobs and assigned women the chore of shopping for the results. In short, men became wage slaves who ran machines and women became shopping cart slaves whose job was to buy whatever came out of the machines. During the industrial age, public opinion came to view crafts like brewing as hopelessly old-fashioned at best, and at worst the domain of the impoverished who couldn't afford to buy factory goods. Engaging in self-sufficient activities like brewing, sewing, or music-making became tantamount to announcing your own poverty. Why soil your own hands when perfectly modern cans of beer are available on the supermarket shelves? Instead of relying on women's creative production to satisfy our needs, they were assigned the meaningless "choice" of selecting one can of beer over another based almost entirely on insights provided to them through clever marketing campaigns. Consumerism replaced creativity and, as a result, Western society transformed its cultural identity. As Westerners, we now view ourselves primarily as consumers and we measure our own worth by the consumer choices we make. Brands give us meaning and identity. As a result, more and more people now feel unfulfilled by this life of passive consumption. Widespread depression and obsessive consumption are just two of the most obvious symptoms of this socially-designed disease.

Seeking the reward that comes from creative work, a growing number of men are discovering homebrewing and other do-it-yourself crafts. Many women, too, are seeking satisfaction in hobbies like gardening and knitting, pursuits once associated with familial nurturing that are now considered leisure activities. But women have been slow to return to the brew kettle. To the delight of many, brewing has begun a fundamental shift back toward craft, but sadly women are peripheral to the trend. The culture of brewing and drinking beer, even within the craft-beer movement, is overwhelmingly masculine. Modern brewing, whether professional or amateur, is for scientists and engineers, and other traditionally male occupations. The craft and homebrewing communities have a great opportunity to break this male domination by removing some of the barriers preventing women from embracing beer. Society would undoubtedly benefit from a renewed female influence in beer culture. Whether by design or acculturation, women and men have some generalizable differences. Women share and cooperate more than men. In a world where the disparity between rich and poor is growing exponentially, we all could do with a hearty dose of these two traits. For beer, the most commonly consumed alcoholic beverage in the world, to be so male dominated, is both an injustice and a tragedy. The injustice is in excluding so many from something so good. The tragedy is that lacking feminine influence, beer is still far from achieving its full potential.

And yet, despite these shortcomings, craft beer culture is at least more gender inclusive than industrial beer culture. Craft brewing is small, community-centered, has lower barriers to entry, and is far more rewarding on a gustatory level. Craft beer cherishes the road rather than the destination. It is warm and emotional where industrial beer is cold and sterile. There are signs that craft brewing is opening up the beer world to women again. In small but growing numbers women are finally returning to the craft as well as the draft.

Take Back the Pint

To the big brewers and marketers, women are an afterthought or a marketing image but never a market unto themselves. As an industry, mainstream brewers are almost unparalleled in their blinkered dismissal of women as a market. Bikinis and puerile humor are the best ideas marketers have for how to sell light lagers to boys. It's little wonder that this advertising approach fails to attract female drinkers. In fact, the insulting barrage of sophomoric advertising is finally starting to wear thin even on the most conventional male audience. Mainstream industrial beers are losing market share to craft beer, imports, wine, and spirits, drinks that are perceived as more sophisticated. Corporate brewers' failure to attract female drinkers is liable to lead to their own demise. As they lose market share, the big companies are finding that the only way to grow is through mergers and acquisitions. In the long run, getting big will not save them because size is part of the problem. Boys tend to think bigger is better. But the market is saying otherwise.

Sophisticated beer drinkers seek authenticity, not sameness. There is no longer such a thing as the mass market. Other industries are experiencing similar revolutions. Take organic food, for example. The market has been growing 25–30 percent annually for the last 5 years. Buyers are looking for local food, produced by small companies, that make unique products. Women are leading the charge in this change. But the craft beer market is solidly male. Craft brewing has barely begun to realize its potential to break down gender barriers by cultivating its female-friendly attributes —some of the same ones embodied by the organic food industry. Unique craft beers are almost certainly more appealing to women than their drab industrial counterparts. To start, craft breweries do little or no advertising to either men or women. Ironically, this may be providing them a marketing edge since it allows the beers to speak for themselves to potential female drinkers rather than letting marketers bungle the job. Furthermore, some evidence suggests that women are more receptive than men to trying diverse beer styles. John Hall, founder of Goose Island Brewing in Chicago, believes his female customers are more apt to try a new style of beer than are his male customers, who tend to stick with tried and trusted styles.

> "Craft-beer-drinking is growing in popularity. We intend to make sure women are also a large factor in continuing this trend."
> — Fred Bowman, co-founder of Portland Brewing

Rebecca Mowling, a beer-drinking advertising copywriter, says that she finds beer packaging dull and that the lack of variety is a turn-off. "You don't have to have a beard and big tummy to enjoy a really good glass of ale," Rebecca says. "The macho approach to beer drinking where quantity is sometimes more important than quality holds little appeal for me," she continues. But when beer succeeds in penetrating the gender divide, "it's the ideal social drink in a pub because it's thirst-quenching and lasts much longer than a glass of wine."

There are other signs pointing to the half of the population that brewers have forgotten as an opening for craft beer. Portland Brewing Co. offered a two-hour Beer Appreciation for Women course that proved to be so popular they had to schedule another one right away. The Tesco supermarket chain in Great Britain has instituted an all-woman panel of beer tasters to try any new brands being considered for the shelves.

As part of its "Ask if it's Cask" promotion, Britain's Campaign for Real Ale (CAMRA) has condemned brewers' marketing departments for failing to make beer appeal to women. CAMRA claims that beer is the only product that is still promoted almost exclusively to men, but that pub owners who have made their establishments friendlier to women have seen sales increase.

Research conducted by CAMRA found that over a fifth of women surveyed said they didn't drink cask ale because it wasn't promoted to them, and 19 percent said they would try it if it were served in more stylish glasses. Because big brewers and advertisers don't spend significant time or money courting smaller market segments, the opportunity exists for brewers on the fringe of the mainstream on both sides of the Atlantic to reach out to women. "Our research suggests that women who try real ale are attracted by the qualities of the product, like its taste and naturalness," said Mike Benner of CAMRA. "But of those who haven't tried it, it is the image of the product that frightens them off. Poor image is created by poor marketing and it's time brewers stepped into the 21st century and made a real effort to make their beers appeal to women." That message doesn't have to be complicated. Shortly after Wisconsin's New Glarus Brewing Co. opened in 1993, President Deb Carey designed a bumper sticker with a message for men and women alike. It read: "Real women don't drink light beer."

Craft brewers would do well to learn from the wine industry, where biology has fueled growth. Kim Caffrey, owner and operator of Wine, Women & Laughs, a Napa Valley-based company offering "entertaining and educational" wine seminars, says: "Women actually have an edge as far as tasting and subtleties because women, anthropologically, are super tasters. They have heightened sensitivity to taste and smell."

> Pliny the Elder, Roman philosopher and author, "mentioned that the spuma or froth of all these brews (presumably the yeasty foam on top of the fermenting beer) 'is used by women as a cosmetic for the face'. If this use of yeast to improve the complexion was a British practice, it is still taking place 1,900 years later. In the 1930s, sufferers from skin complaints would collect excess yeast from Adey and White's brewery in St. Albans, Hertforshire, making a small donation to St. Albans City Hospital at the same time."
>
> — Martyn Cornell, *Beer: the Story of the Pint*

Cultural Creatives

Women are leading some of today's biggest trends. Europe and North America are experiencing an explosion of interest in all things natural. Organic and natural foods are experiencing exponential growth. As the food providers in most households, women are leading the organic charge. Women are concerned about what their children eat, so it's no wonder that they want their food to be natural, wholesome, fresh, and locally produced.

Organic food trendsetters are part of what Paul Ray, a leading market researcher, terms "Cultural Creatives," a population of about 50 million Americans that, among other behaviors, tends to choose natural, organic foods for themselves and their families. They want authentic experiences and they shy away from mass-produced, anonymous commodities. They like the real thing. That sounds like the craft beer demographic to me, but there is one exception. The majority of Cultural Creatives are women. Here is where the better beer movement has enormous potential. Women could become (and already are in some cases) flag-bearers in the struggle to reestablish a healthy, authentic, natural, and family-friendly beer-drinking culture.

The explosion in the popularity of yoga is another one of the signs of the strength of the Cultural Creatives market. And it should be made clear that there is nothing inconsistent with practicing yoga and drinking beer. In fact, I have known more than one (well, only two, but still) beer-drinking female yoga instructors. They keep their bodies fit and they drink in moderation. How sexy is that! And yet the men who make and drink beer either don't know women like these or else they are ignoring them. I can't figure out why.

Drafting Women

It may be a Catch-22, but if more women were brewers, beer would appeal to more women. The Queen of Beer is an annual homebrew competition sponsored by the Hangtown Association of Zymurgy Enthusiasts, a California-based homebrew club. The competition attracts entries from all over the country and is open to women only. Recent best-of-show competition winners included a Russian Imperial Stout, an ale spiced with sweet chocolate espresso beans, and a Belgian specialty brew. Results like that suggest that women may be just as adventurous beer brewers as they are beer tasters.

Professional female brewers are still pretty rare, but the few that exist stand out for their excellence. A number of the leading craft breweries owe their success to women, including the likes of New Belgium, New Glarus, Stoudt's, and Lost Coast. In all these cases, the women involved are half of a husband-wife team, with the exception of Lost Coast which goes a step further and is run by a team of two women. This illustrates one way women are

Viking women were the exclusive brewers in Norse society near the end of the first millennium and law dictated that all brewhouse equipment remained the property of women only.

influencing the industry. To generalize, women are more collaborative and group-oriented than men. They're less likely to be egotistical and want all the attention. By definition, they are not the "alpha male" types that run so many craft breweries. "Alpha male" is a biological term that refers to men who dominate their community, usually through physical prowess, and constantly demand ceremonial respect. Women are less often like this, even when they run beer companies. The number of breweries named after their male founders may be evidence of this difference. Sure, there's nothing wrong with naming a brewery after the person who founded it, but it demonstrates how men demand recognition for their efforts, and sometimes act like success is due exclusively to their own labors, when usually lots of people were involved. Women, on the other hand, generally tend to share the credit with others. Sharing is a good thing — especially when it comes to beer.

A Stout in Stoudtburg

In 1987, Carol Stoudt became the first woman to found her own microbrewery. Then, along with her husband Ed, she literally built a community.

Carol Stoudt surveys the cheese selection in the Black Angus Restaurant and Brew Pub owned by the Stoudt family. Family artwork and history adorns the classically decorated dining rooms and the wall of the German style bier garden depicting the Stoudt family history since they first arrived in America in 1733.

Stoudtburg Village is designed as a mixed-use town where eventually 150 store-front homes are planned to line the town streets. Carol says she is "committed to the artisanal renaissance sweeping the nation," and this unique experiment in community is proof. Naturally, the brewery is the heart of the community, but other businesses include a bakery (that makes bread with spent brewing grains, of course), a music shop, art gallery, coffee shop, and dozens of antique dealers. Black Angus is Carol and Ed's pub and restaurant where they serve locally grown organic produce and free-range chickens raised just up the road. The buildings are all Energy Star rated, which means they were designed with energy efficiency in mind. The Stoudts pay attention to quality and detail in everything they do, and their award-winning beers are the best proof. Carol received the 2005 Brewers Association Recognition Award in honor of her outstanding beers, including ones like Scarlet Lady ESB and Fat Dog Stout, and for her dedication to furthering the cause of the craft-brewing movement as a whole.

Return of the Beer Chalice

Kim Jordan is part of another husband-wife team. She and Jeff founded New Belgium Brewing in 1991. They must have already known what the

A female-friendly New Belgium beer chalice.

CAMRA research later found — that women want nicer glassware than the usual heavy beer mugs. A stemmed chalice would do nicely, just like Belgian brewers use to serve their unique creations. Brewing exclusively Belgian-style ales, and serving them in refined and delicate glasses, the couple launched what has become one of the most successful craft breweries in the country. And it is decidedly eco-friendly too. The brewery is certified by the US Green Building Council, runs on 100 percent wind power, and has on-site wastewater treatment ponds that clean the brewery's used water and produce energy at the same time. Kim has a philosophy of community and sharing that comes through in the business model. Since their first employee was hired, New Belgium has always been worker-owned. "It's important that we share in all the benefits," says Kim "and, frankly, in the risks too. We have tried to make our relationship with our co-workers — in terms of the business of running the business — very transparent, and I think that's a foundational piece of who we are."

Deborah Carey is founder and president of the New Glarus Brewing Company. She sums up her outlook quite succinctly: "Our philosophy is based on individuality, cooperation, and the employment of 100 percent natural ingredients to produce world-class, handcrafted beers for our friends in Wisconsin." It should be noted that Deborah refuses to sell beer outside of her home state of Wisconsin — opposing business growth for its own sake and instead paying attention to her customers, community, and the craft of brewing.

Women like Carol, Kim, and Deborah exemplify the traits Charlotte Bunch, executive director of Center for Women's Global Leadership, attributes to female leaders. Women tend to make the biggest impact, she says, in the area of social cohesion, "They tend to pay more attention to the things that keep people's daily lives together ... to bring people together and to move communities forward." Sounds exactly like what a good brewpub does.

Women of the World, Greedy Men Have Stolen Your Beer and It Is Time to Take It Back

My brother-in-law is a home brewer. One day his seven-year-old daughter Meg brought her journal home from school. Her parents got a great deal of joy reading their daughter's account of her life. That is until they read the entry where she wrote, "I helped my dad put bear in bear bolds (sic)." Her parents were mildly concerned. Not because of the spelling errors, but because they were afraid of what the teacher might think

CRANNOG ALES

Rebecca MacIsaac drives the tractor at Crannog Ales, a zero-waste organic farm brewery in Sorrento, British Columbia.

Amelia Slayton, founder of Seven Bridges Cooperative, supplier of all-organic homebrewing ingredients, as well as fair trade and organic green coffee beans for home-roasting.

about their parenting practices — imagine teaching an innocent young girl to make beer! For millennia women have proudly taught their daughters to brew. It was a celebrated tradition, a creative outlet, and even an honor. Today it is a social faux pas at best, criminal at worst. My solution? Organize a "Take Your Daughter to the Brewery" day. Teach your kids how to brew by involving them in the process. Gather your girl friends for an educational beer tasting. Have a group brew. Femaleists of the world, whatever you do, get more beer into your life.

Eco-femaleism

Ecofeminism is an environmental movement with social concerns. Ecofeminist theorists connect the oppression of women with the degradation of nature. The emergence of environmentally focused female brewers might best be called Ecofemaleism. Women like Amelia Slayton and Rebecca MacIsaac might be called the unwitting leaders of this nascent movement. Slayton founded the Seven Bridges Cooperative as the world's first supplier of all organic homebrewing supplies. Rebecca, with her husband Brian, built an ecologically integrated farm brewery that produces all organic beers for their local market around Sorrento, British Columbia, near Canada's left coast.

CHAPTER 17

How to Drink Beer and Save the World: A Twenty-Four-Point Action Plan

> "The success of the consumer revolt is important not just to beer drinkers but to everybody who is concerned about the quality of life. If it can be done with beer it can be done with other things. We do not have to behave as accountants and economists think we ought to behave. You can stand in the way of progress."
>
> — Richard Boston, *Beer and Skittles*

Consumers are powerful. But so are corporations and their ability to coerce consumers into buying stuff. Britain's large and well-organized group of beer drinkers are fighting back and winning. The Campaign for Real Ale (CAMRA) has been described as "Europe's most successful campaigning consumer organization." The group's main objective is to protect and promote independent breweries and pubs. Among their many victories is their defeat of Watney's Red. This large brewing concern spent millions of dollars on branding and positioning their product as England's national keg beer of choice, sort of a Budweiser of Britain. CAMRA set to work opposing the behemoth's attempts to monopolize part of the market and the small band of beer activists managed to catalyze its demise.

This can be a model for other consumer activists. When despicable trends emerge, it is often the result of marketing, not public demand. Consumer movements, on the other hand, often begin with a humble group of citizens sitting around the kitchen table discussing a grievance. They are successful when they articulate a thought that is already widely shared but has yet to be formulated in a public way. When the idea is given form by a group of advocates, it can spark a wildfire of focused public sentiment able to topple even the most entrenched and well-financed corporations.

Consumers have the power to reject the status quo and demand something better. By making wise choices, beer activists can help restore ecological balance, build stronger communities, and help create a more rewarding lifestyle for people all over the world. The American brewing renaissance was started by dissatisfied beer drinkers who took their disgruntled palates to the marketplace and brewed up small businesses that quenched their thirst. The growth of the craft beer movement is not a consequence of its marketing prowess. Most small breweries have little or no money allocated to advertising. The better beer movement grows because people genuinely want better beer and better beer–drinking experiences. Beer drinkers fermented the American brewing revolution. So, in testament to the power people have to change the things that matter to them, and because beer clearly matters to me, and apparently to you as well, here is, in no particular order, a case worth of ways to get started fermenting your own beer revolution.

1. Buy Local Beer

According to the Brewer's Association, the majority of Americans now live within ten miles of a brewery. Simply put, buying locally-made beer is better for the environment and helps to strengthen local communities.

A popular bumper sticker from Stoudt Brewing in Adamstown, Pennsylvania.

2. Walk Lightly and Carry a Cloth Sack

The perennial conundrum: paper or plastic? Which is better for the environment? The answer is surprisingly easy — they both suck pretty bad. The solution? Use a cloth bag. Here's why.

Plastic Is Drastic

Factories churned out between four and five trillion plastic shopping bags in the year 2002. They start life as crude oil, natural gas, or other petrochemical derivatives and mostly end up in landfills or the ocean. Stray plastic bags also clog sewer pipes, and the resulting stagnant water causes health hazards. In 2002, Bangladesh banned plastic bags after drains blocked by bags contributed to widespread monsoon flooding in 1988 and 1998. The Irish imposed a consumer tax on plastic bags and have since stopped using them almost entirely. In the Indian province of Himachal Pradesh, people caught with plastic bags are fined up to $2,000.

Americans recycle less than 1 percent of our plastic bags and throw away about 100 billion of them a year. North America and Western Europe account for nearly 80 percent of plastic bag use. Some manufacturers have introduced biodegradable or compostable plastic bags made from starches, polymers, or polylactic acid, and no polyethylene, but these remain prohibitively expensive and account for less than one percent of the market.

Surprisingly, despite all these problems, research conducted by the Institute for Lifecycle Environmental Assessment suggests that plastic bags are a superior choice over paper. Comparatively, producing plastic bags uses less energy and water and generates less air pollution and solid waste, taking up less landfill space. But many never make it to landfills, instead going airborne and getting caught in fences, trees, the throats of birds, and clogging gutters, sewers, and waterways.

So if plastic is this bad and still better than paper, what does that say about paper bags?

Paper Is a Waster

According to the Environmental Protection Agency, Americans recycle about one in five paper bags. Compared to the plastic bag recycling rate, that's pretty good, especially because it takes approximately seven trucks to transport the same number of paper bags that would fill one truck with plastic bags. One paper bag requires more than twice as much energy, produces 15 times as much waterborne waste and twice as much atmospheric waste, as one plastic bag.

So if plastic is drastic and paper is worse, what's a concerned beer drinker to do when faced with the worrisome task of carrying home a six-pack?

He Doth Tote Cloth

Keep canvas bags in your home, office, car, on your bike, and wherever else is convenient, so that you always have one handy when you go to the store. Reuse your own durable cloth bags over and over again. Try to go a week without accumulating any new plastic bags. If every shopper took just one less bag each month, this could eliminate the waste of hundreds of millions of bags each year. Reusable sacks come in a variety of sustainable choices, like organic cotton, hemp, and even recycled plastic that looks and feels like cloth.

Supermarkets around the world are voluntarily encouraging shoppers to forgo bags or bring their own by offering a small per-bag refund or charging extra for each bag they give out. That means bringing your own bag saves you money too!

3. Recycle Your Empties

Aluminum can manufacturing takes a heavy toll on the environment, including deforestation, open-cast mining, road building, and consuming huge amounts of energy. Recycling aluminum cans has immense savings though, and beer drinkers sure can recycle. Americans use about 392 aluminum cans per person per year. These cans typically have a recycled content of about 55 percent. In all, 62.8 billion or 63.5 percent of aluminum cans are recycled every year. Recycling aluminum saves about 95 percent of the energy it takes to produce new aluminum from bauxite. Recycling one aluminum can saves enough electricity to run a TV for three hours. Aluminum recycling is so efficient that it can take as few as 60 days for a can to be collected, melted down and made into a new can sitting on a grocery store shelf. *Can* you believe it?

People in beer houses shouldn't throw glass bottles in the trash. Glass bottle manufacturing is less energy and resource intensive than making aluminum cans, but because glass weighs more it requires more fuel to ship it around. Still, a ton of glass produced from virgin materials produces 27.8 pounds of air pollution, and recycling cuts that amount by over 5 pounds. Ideally, breweries would just reuse glass bottles, but if they don't, they should use bottles produced locally from recycled glass. They can't do that if there isn't a local supply of recycled glass, so drinkers need to recycle their bottles. Americans only recycle about a third of the 12.5 million tons of glass we produce in a year, disposing of over 28 million glass bottles and jars, which is about 7 percent of our municipal solid waste. Glass recycling employs over

30,000 workers in 76 plants in 25 states, and saves more than 25 percent of the energy needed to make glass from virgin materials.

4. Get Thee to a Brewpubbery

Who needs cloth bags and recycling when you can plant yourself on a stool at the shiny wooden bar of your favorite local brewpub? Most of the packaging is eliminated when you drink at a brewpub. Sometimes they don't even keg their beer, instead dispensing it straight out of the big storage tanks behind the bar. From brew tank to beer glass to mouth — now that's efficient!

5. Fill a Growler

The term "growler" is just a fancy way of saying "big glass jug." Most brewpubs and many breweries offer these nowadays. Simply bring your empty jug and they'll fill it straight out of the tap. This offers all the same benefits as number four above; it's just that sometimes you want to have beer at home with your family.

6. Brew Your Own

Unfortunately, no scientific studies seem to exist on whether homebrewing is more eco-friendly than buying locally-brewed craft beer. However, making beer at home does offer some clear benefits. First of all, most of the weight of beer is water, as much as 95 percent or more. Transporting all this weight from a brewery to a distributor to a store to your house requires a lot of fuel. The water in homebrew goes from the kitchen tap to the kitchen table. Moreover, homebrewing can be highly efficient in terms of packaging and helps build social bonds with other homebrewers and family members. My nine-year-old niece Meg usually helps her father and me bottle our homebrew. It's amazing how homebrew draws people together in ways that regular beer doesn't. Every batch of homebrew provides a new excuse to invite friends and family over for socializing. I should know, I've been to more homebrew-as-excuse-to-hang-out gatherings than I can count. Plus homebrewing helps reduce the number of times you need to drive to the store or brewpub. It's also a great way to relax by using creative energy for something outside of your job.

7. Teach a Friend to Homebrew

If one person homebrewing is eco-positive, imagine the impact of a whole group of friends homebrewing.

8. Compost Packaging

Most people do not live on homebrew alone and like to sample the offerings from their local breweries. Unfortunately, those purchases usually come packed in a cardboard carton with four individual six-pack carriers inside. Many of these cartons and carriers contain significant recycled content, which is obviously a good thing. But what are you going to do with it once you've gotten it home? Recycling it again is an option in some places, but even recycling requires energy inputs. A different option is to rip it into strips and chuck it on the compost heap. Composting is very rewarding, especially if you have a garden where you grow some of your own homebrew supplies and beer snacks. But even if you don't have a green thumb, composting is easy, and the rich soil it creates can also be used to grow a pretty lawn.

9. Enjoy Organic

When possible, buy organic beer or organic homebrewing ingredients. When it's not available, ask for it. One of the benefits of visiting brewpubs is the straight line of access to the brewer. Usually he (unfortunately — or fortunately, depending on your agenda — it is almost always a guy) is poking around behind the bar or near some of those big copper or stainless steel tanks. Sometimes he's even the guy pouring your beer. Nearly always, he is available to chat if you just ask a staff person for the brewer. Tell him you'd really be glad if he would brew with organic ingredients. Lots of brewpubs are brewing an organic beer or two these days, and brewers are often glad to respond to customer suggestions.

The same thing goes for retailers. There is a growing number of organic beers available in bottles, but if your retailer doesn't stock them, just tell them you would buy them if they did. Simple customer feedback like this can affect the store buyer's decisions about what to carry. Business owners usually appreciate customer feedback like this because it helps them understand what people want, and if they have what people want then they make more money to support their small business. So just ask for what you want.

"Thanks to genuine consumer demand, organic beers will be made at an even faster rate as English-grown hops are produced on a wider scale. The lights are on green ... Consumers found their voice and voted with their wallets."

— Roger Protz, *Organic Beer Guide.*

The Black Isle Brewery in Scotland brews all organic beers.

10. Take Care of Yourself

People are part of the environment too. Healthy people help make for a healthier environment. Be happier and healthier by drinking in moderation, which in turn will keep you healthy longer and also help you avoid painful hangovers. See Chapter 14 for details.

11. Try Beers Made with Local Ingredients

Lots of craft breweries are experimenting with crazy ingredients. This is part of what makes the American brewing scene so vibrant and exciting. I've had beers brewed with oysters, fresh cranberries, juniper berries, and so much more. Local ingredients are fresh. They support the local economy and they can contribute to making some really intriguing and tasty brews. Beers that use local ingredients help create a local identity and feeling of belonging to a place. Try a pint of oyster stout and I'll bet you'll always remember you had it in Baltimore. Have a glass of wheat beer with fresh blueberries floating in it and you'll recall that it was in Boston. What's the point of traveling if you don't feel like you have gone anywhere? What's the point in being from *some-where* if it feels like *anywhere?* Think globally, drink locally.

12. Keep the Fridge Stocked

A relatively full refrigerator is more efficient than a relatively empty one because the cold mass of products helps maintain the temperature when the door is open. So keep yours stocked with homebrew and craft beers. However, overstocked fridges can be a problem since they inhibit airflow, thus making the refrigerator work harder to maintain proper temperature. As long as you maintain a moderate beer-drinking diet, it shouldn't be much of a challenge to keep the stock rotating.

More important than keeping it stocked though is making sure your refrigerator is energy efficient. Refrigerators are usually the biggest energy hogs of all the kitchen appliances. They can account for as much as 15 percent of a home's total energy usage. According to recent sales statistics, the typical refrigerator costs about $1,140 to operate over its lifetime. The older the model, the more electricity it uses, the more it costs you. If your present refrigerator is more than 15 years old, the US Department of Energy says you'll save money on your electric bill if you replace it with a new, more efficient unit. New models can be as much as 50 percent more energy efficient than older refrigerators. If every household in the United States had the most efficient refrigerators available, the electricity savings would eliminate the need for more than 20 large power plants.

Federal law now requires all new refrigerators to be labeled with an EnergyGuide. These are bright yellow tags that usually appear right on the front of the product and show how much electricity a particular model uses compared to other similar models. When you're shopping for the best buy in a new appliance, using EnergyGuide can save you money. The smaller the number, the less energy the refrigerator uses and the less it will cost you to operate. And although some energy-efficient products are more expensive to purchase, they cost less to operate over their useful lifetime. Some of the more expensive models pay for themselves in a little over three years. Over the 15-year lifetime, a more expensive refrigerator can save up to $750. That's a lot of homebrew supplies.

In addition to the EnergyGuide, look for the Energy Star label. This tells the consumer that the product was designed with efficiency in mind and meets certain federal standards for being highly efficient. A new refrigerator with an Energy Star label saves between $35 and $70 per year compared to models

Look for the Energy Star logo and check the EnergyGuide when you buy a new fridge.

designed ten years ago. This adds up to as much as a thousand dollars over the average life of the unit.

Tips for Lowering Your Refrigerator Energy Usage

- Keep your refrigerator between 37–40°F and the freezer between 0–5°F. Use a thermometer to check inside temperatures.

- Regularly defrost manual-defrost refrigerators and freezers; don't allow frost to build up more than one quarter of an inch.

- Make sure your refrigerator and freezer door seals are airtight. Check the seal on door gaskets periodically by closing the door on a dollar bill. If it pulls out easily, you may need a new gasket.

- Keep the doors closed as much as possible and make sure they are closed tightly. Help your fridge run more efficiently by not leaving the door open for long. Every time you open the door, the compressor has to run for eight to ten minutes to re-chill the fridge.

- Don't overcrowd. Overstuffing obstructs air circulation, forcing the fridge to work harder.

- Cover liquids and wrap foods stored in the refrigerator. Uncovered foods release moisture and make the compressor work harder.

- Replace paper wrappings on food items with aluminum foil or plastic wrap. Paper is an insulator so it requires more energy to cool the contents inside the paper wrapping.

- Experiment with the "energy saver" switch in your refrigerator — it allows you to adjust the heating coil under the "skin" of the refrigerator (the purpose of the heating coil is to prevent condensation on your refrigerator).

- Place the refrigerator properly. Direct sunlight and close contact with hot appliances make the compressor work harder. Don't suffocate the refrigerator by enclosing it tightly in cabinets or against the wall because heat from the compressor and condensing coil needs to escape freely. A rule-of-thumb is to allow two inches of air flow around the refrigerator — something important to know before the cabinets are redesigned to fit your growing stock of homebrew supplies.

- Regularly brush off or vacuum the refrigerator coils on the back or bottom of the unit. Be sure to unplug the fridge first and be careful not to bend or break the coils while cleaning them.

- Don't keep that old, inefficient fridge running day and night in the garage for those few occasions when you need extra refreshments. Running a 15-year-old refrigerator can cost $150 per year.

Tips for Buying a New Refrigerator

- If your fridge is over ten years old, consider replacing it with an Energy Star refrigerator. This can save over 2,000 kWh and reduce carbon dioxide emissions by over 2,000 pounds every year. However, you must balance these savings against the raw materials and energy consumed in producing a new refrigerator — or any new product.

- The most energy-efficient models are in the 16–20 cubic foot sizes. Generally, the larger the refrigerator, the greater the energy consumption. Too large a model will waste space and energy; too small a model could mean extra trips to the supermarket.

- It is usually less costly to run one larger refrigerator than two smaller ones. If you're debating between two different sized refrigerators and each uses the same amount of energy, the larger model is more efficient since it keeps more space cold with the same amount of electricity.

- Top freezer models are about a tenth more efficient than side-by-side models and bottom freezer models are in between.

- Automatic defrost, once considered an energy vice, has improved and is now just about as efficient as manual defrost models.

- Automatic ice-makers and through-the-door dispensers increase energy use by up to 20 percent and increase the purchase price by about $75–$250. Even though this feature reduces the number of times the door opens, opening both freezer and cooler compartment doors accounts for only six percent of total energy use. So through-the-door features are a net energy waster.

- Models with an anti-sweat heater consume five percent to ten percent more energy. Look for a model that has an "energy saver" switch that allows you to turn off or turn down the heating coils.

13. Make or Buy Recycled Beer Glasses

Tossing your beer bottles in the recycle bin is only the first step in the recycling loop. There must be a market for products made from recycled materials for recycling to work. Beer-drinking vessels made from recycled glass and plastic are available. Green Glass <www.greenglass.com> makes some of my favorites. They actually convert used wine and beer bottles into drinking glasses without even re-melting and remanufacturing the glass.

GREEN GLASS

By Green Glass Inc.

Green Glass remanufactures wine and beer bottles into drinking glasses.

All that is required to make glass is a little sand, soda, and lime, but most importantly, a lot of heat. The amount of energy needed to melt recycled glass is considerably less than that which is needed to melt virgin raw materials. Glass-making workshops are available in lots of communities, often at local colleges and technical schools. Check the course listings in advance and sign up to make some beautiful and unique beer glasses.

14. Buy a Keg for Your Next Party

Kegs are far more packaging-efficient than 165 individually packaged beers (almost seven cases, which is how much a standard half-barrel keg holds), and much cheaper too. Many small breweries and brewpubs offer kegs these days, including smaller sizes as well. Some even offer delivery service. Kegs help reduce clean up time after the party too, since there aren't all those bottles and cans laying around. Ask people to bring their own favorite beer glasses and you've really reduced your clean up time. Or buy disposable cups made from biodegradable, compostable cornstarch. Check out <www.ecoproducts.com> to find some of these products.

15. Build a Root Cellar

I won't pretend that this is the simplest way to drink beer and save the world. Building a root cellar is definitely a project for the advanced beer activist, but it can be really fun and will surely make you the envy of all your neighbors.

A root cellar is a structure that is built partly or entirely underground so as to benefit from the cool natural temperature of the earth. During the summer, underground temperatures can be 30–40 degrees cooler than the outside air temperature, often right in the range of the ideal serving temperature for most beers. Voila, all-natural energy-free refrigeration for a giant beer collection! Easier than building a root cellar is just using the basement to store extra beer instead of getting a second fridge to house that blossoming beer collection.

16. Walk or Bike to the Store

This one should be pretty self-explanatory. Leave the car in the garage, save some gas, keep the air cleaner, reduce your contribution to global warming and exercise off some of the calories that you are about to consume in the form of malted beverages.

17. BYO Beer Mug

Going to a keg party where the host is probably going to be using disposable plastic cups? Bring your own favorite pint glass, beer mug or fancy tulip-shaped Belgian beer glass. The really fancy ones may impress your friends and will in any event avoid the unnecessary use of disposable plastic cups.

18. Don't Buy Your Beer at Wal-Mart

Ranked among the ten worst corporations of 2004 by the *Multinational Monitor*, this colossus of US — and increasingly global — retailing registers more than a quarter trillion dollars in sales. Wal-Mart's revenues account for two percent of US Gross Domestic Product. It is arguably the defining company of the present era. A key component — arguably *the* key component — of the company's business model is under-compensating employees and externalizing costs onto society. A February 2004 report issued by Representative George Miller, a California Democrat, tabulated some of those costs. The report estimated that one 200-employee Wal-Mart store may result in a cost to federal taxpayers of $420,750 per year — about $2,103 per employee. These public costs include free and reduced lunches for 50 Wal-Mart families, Section 8 housing assistance, federal tax credits and deductions for low-income families, and federal contributions to health insurance programs for low-income children. Wal-Mart likes to tout how it provides jobs in communities, but according to the statistics, average income drops in communities immediately after a Wal-Mart opens in it. Another common defense of Wal-Mart is that it serves low-income people by offering them cheap products. But it also creates low-income people all over the world by relying on goods made in factories that many people call sweatshops where workers are desperately underpaid. Skip Wal-Mart and support your local independent retailer.

19. Teach Young People to Drink Responsibly

I can't encourage you to drink beer with your kids since it is illegal. But if it were legal, that would be the best way to teach them how to drink responsibly. Instead, you'll have to settle for honest, open communication. Demystify beer for them as best you can so that they are capable of integrating beer-drinking into their lives as a normal, everyday activity, rather than as a binge phenomenon.

20. Encourage Mega-Brewers to Do Better

Wouldn't it be amazing if one of the big brewing corporations started using organic ingredients? Stranger things have happened. Customer feedback for the big brewers is usually as simple as filling out a form on their website. Shoot them an email and tell them you want organic beers.

    *** Stop the presses! Just as this book was going off to printer, Anheuser-Busch began test marketing a line of organic beers, cleverly labeled as coming from the Green Valley Brewing Company, a name created to distance the products from their corporate origins. A-B has strategically avoided any public affiliation with the new line in an attempt to lend the beers credibility as artisanal creations. If the pilot markets do well, consumers around the country may soon see Wild Hop Lager and Stone Mill Pale Ale on their shelves. ***

21. Drink in Season

Until fairly recently, brewers in northern climes brewed only during the cooler months because it was easier to keep the yeasts active that produce the alcohol in beer. To make a long technical story short, this helped create a variety of beer styles that were brewed according to the season, like Marzen/Octoberfest. Many craft brewers now make seasonal beers and some use fresh, seasonally available ingredients. When you go to a brewpub, just ask "What's your seasonal tap?"

22. Encourage Your Local Bar or Restaurant to Stock Local and Organic Brews

Brewers are making organic beers but they are still hard to find. Tell your local beer shop or favorite bar what you want. If they can get it, they usually will.

23. Party to Save the Planet

When you're hosting a beer bash, integrate some do-goodism into the event. For example, if it's a Saturday night party you're holding, invite your guests to join you in the afternoon to clean up a local area — it could be a stream, or park, or it could be planting trees on the block where you live. Or ask your guests to simply bring a donation to the party — collect books for the local school library, or food for the local soup kitchen. It doesn't really matter, just pick your favorite issue and invite your friends to help out. Invite a speaker from an organization you like. Afterwards, party down!

24. Don't stop with beer. Follow these same principles with other products and other areas of your life!

Beer Activist Guide

Drink Beer. Save the World. Enjoy these Beers.

This directory includes many of the breweries playing a part in the ferment-ing revolution. In the last twenty-five years, the number of breweries in the US has grown from fewer than fifty to over 1,500. More are opening every day, both in the US and abroad. Therefore, it is impossible to compile a comprehensive list. For updates, check the website <www.beeractivist.com>.

In assembling this list, I tried to adhere to a few criteria. But defining "sustainable breweries" is a bit of a moving target. It's kind of like defining jazz — jazz has certain measurable characteristics, it should swing and have some syncopation and improvisation, but it also has intangible attributes, such as jazz by association. Plus, the definition evolves over time. Similarly, *sud*stain-ability includes energy efficiency, water efficiency, and zero-waste design. But it also includes elusive attributes like community building, the ability to deliver sublime experiences, and deliciousness. Sustainable breweries help to educate and uplift their customers and their community rather than pander to the lowest common denomi-nator by dumbing down their product. Taking the time to educate a customer is a sign of

"In a world as free as we have ever known, do we want real diversity or an endless 'choice' of same, bland beers? That will be determined not by the marketer but by the consumer. It is for us to decide."

— Michael Jackson

respect. A customer is an equal, whereas a consumer is a passive target in the sights of a selfish businessperson. Good breweries treat their customers with respect by giving them good beers that echo the depth and complexity of the customers themselves.

Because it is difficult to measure such inherently subjective qualities, this list is not meant to be comprehensive. I have included brief notes on why these particular breweries have been included, but this is not a checklist. The best way to discover beers that are saving the world is to explore your local brewpubs and breweries and decide for yourself.

North America

5 Seasons Brewery Atlanta Georgia. The Big O, certified organic English Strong Ale.

Anderson Valley Brewing Company Bootville, California. A leading eco-friendly brewery featuring solar panels, a wind-powered "living machine" pond system for wastewater treatment, and a horse-drawn delivery carriage. Customers and workers speak a unique local language called Boontling, spoken exclusively in the brewery's native Boont Valley. The 3-acre farm-brewery includes an 18-hole disc-golf course with baskets handmade from salvaged scrap materials. Organic beers are occasionally featured, like their Raspberry Wheat.

Bison Brewing Berkeley, California. Organic beers.

Blackfoot River Brewing Company Helena, Montana. Organic beers.

Brooklyn Brewery Brooklyn, New York. One hundred percent wind-powered, brews Sustainable Organic Porter.

Butte Creek Brewing Company Chico, California. Organic beers.

Caldera Brewing Ashland, Oregon. Hemp and organic beers.

C'est What? Toronto, Ontario. A community center buzzing with Canadian culture, this brewpub hosts a radio station, live music venue, and art gallery that all highlight local Toronto flavors, and a bar that features radical brews like the Homegrown Hemp Ale.

Coastline Brewery Capitola, California. All organic brewpub.

Crannog Ales Sorrento, British Columbia. All-organic, zero-waste, farm and draught-only microbrewery.

Diamond Knot Brewery and Alehouse Mukilteo, Washington. Hemp beer.

Dogfish Head Lewes, Delaware. Renowned for their experimental, huge-bodied, historic, and otherwise completely radical beers, including Chicory Stout, a beer brewed with organic coffee, St. John's Wort, licorice root and chicory. The brewpub menu offers fresh, local, and organic produce; and houses one of the first of America's new micro-distilling operations.

Dragonmead Microbrewery Warren, Michigan. Hemp beer.

East End Brewing Company Pittsburgh, Pennsylvania. Eco-conscious production brewery.

Eel River Brewing Company Fortuna, California. Certified organic beers from the first certified organic brewery in the US, also served in an eco-friendly pub made from recovered Redwood and Douglas fir woods.

Elliott Bay Brewery Pub Seattle, Washington. Organic malts used in all their beers.

Eske's Brew Pub and Eatery New Taos, New Mexico. Organic bitter.

Estes Park Brewery Estes Park, Colorado. Organic Staggering Elk Lager.

Fish Brewing Company Olympia, Washington. Organic beers and food.

Fitger's Duluth, Minnesota. Homegrown Hempen Ale and organic Pale Ale.

Flat Branch Pub and Brewing Columbia, Missouri. Organic Alt Bier.

Full Sail Brewing Company Portland, Oregon. Worker-owned.

Great Barrington Brewery and Restaurant Barrington Maine. Organic English Pale Ale.

Great Lakes Brewing Company Cleveland, Ohio. Zero-waste brewery and brewpub, and the best Dortmunder style beer this side of Germany.

Kettle House Brewing Company Missoula, Montana. Hemp beer.

Lakefront Brewery Milwaukee, Wisconsin. Organic beer.

Laurelwood Public House and Brewery Portland, Oregon. Extensive line of organic beers.

Leopold Brothers Brewery Ann Arbor, Michigan. Eco-friendly brewpub.

Lucky Labrador Brewing Company Portland, Oregon. Organic Golden Ale.

Mad River Brewing Company Arcata, California. Nearly zero-waste brewery.

McMenamins Oregon and Washington. This northwestern chain of breweries, pubs, hotels, restaurants, and theatres has renovated dozens of historic buildings, supports local artists, and features occasional organic beers.

Millstreet Brewery Toronto, Ontario. Organic lager and pilsener.

New Belgium Brewing Company Fort Collins, Colorado. The first wind-powered brewery in America, employee-owned.

Pacific Western Brewing Company Prince George, British Columbia. Organic Natureland lager.

Pearl Street Brewery La Crosse, Wisconsin. Hemp, organic, locally-grown ingredients.

Peak Organic Brewing Company Portland, ME. All organic beers.

Pisgah Brewing Company Black Mountain, North Carolina. Exclusively organic beers.

Roots Organic Brewing Portland, Oregon. This organic brewery organizes the annual North American Organic Brewers Festival.

Santa Cruz Mountain Brewing Santa Cruz, California. This brewery rounds out Santa Cruz's hat trick of organic beer resources, which includes Seven Bridges, a cooperative purveyor of all organic homebrew supplies, and the all-organic brewpub Coastline Brewing.

Squatters Pub Brewery Salt Lake City, Utah. Eco-friendly.

Uinta Brewing Company Salt Lake City, Utah. Wind-powered.

Ukiah Brewing Company Ukiah, California. The first certified organic brewpub.

Wild Rose Brewery Calgary, Alberta. Organic beer.

Wolaver's/Otter Creek Middlebury, Vermont. America's first nationally distributed line of organic beers.

World

Arkells Britain. Bees Organic Ale.

Batemans Britain. Yella Bally organic golden ale.

Bath Britain. Organic Lager.

Black Isle Scotland. Organic brewery.

Brakspear Britain. Organic beers.

Broughton Ales Scotland. Organic beers.

Bunker Britain. Organic beer.

Caledonian Scotland. Organic beers.

Cantillon Belgium. Organic brewery making wild fermented beers.

Charles Wells Britain. Fair trade banana beer.

Daishichi Japan. Organic sake.

Dublin Brewing Dublin Ireland. Organic cider.

Duchy Britain. Organic beers, benefits charity.

Dunkertons Britain. Organic ciders and perry.

Echigo Japan. Organic Pilsener.

Eisenbahn (Cervejaria Sudbrack) Brazil. Organic beer.

Emersons New Zealand. Organic beer.

Feral Australia. Organic Pils.

Founders New Zealand. Organic beers.

Greenleaf Hemp Ale Britain. Hemp beer.

Heather Ale Scotland. Reviving endangered beer species.

Hitachino Nest Japan. Organic beers.

Locher Switzerland. Hemp and organic beers.

Marble Beers Britain. Organic beers.

Meantime Britain. Fair trade coffee beer.

Mongozo Belgium. Organic and fair trade beers.

Neumarkter Lammsbrau Germany. Eco-friendly brewery.

Niigata Japan. Hemp beer.

Pitfield Beer Shop Britain. Certified organic brewery, homebrew shop, and beer shop.

The 4 Elements Germany. Organic beer.

Wadi Brau Hanf Switzerland. Hemp and organic beers.

Vocabrewary

A Glossary of Revolution*aley* Terminal*eogy*

Aleienated – how a person feels when there is no good beer around, or when there is no one with whom to drink it.

Beerate – to scold someone for drinking bad beer.

Beergoiesie – high-class beer snobs.

Beerhemoth – a corporate industrial brewing behemoth.

Beeracle – a beer miracle, popular with Saints in the Middle Ages.

Beeriod – a beer epoch.

Beeriodicals – magazines read by beer drinkers.

Beerocracy – 1) the global brewing giants 2) the imbroglio of contradictory; and asinine laws governing the brewing, transport, marketing, sale, and drinking of beer.

Beerodiversity – a measure of the diversity of beer in a given community.

Beerological hotspot – A place with exceptionally good *beer*-odiversity, like the Brickskeller Saloon in Washington, D.C.

*Beer*oregion – an area in which a unique overall pattern of brewing characteristics can be found.

*Beer*oregionalism – the idea that we can evolve human activities to be sustainable by adapting our activities to a *beer*oregion.

Blandardization – the *beer*ocracy's hegemonic quest to make bland, standardized and crappy beers.

*Brew*icide – the death of a beer brand or style.

*Brew*pie – contraction of "brewery groupie," someone who likes beer so much that they hang around breweries and help out for free.

*Brew*spaper – newspapers read by beer drinkers.

*Brew*tiful – as pretty as a beer.

Brid*eale* – before weddings, a nuptial beer was brewed and sold, the proceeds going to the bride on her wedding day. These "bride-ales" survive in the contemporary word "bridal."

Cons*beer*acy – 1) a plot to get beer 2) the government plot controlling beer.

Evang*ale*ist – one who proselytizes about how beer is saving the world.

Fem*ale* – a righteously beer-empowered woman.

Festiv*ale* – beer festival.

Glo*beer*ization – 1 the spread of beer throughout the world 2 the growth of breweries to a world wide scale.

Lab*brew*tory – the place where cool beer stuff is investigated and invented.

Li*beery* – where *beer*iodicals and *brew*spapers are stored.

Mem*beer*ship – what you get when you join a li*beery*.

S*beer*itual – of or relating to beer and spirituality.

*Sud*stainability – sustainability as practiced by beer activists.

Bibrewography

22nd FAO Regional Conference for Europe, Porto, Portugal. "Food Safety and Quality as Affected by Organic Farming." Agenda Item 10.1. July 24–28, 2000.

Aidells, Bruce and Denis Kelly. *Real Beer and Good Eats: The Rebirth of America's Beer and Food Traditions.* Alfred A. Knopf, 1995.

Aluminum Association. "Facts and History about Aluminum Recycling" [online]. [Cited April 8, 2006]. <www.earth911.org/master.asp?s= lib&a=aluminum/history.asp>

Aminov, Rustam. *Applied and Environmental Microbiology,* Vol. 67. University of Illinois, 2001.

Anderson, Ray C. *Mid-Course Correction.* Chelsea Green, 1998.

"Atmospheric Deposition of PAH, PCB, and Organochlorine Pesticides to Corpus Christi Bay." *Science Daily Magazine,* Sept. 21, 2001.

Bacon, Selden D. "Alcohol and Complex Society." In *Society, Culture, and Drinking Patterns.* David J. Pittman and Charles R. Snyder, eds. Wiley, 1962.

Baron, Stanley. *Brewed in America: A History of Beer and Ale in the United States.* Little, Brown and Company, 1962.

Barstow, Cynthia. *The Eco-Foods Guide: What's Good for the Earth Is Good For You.* New Society Publishers, 2002.

Baum, Dan. *Citizen Coors: An American Dynasty.* HarperCollins, 2000.

Beach, David R. *Homegrown Hops: An Illustrated How to Do it Manual.* David R. Beach, 1988.

Bede. *The Life and Miracles of St. Cuthbert, Bishop of Lindesfarne, 721* [online]. [Cited April 8, 2006]. J.A. Giles translator. <www.fordham.edu/halsall/basis/bede-cuthbert.html>

Begon, Michael, John L.Harper, and Colin R. Townsend. *Ecology.* Blackwell Scientific Publications, 1990.

Benbrook, Charles, PhD. "Elevating Antioxidant Levels Through Organic Farming and Food Processing" [online]. [Cited April 8, 2006]. The Organic Center, 2005. <www.organic-center.org/science.htm?articleid=54>

Bennett, Judith M. *Ale, Beer, and Brewsters in England: Women's Work in a Changing World, 1300–1600.* Oxford University Press, 1996.

Bennett, Judith M. *Women in the Medieval English Countryside: Gender and Household in Brigstock before the Plague.* Oxford University Press, 1987.

Beyond Pesticides. "Technical Report." April, 2001.

Beyond Pesticides. "Technical Report". August–September, 2001.

Boesch, Dr. Donald. "Marine Pollution in the United States: Significant Accomplishments, Future Challenges." University of Maryland Center for Environmental Science, Pew Oceans Commission, 2001.

Boston, Richard. *Beer and Skittles.* William Collins Sons and Co., 1976.

Brewers Company. "The Master and Keepers or Wardens and Commonality of the Mystery or Art of Brewers in the City of London" [online]. [Cited April 8, 2006]. <www.brewershall.co.uk/history.htm>

Buhner, Stephen Harrod. *Sacred and Herbal Healing Beers: The Secret of Ancient Fermentation.* Siris Books, 1998.

Burgess, Robert J. *Silver Bullets: A Soldier's Story of How Coors Bombed in the Beer Wars.* St. Martin's Press, 1993.

Calagione, Sam. *Brewing Up a Business.* Wiley, 2005.

Calvin, John. "Commentary on Psalms 104:15". *Institutes of the Christian Religion, III, XIX, 9.* McNeill, John T., ed. Westminster John Knox Press, n.d.

Cornell, Martyn. *Beer: The Story of the Pint: The History of Britain's Most Popular Drink.* Headline Book Publishing, 2003.

Daniels, Ray. *101 Ideas for Homebrew Fun.* Brewers Publications, 1998.

Daniels, Ray and Geoffrey Larson. *Smoked Beers: History, Brewing Techniques, Recipes.* Brewers Publications, 2000.

Dornbusch, Horst. "Born to Be (Beer) King" [online]. [cited April 8, 2006]. Beeractovate.com, 2004. <http://beeradvocate.com/news/stories_read/604/>

Dunkling, Leslie. *The Guinness Drinking Companion*. The Lyons Press, 2002.

Dunster, Bill. Personal communication, June 2004. Zedfactory.com

Eames, Alan D. *The Secret Life of Beer: Legends, Lore & Little Known Facts.* Storey Publishing, 1995.

The Endocrine Society. "Study Reveals Drinking Alcohol Reduces Breast Milk Supply in Women. Alcohol and Lactation: Myth vs. Science." *The Journal of Clinical Endocrinology & Metabolism*. April, 2005.

Environmental Defense. "Chemical Profile for ENDOTHALL (CAS Number: 145–73-3)" [online]. [Cited April 8, 2006]. <www.scorecard.org/chemical-profiles/summary.tcl?edf_substance_id=145-73-3>

Environmental Illness Society of Canada. "Pesticides: Their Multigenerational Cumulative Destructive Impact on Health, Especially on the Physical, Emotional and Mental Development of Children and of Future Generations — Canadian Government Responsibilities and Opportunities" [online]. [Cited July 2005]. February 2000,

<www.eisc.ca/pesticide_moratorium.html>

Estes, Priscilla A. "What Have You Done for Your Liver Lately?" *American Brewer*, March–April, 1999.

Farm Aid. "Why Family Farmers Need Help" [online]. [Cited April 8, 2006]. <www.farmaid.org/site/PageServer?pagename=info_facts_help>

Fisher, Joe and Dennis Fisher. *The Homebrewer's Garden*. Storey Publishing, 1998.

Fodor, Eben. *Better Not Bigger*. New Society Publishers, 1999.

Ford, Gene. *The Benefits of Moderate Drinking: Alcohol, Health and Society*. Wine Appreciation Guild, 1988.

Forget, Carl. *Association of Brewers' Dictionary of Beer and Brewing*. Brewers Publications, 1988.

Forster, Adrian, B. Beck and R. Schmidt. *Problematic Substances of Hops.* Presented at the 76th October meeting of the VLB in Berlin, 1989. <www.vlb-berlin.org/english/index.html>

Foster, Terry. *Porter, Classic Beer Style Series No. 5*. Brewers Publications, 1992.

French, Richard Valpy. *Nineteen Centuries of Drink in England: A History*. National Temperance Publication Depot, 1884.

Glaser, Gregg. "You're Better Off With Beer: Beer and Your Health." *All About Beer Magazine*, Volume 23, Number 3, July 2002.

"The Global Market for Organic Food and Drink." *Organic Monitor*, July 2003.

Goldman-Armstrong, Abrahm. "Organic Beer Update." *Northwest Brewing News*. April–May 2004.

Grant, Bert. *The Ale Master*. Sasquatch Books, 1998.

Griffith, Ralph. *The Rig-Veda* [online]. [Cited April 8, 2006]. The Internet Sacred Texts Archive, 1896. <www.sacred-texts.com>

Griffith, Ralph. *Hymns of the Samaveda* [online]. [Cited April 8, 2006]. The Internet Sacred Texts Archive, 1896. <www.sacred-texts.com>

Guinard, Jean-Xavier. *Lambic, Classic Beer Style Series No. 3*. Brewers Publications, 1990.

Harper, Timothy and Garrett Oliver. *The Good Beer Book*. Berkley, 1997.

Hawken, Paul. *The Ecology of Commerce*. HarperBusiness, 1993.

Headden, Susan. "A Heavy Footprint." *US News and World Report*. May, 2004.

Heath, D. B. "A Decade of Development in the Anthropological Study of Alcohol Use: 1970–1980". Douglas, M., (ed.). *Constructive Drinking: Perspectives on Drink from Anthropology*. Cambridge University Press, 1987, pp. 16–69.

Heinberg, Richard. *The Party's Over*. New Society Publishers, 2003.

Hightower, Jim. Thieves in High Places. Viking, 2003.

Illich, Ivan. *Shadow Work*. Open Forum, 1981.

Jackson, Michael. *Great Beers of Belgium*, 3rd ed. Running Press, 1998.

Korten, David C. *The Post-Corporate World*. Kumarian Press and Berrett-Koehler Publishers, 1999.

Lawrence, Margaret. *The Encircling Hop: A History of Hops and Brewing*. SAWD, 1990.

Leake, Chauncy D. *Alcoholic Beverages in Clinical Medicine*. 1966.

Leick, Gwendolyn. *The Babylonians: An Introduction*. Routledge, 2003.

Lender, Mark Edward and James Kirby Martin. *Drinking in America: A History, The Revised and Expanded Edition*. Free Press, 1987.

Long, John S. "Beer and Food - A Heady Combination: Good brews can be matched with all sorts of dishes, even desserts, to make dynamic duos." *The Cleveland Plain Dealer*, May 8, 2002.

Mares, William. *Making Beer*, revised edition. Alfred A. Knopf, 1995.

Marr, Peter and Stephen Fineman. "Mergers: Why the Bigger Isn't the Better," *Marketing*. University of Sheffield, November 1970.

Mason, John. "Agriculture is depleting gene diversity of animals." *Financial Times*. March 31, 2004.

Mennella, Julie, PhD. "Alcohol's Effect on Lactation." *Alcohol Research and Health*. Fall 2001.

Merchant, Carolyn. *The Death of Nature: Women, Ecology and the Scientific Revolution*. HarperSanFrancisco, 1980.

Metzger, Bill and Barbara Block. *The Beer Diet Book: Losing Weight and Gaining Strength the Beer Diet Way*. Beerly Legible Press, n.d.

Metzner, Jim. "Antibiotics in Ancient Bone: Tetracycline" [online]. [Cited April 8, 2006]. *Pulse of the Planet*. <www.pulseplanet.com/archive/May05/3448.html>

Nachman-Hunt, Nancy. "Bill Coors: There's Nothing Like the Original." *LOHAS Journal*, Vol 2, No 1, Spring 2001.

Noonan, Gregory J. *Scotch Ale Classic Beer Style Series No. 8*. Brewers Publications, 1993.

Oikos. "Refrigerator Efficiency Improves." *Energy Source Builder #31*. February 1994.

Roper Public Affairs and Media. "Food and Farming 2004." Organic Valley Family of Farms, April 2004.

O'Shea, Theresa. "Beer Saints: With Beer On Their Side." *Brew Your Own*. Volume 22, Number 6, January 2002.

Papazian, Charlie. *The New Complete Joy of Home Brewing*, 2nd ed. Avon Books, 1984.

Parry, Martin. *Climate Change and World Agriculture*. Earthscan Publications, 1990.

Pauli, Gunter. *UpSizing: The Road to Zero Emissions, More Jobs, More Income and No Pollution*. Chelsea Green, 2000.

Pesticide Action Network. "Demise of the Dirty Dozen 1995 Chart" [online]. [Cited April 8, 2006]. <www.panna.org/resources/documents/dirtyDozenChart.dv.html>.

Petrini, Carlo, ed. *Slow Food: Collected Thoughts on Taste, Tradition and the Honest Pleasures of Food*. Chelsea Green, 2001.

Protz, Roger. *The Organic Beer Guide*. Carlton Books, 2002.

Protz, Roger. *The Ale Trail*. Eric Dobby Publishing/Verulam, 1995.

Romm, Joseph J. *Cool Companies: How the Best Businesses Boost Profits and Productivity by Cutting Greenhouse Gas Emissions*. Earthscan Publications, 1999.

Rowe, Vicky. "Gift of God, Drink of Kings" [online]. [Cited April 8, 2006]. Realbeer.com <www.realbeer.com/edu/mead/giftofgods.php>

Sandars, N.K. *The Epic of Gilgamesh*. Penguin Books, 1972.

Schlosser, Eric. *Fast Food Nation*. Perennial, 2002.

Sclove, Richard E. *Democracy and Technology*. Guilford Publications, 1995.

Shute, Nancy and Charles W. Petit. "Preparing for a Warmer World. The Future of Earth." *US News & World Report Special Edition*. May 2004.

Skilnik, Bob. *The History of Beer and Brewing in Chicago 1833–1978*. Pogo Press, 1999.

Slaughter, Thomas P. *The Whiskey Rebellion: Frontier Epilogue to the American Revolution*. Oxford University Press, 1986.

Smith, Gregg and Carrie Getty. *The Beer Drinker's Bible: Lore, Trivia & History: Chapter & Verse*. Brewers Publications, 1997.

Smith, Gregg. *Beer: A History of Suds and Civilization From Mesopotamia to Microbreweries*. Avon Books, 1995.

Starke, Linda, ed. *Vital Signs 2003*. Worldwatch Institute. W.W. Norton, 2003.

Steinkraus, Keith H. *Industrialization of Indigenous Fermented Foods: Food Science and Technology*. Marcel Dekker, 1989.

Steinkraus, Keith H. *Handbook of Indigenous Fermented Foods (Food Science and Technology)*. CRC, 2nd edition, 1995.

Tominack, R.L., G.Y. Yang, W.J. Tsai, H.M. Chung, and J.F. Deng. "Taiwan National Poison Center survey of glyphosate-surfactant herbicide ingestions." *Journal of Toxicology and Clinical Toxicology*, 29 (1), 1991.

"Uganda's Homebrew Hit." *Capital Ethiopia*. Vol 6 No 270. February 8–14, 2004.

US EPA. "Municipal Solid Waste in the United States: 2000 Facts and Figures." June 2002. <www.epa.gov/garbage/msw99.htm>

Van Munching, Philip. *Beer Blast: The Inside Story of the Brewing Industry's Bizarre Battles for Your Money*. Times Business, 1997.

Webb, Anne. *CAMRA Dictionary of Beer*. CAMRA, 2001.

Weida, William J. "Considering the Rationales for Factory Farming" (PDF). The Global Resource Action Center for the Environment. February 2004. <www.factoryfarm.org/docs/Foundations_of_Sand.pdf>

Wells, Ken. *Travels with Barley*. Wall Street Journal Books, 2004.

Woods, Shirley E. *The Molson Saga: 1763–1983*. Doubleday Canada, 1983.

Zuckerman, Jocelyn. "Mother Africa: Across the continent, women are taking power." *Utne Magazine* No. 134. March–April 2006.

Index

bold numbers indicate illustrations

A

Abramson, Jerome L., 204–205

Adams, Patch, 203

Adams, Sam, 79, 80

Africa (*see also* Egypt): brewing tradition in, 50–51, 110–112, 225; masculinization of brewing, 68–69; prohibition, 31–32; women brewers, 68–**69**, 74, 111–112, 113–114

agave drinks, 13

agriculture: and ancient beverages, 13; conventional, 167–169, 170–173, 181; evolution of, 8–9; and plant diseases, 124, 174–176; and toxic chemicals, 168–169, 171, 174–180, 182

air pollution, 124–125, 211, 239, 240

Aitken, John, 182

Akita Research Institute, 220

Alaskan Brewing Company, 145

alcohol content, 56, 192–193

alcoholism: and Islam, 30; true level of, 196, 212; in US, 93–94, 96

ales, 56

alewives, 126

Altbier, 47

aluminum cans, 219–220

Amazon, Inc., 145

AmBev, 103, 225

Aminov, Rustam, 168

Anchor Brewing Company, **141**, 142

Anderson Valley Brewing Company, 252

Anheuser-Busch: global reach, 104, 217, 222; organic beer, 249; politics, 82, 83; sustainability, 222–224; water conservation, 157

antibiotics, 168–169, 197–198

apple farming, 181

architecture, green, 151–152, 154, 158–162

Armelagos, George, 197–198

Arnold of Metz, Saint, 43, **49**

Arnold of Soissons, Saint, 43–45

Arnoldus the Strong, 45

art, **22, 37, 50, 92, 161**–162

Arthur, Tomme, 146, 192

Augustine of Hippo, Saint, 41

B

Babylonia, 11–12, 24, 32, 198

Bacchus, 37

Bacon, Selden D., 200

Baer, David J., 210

bags, shopping, 238–240

Bamburg brewery, 39

banana beers, 112, 116

barley: based beers, 30, 36, 54; in brewing process, 88, 145, 216; as currency,

About the Author

Chris O'Brien dedicates his life to drinking beer and saving the world.

As Director of the Responsible Purchasing Network, at the Center for a New American Dream, he helps large institutions like governments and corporations shift their purchasing to socially and environmentally superior products. He also directed the Co-op America Business Network and the Fair Trade Federation, two trade associations that use business as a force for social change.

Beer dominates his pursuits outside the office. He did a stint as head brewer at Zululand Brewing Company in South Africa, and is part-owner of Seven Bridges, the world's only exclusive purveyor of organic brewing ingredients, and fair trade, home coffee-roasting supplies. His column "Brewing a Better World", appears in *American Brewer* magazine, and he frequently contributes to *New Brewer*, and *Zymurgy*. His own brewsletter is online at Beeractivist.com. *Fermenting Revolution* is his first full-length book.

If you have enjoyed *Fermenting Revolution* you might also enjoy other

BOOKS TO BUILD A NEW SOCIETY

Our books provide positive solutions for people
who want to make a difference. We specialize in:

**Environment and Justice • Conscientious Commerce • Sustainable Living
Ecological Design and Planning • Natural Building & Appropriate Technology
New Forestry • Educational and Parenting Resources • Nonviolence
Progressive Leadership • Resistance and Community**

New Society Publishers

ENVIRONMENTAL BENEFITS STATEMENT

New Society Publishers has chosen to produce this book on Enviro 100, recycled paper made with **100% post consumer waste**, processed chlorine free, and old growth free.

For every 5,000 books printed, New Society saves the following resources:[1]

29	Trees
2,604	Pounds of Solid Waste
2,865	Gallons of Water
3,737	Kilowatt Hours of Electricity
4,734	Pounds of Greenhouse Gases
20	Pounds of HAPs, VOCs, and AOX Combined
7	Cubic Yards of Landfill Space

[1]Environmental benefits are calculated based on research done by the Environmental Defense Fund and other members of the Paper Task Force who study the environmental impacts of the paper industry.

For more information on this environmental benefits statement, or to inquire about environmentally friendly papers, please contact New Leaf Paper – info@newleafpaper.com Tel: 888 • 989 • 5323.

For a full list of NSP's titles, please call **1-800-567-6772** *or check out our website at:*

www.newsociety.com

NEW SOCIETY PUBLISHERS